Inspiring Academics

Learning with the World's Great University Teachers

Inspiring Academics

Learning with the World's Great University Teachers

Iain Hay

Open University Press

Open University Press
McGraw-Hill Education
McGraw-Hill House
Shoppenhangers Road
Maidenhead
Berkshire
England
SL6 2QL

email: enquiries@openup.co.uk
world wide web: www.openup.co.uk

and Two Penn Plaza, New York, NY 10121-2289, USA

First published 2011

A catalogue record of this book is available from the British Library

ISBN-13: 978-0-33-523742-5 (pb) 978-0-33-523741-8 (hb)
ISBN-10: 0335238157 (pb) 033523741-X

Library of Congress Cataloging-in-Publication Data
CIP data applied for

Typeset by RefineCatch Limited, Bungay, Suffolk
Printed in the UK by CPI Antony Rowe, Chippenham and Eastbourne

The **McGraw-Hill** Companies

Contents

List of boxes, figures and tables

Boxes

Figures

Tables

Notes on contributors

Gerlese Åkerlind is Director of the Centre for Educational Development and Academic Methods at the Australian National University (ANU). The Centre provides professional development support for ANU academics, and Gerlese teaches into the Centre's Graduate Certificate and Masters of Higher Education. Her research focuses on the nature of academic practice, including academics' experiences of teaching, research and their own growth and development as academics. She is an honorary Research Associate of the Oxford Learning Institute, Oxford University, and a member of the Editorial Boards for *Educational Research Review, Learning and Teaching in Higher Education* and *International Journal of Researcher Development.*

Donna Boyd is Eminent Professor and Head of Anthropological Sciences at Radford University and Co-Director of the Radford University Forensic Science Institute. She is a Diplomate of the American Board of Forensic Anthropology and an adjunct member of the Virginia Office of the Chief Medical Examiner, Western District. Her research interests include the skeletal biology of historic African-Americans, theory in forensic anthropology, and distinguishing blunt force and sharp force perimortem trauma in human remains. She received the Virginia State Council of Higher Education Outstanding Faculty Award and the CASE/Carnegie US Professor of the Year award in 2006.

Ian Cameron is the former head of Chemical Engineering at the University of Queensland, an inaugural Senior Fellow of the Australian Learning and Teaching Council (ALTC) and ALTC Discipline Scholar in Engineering and Technology. He completed Chemical Engineering degrees at the University of New South Wales and the University of Washington. After ten years working in diverse industry sectors he obtained his PhD from Imperial College London in the area of Process Systems Engineering. He worked for a nine-year period as a UNIDO process engineering consultant in Argentina and Turkey. He has spent the last 20 years in research, consulting, teaching and learning innovation at the University of Queensland, having received numerous research and teaching awards, including the Australian Prime Minister's Award for University Teacher of the Year in 2003.

Jane Dahlstrom is Professor of Anatomical Pathology at the Australian National University Medical School and Senior Staff Specialist in Anatomical

Pathology at ACT (Australian Capital Territory) Pathology, Canberra Hospital, Australia. Her job involves an interesting mix of undergraduate and postgraduate teaching in pathology, surgical and autopsy pathology, and research. Her principal research interests revolve around breast and perinatal pathology. She is the immediate past chair of the Board of Education for the Royal College of Pathologists of Australasia. In 2007 Jane received a Carrick Award for Australian University Teaching Excellence.

Brian Detweiler-Bedell is Associate Professor of Psychology at Lewis and Clark College in Portland, Oregon, USA. His principal area of research examines the influence of emotion on social judgement and decision-making. Together with his wife, Jerusha, he directs the Behavioral Health and Social Psychology laboratory, which provides an immersive research experience to over a dozen undergraduate student collaborators each year. Brian received the William Kessen Teaching Award in 2000 for excellence in graduate student teaching at Yale University.

Jerusha Detweiler-Bedell is Associate Professor of Psychology at Lewis and Clark College in Portland, Oregon, USA. Her programme of research brings together investigations of human decision-making, health psychology and clinical psychology, with the goal of promoting health behaviours by understanding better why people fail to do 'what's best' for their physical and mental well-being. She co-directs the Behavioral Health and Social Psychology laboratory, where she conducts research with undergraduate student collaborators. In 2008 Jerusha was named the United States Professor of the Year for Baccalaureate Colleges.

Lisa Emerson is an Associate Professor in the School of English and Media Studies at Massey University in New Zealand with research and teaching interests focused on writing in a tertiary context. She teaches science writing, academic writing and writing centre theory and practice, and has also taught creative writing and life writing. Her research interests include writing in the disciplines, plagiarism, online learning and tertiary teaching. She has published a range of writing handbooks for students (the *Writing Guidelines* series, published by Cengage) as well as many academic articles on teaching and writing. She won the New Zealand Prime Minister's Supreme Award for Tertiary Teaching and Massey University's teaching award for elearning in 2008.

Sally Fincher is Professor of Computing Education in the School of Computing at the University of Kent, where she leads the Computing Education Research Group. Her work is centrally concerned with the teaching and learning of computing, with particular emphasis on teachers and teaching practices. She has worked on several major computing education projects, such as the *Bootstrapping Research in Computer Science Education* series, and currently manages the UK 'sharing practice' project (http://www.sharingpractice.ac.uk). She is Editor-in-Chief of the journal *Computer Science Education* jointly with Laurie Murphy, a National Teaching Fellow, a Senior Fellow of the UK Higher Education Academy and a Fellow of the Royal Society of Arts.

Rhona Free is Vice President of Academic Affairs at Eastern Connecticut State University. From 1983 to 2007 she taught and did research in labour and political economy in the Economics Department at Eastern. She was honoured in 2004 as a Professor of the Year National Winner by the Carnegie Foundation for the Advancement of Teaching and the Council for Advancement and Support of Education. A founding member of the Connecticut Consortium for Learning and Teaching and of Connecticut Campus Compact, a coalition of universities that promote service-learning, Rhona is the editor of Sage Publications' *21st-Century Economics: A Reference Handbook* (2010).

Iain Hay is Professor of Human Geography at Flinders University, South Australia and the Australian Learning and Teaching Council's Discipline Scholar for the Arts, Social Sciences and Humanities. His principal research interests revolve around geographies of domination and oppression. He is author or editor of eight books – several of which have gone into multiple editions. In 2006 Iain was named Australian University Teacher of the Year. He was admitted as a Senior Fellow of the Higher Education Academy in 2008 and as a Fellow of the Australian College of Educators in 2009. He is also President of the Institute of Australian Geographers.

Mick Healey is formerly Professor of Geography and Director of the Centre for Active Learning, University of Gloucestershire, UK. He is now a higher education consultant. He was one of the first people to be awarded a National Teaching Fellowship and a Senior Fellowship of the Higher Education Academy. Mick is known internationally for his work on linking research and teaching, developing the scholarship of teaching and learning, active and inquiry-based learning, and designing an inclusive curriculum. He has twice won the *Journal of Geography in Higher Education* biennial award for the best peer-reviewed paper on geography in higher education.

Welby Ings is Associate Professor in Design at AUT University (Auckland University of Technology). He is an elected Fellow of the British Royal Society of Arts, and holds a PhD in applied narratology. He has been a consultant to many international organizations on issues of creativity and learning. Welby is also an award-winning designer, filmmaker and playwright. His film *Boy* was shortlisted for the 2006 Oscars after winning numerous international awards. He has taught at all levels of the education system and has remained an outspoken critic of dehumanized and fragmented systems of learning. In 2002 he was awarded the New Zealand Prime Minister's inaugural, Supreme Award for Tertiary Teaching Excellence.

David Kahane is Vargo Distinguished Teaching Chair in the Department of Political Science at the University of Alberta. His teaching awards include the 3M Fellowship (Canada's highest award for undergraduate teaching), the Alan Blizzard Award (a yearly national prize for collaborative teaching projects), and the University of Alberta's Award for Excellence in Graduate Supervision, Rutherford Award for Undergraduate Teaching, and Teaching Unit Award. His research focuses on citizen participation, democratic deliberation and social change, and he is especially interested in how models of inclusive, collaborative citizen action can inform what we do in university classrooms and university governance.

Sally Kift is a Professor of Law at Queensland University of Technology (QUT), where she served as Law Faculty Assistant Dean, Teaching and Learning (2001–06) and QUT's foundational Director, First Year Experience (2006–07). She received a National Teaching Award (AAUT) in 2003 and in 2006 was awarded one of three inaugural Australian Learning and Teaching Council (ALTC) Senior Fellowships to investigate first-year curriculum design. In 2007, Sally led a Law Project Team to the award of an ALTC National Program Award for Assessment and Feedback practices. Her research interests include criminal law, legal education, student transition and the first-year experience, and curriculum design to embed and assess graduate attributes.

Dennis Krebs is a Professor of Psychology at Simon Fraser University in British Columbia, Canada. He obtained his PhD from Harvard University, where he taught for several years, and is a Fellow of the Center for Advanced Study in the Behavioral Sciences. He has devoted his career to improving the quality of education and our understanding of altruism and morality, having published more than 90 articles and several books on these and other topics. His latest book, *Origins of Morality: An Evolutionary Framework* is scheduled for publication in 2011. He has won his university's excellence in teaching award and Canada's 3M Teaching Fellowship.

TA Loeffler brings 20 years of expertise leading students through significant life-changing experiences to her teaching. As Professor of Outdoor Recreation at Memorial University of Newfoundland, TA has developed a reputation for excellence in experiential education because her students are more likely to be outside chasing icebergs than sitting in a classroom. In 2008, TA was awarded a prestigious 3M Canada National Teaching Fellowship. In 1999, the Association for Experiential Education named TA the Outstanding Experiential Teacher of the Year. TA has authored numerous articles and books on her research related to outdoor education, hockey, competency and gender.

Ursula Lucas is Professor of Accounting Education at the Bristol Business School, University of the West of England and Senior Fellow of the Higher Education Academy. Her research is concerned with the development of a reflective capacity by students and teachers within degree and professional learning. Ursula serves as Senior Associate Editor for *Accounting Education: An International Journal*. In 2001 she was awarded a Higher Education Funding Council for England (HEFCE) National Teaching Fellowship for excellence in teaching. Further information about her research and activities is available at http://www.uwe.ac.uk/bbs/acad/accfin/lucas.shtml.

Roger Moltzen is a Professor and Deputy Dean of the University of Waikato School of Education. He is widely published in special and inclusive education, and giftedness and talent. His current research focus is on the life stories of eminent adults. Roger is Patron of the New Zealand Association of Gifted Children and co-editor of *APEX: The New Zealand Journal of Gifted Education*. In 2005 Roger was awarded the Prime Minister's Supreme Award for Tertiary Teaching Excellence.

Bernard Moss is Emeritus Professor of Social Work Education and Spirituality at Staffordshire University, UK, where he has been instrumental in developing innovative approaches to learning and teaching in social work. His particular interests include the teaching of communication skills, where he has pioneered the involvement of service users and carers in a skills lab programme for which they received a prestigious UK Community Care Excellence award in 2009. His teaching excellence was recognized by the UK Higher Education Academy in 2004 with a National Teaching Fellowship, and then in 2008 with Senior Fellowship status. www.bernardmoss.org.uk.

Kathleen Regan is Chair of the Foreign Languages department and Professor of Spanish at the University of Portland. Her numerous awards for excellence in teaching include the prestigious Carnegie and CASE Foundation US Professor of the Year for Masters and Comprehensive Universities in 2000. She conducts research in areas including Sephardic culture of Medieval Spain, gender and cross-dressing in the Spanish Comedia, Spanish for business purposes, and Spanish cinema. Recently, Kate's work has included digital film technology and documentary film-making. She has given presentations on using film-making in humanities scholarship, released a short digital video piece on entrepreneurship, and completed two documentaries: *The Sephardic*

Legacy of Segovia, Spain: Pentimento of the Past (2006) and *Fiestaremos: Judy Frankel and the Sephardic Music Tradition* (2008).

Wendy Rogers is Professor of Clinical Ethics at Macquarie University, Australia. She trained in medicine (Flinders University) and general practice (UK) before completing her PhD in medical ethics. Her first academic appointment was to develop ethics, law and professionalism teaching in the Flinders University medical school. Wendy's teaching programme won university and national awards. Simultaneously, she served on the Australian Health Ethics Committee, the Medical Board of South Australia, and as Co-coordinator of the International Network on Feminist Approaches to Bioethics. Her research interests include public health ethics, organ donation, feminist ethics and conflicts of interest in medicine. She has published widely and is the co-author of *Practical Ethics for General Practice* (OUP, 2nd edition 2009).

Peter Schwartz still teaches medical students at Otago Medical School, Dunedin, New Zealand, in the subjects clinical biochemistry and endocrinology even though he supposedly 'retired' several years ago. Originally American, he discovered in medical school that he wasn't cut out to be a practising doctor. During a fellowship in Australia after medical school he got a taste of teaching medical students, igniting a passion that has consumed him since then. His research and publication have been mainly on medical education. He has received numerous teaching awards and he was awarded the Prime Minister's Supreme Award in the New Zealand National Tertiary Teaching Excellence Awards in 2003.

Fred Singer is Professor of Biology at Radford University, Virginia. His research has investigated sex and fighting of small animals such as dragonflies, spiders and zebrafish. His current research investigates thinking and learning in humans of all sizes. He received the Radford University Award for Creative Scholarship in 2000.

Michael Wesch, dubbed 'the explainer' by *Wired* magazine, is a cultural anthropologist exploring the effects of new media on society and culture. After two years studying the implications of writing on a remote indigenous culture in the rain forest of Papua New Guinea, he has turned his attention to the effects of social media and digital technology on global society. His videos on culture, technology, education and information have been viewed by millions, translated into more than 15 languages, and are frequently featured at international film festivals and major academic conferences worldwide. Wesch has won several major awards for his work, including a *Wired* Magazine Rave Award and the John Culkin Award for Outstanding Praxis in Media Ecology, and he was recently named an Emerging Explorer by *National Geographic*. He has also won several teaching awards, including the 2008 CASE/Carnegie US Professor of the Year for Doctoral and Research Universities.

Carl Wieman, recipient of the Nobel Prize in physics in 2001, currently directs the Carl Wieman Science Education Initiative at the University of British Columbia and the Science Education Initiative at the University of Colorado. Prior to joining UBC, he served on the faculty at the University of Colorado from 1984 to 2006 as a distinguished professor of physics and presidential teaching scholar. He is a recipient of the National Science Foundation's Distinguished Teaching Scholar Award (2001), Carnegie Foundation's US University Professor of the Year Award (2004), and the American Association of Physics Teachers' Oersted Medal (2007).

Susan Wurtele is Associate Professor of Geography at Trent University, Peterborough, Ontario, Canada. Her research interests include gendered cultural geographies of agrarian communities of the Canadian prairies in the early twentieth century. She is the recipient of Trent University's Symons Award for Excellence in Teaching (1999), the Ontario Confederation of University Faculty Associations Teaching Award (2005), the national 3M Teaching Fellowship (2006), and the Canadian Association of Geographers Teaching Award (2008). In addition to her research and teaching, Susan has been active with the faculty union as President of the Trent University Faculty Association from 2007 to 2010.

Acknowledgements

I would like to thank Barry Johnston, Keith Thomson, Richard Le Heron, Morgan Thomas, Murray Wilson and Murray McCaskill for long ago having enough faith in me to help open doors to a career about which I could never have dreamed.

Thank you Mark Israel for so generously sharing your enthusiasm, intellect and understanding over the past 15 years! And thank you to my niece, Alyce Hay, who offered such prompt and perceptive comments on my writing.

My remarkable wife, Tania: thank you for everything – for listening, lunches and loving me.

And finally, to the contributors to this volume, thank you very much for your passion for teaching, your commitment to this project, and your forbearance with my editing!

1 Opening doors

Iain Hay

It was 1983. I was a 23-year-old brand new Junior Lecturer at New Zealand's Massey University in the provincial city of Palmerston North. And before me sat a class of about 30 extramural (distance education) students who had taken a week away from work or family to attend a series of intensively delivered classes in a second-year geography subject I'd been asked to teach about four weeks earlier. These students came from all across the country. Probably without exception they were older than me. And they brought to the class a wealth of knowledge gained through diverse personal and professional lives that made my experiences as a student and military officer seem limited. My hands were shaking and my pulse was racing. I had prepared extensive notes. I sat on a high stool behind a high desk and, quite terrified and hesitatingly, read those notes aloud. Compounding my deep-seated and lifelong fear of public speaking was the deeply disconcerting realization that my father – yes, my father – was sitting in the back row of this class watching intently. For the life of me I had no idea why he was there, given that he lives some five hours' drive away and had never expressed any particular interest in coming to my classes. Racking my brain as to why he was there and what he was thinking, I continued to wade through my notes before realizing after about an hour that my 'father' was, in fact, a student who simply bore a quite uncanny resemblance to my dad.

Although I did not realize it immediately, I believe that dreadful experience – for both the students and me – shaped much of my own approach to university teaching. It was apparent first that as someone not naturally inclined to speaking in public I not only needed to improve that kind of 'performance', but more importantly I had to find other ways of communicating that were less destructive to my ego and more constructive of student learning. It also struck me that there might be much greater pedagogic value, not to mention some kind of moral imperative, in finding ways to draw out and build on students' expertise rather than presenting myself as the 'expert'. That latter lesson was compounded over the following five to six years as I moved to the United

States to complete a PhD and then to Australia to take up another academic role. In each case I moved to places of which I had no prior direct experience. My new students were interested in examples drawn from jurisdictions with which I was familiar – but only up to a point. They were more interested in making sense of *their* worlds – not mine. So as a geographer and teacher I made it my long-term job to find ways of doing that.

In the years that followed I stumbled my way through teaching. As was my nature I tried to do the best I could. I went to professional development classes. I learned from student evaluations of my teaching. I never wanted to repeat awful, fearful days like that first one in 1983. Instead I wanted to preserve my own self-worth. I wanted to help students. And I sought ways to teach effectively while maintaining the enduring and deep-seated interests in research and serving scholarly communities that, with teaching, continue to hold me to academia. That commitment to learning-and-teaching took some form in research and a range of publications supporting more 'effective' and 'efficient' teaching (Hay *et al.* 2000, 2006; Hay 2001).

Eventually I was encouraged to prepare exegeses of my teaching and related scholarly work for some major teaching honours. In the process of putting these documents together my attention was forced away from my customary focus on well-organized learning-and-teaching practices and high-quality resources to a new emphasis on opinion and experience. Commenting on one exegesis, a close colleague made some telling remarks. He pointed out that my discussion was somewhat bloodless and encouraged me to try to answer the question, 'What is it really like to be in your class?' As someone with a long-standing interest in qualitative research methods and humanistic approaches to my own discipline (see, for instance, Hay 2010), these observations, coming from a physical scientist, were something of a revelation. His comments led me to rethink my self-analysis dramatically. My statements shifted from rather anodyne accounts of teaching practice to bolder disclosures about my identity and motivations as a university teacher, all structured around a five-part framework identified by Australia's premier university teaching agency as constituting the elements of good practice.

That 'formula' proved personally successful. I received some teaching honours. But I also wondered what others had presented in this process, or might say if similarly prompted? What insights to learning and teaching might this kind of approach offer when taken up and made public by people identified as high-quality teachers? Could I use the approach to find out what thinking and reflection – as well as practices – actually lie behind good teaching? And might I use that approach to find out why great teachers adopt particular strategies and how they reshape themselves to teach better? As I had already discovered in my own career, and perhaps remarkably, teaching remains one of the most privatized of the public professions (Palmer 2007) – despite streaming lectures, www.RateMyProfessors.com, and increasing emphasis on peer review of teaching. Showalter (2003: 9) notes: 'It is not always easy to find out what our colleagues are doing behind . . . closed classroom doors.' Nevertheless, I wanted to 'open the doors' of distinguished colleagues' classrooms, offices and indeed their lives to find out more about the kind of learning that goes on there – by the teachers as well as by students. What has inspired great teachers? And what has made them inspiring?

Although this book talks of practices of great university teaching, one of its key ambitions is to offer reflective insights to such teaching that are not disembodied, dislocated, dehistoricized or dispassionate. For the selfish reason of simple curiosity I wanted to hear directly from people identified as great teachers about matters that have motivated and guided them. And I thought that perhaps a few other people might wish to as well. And so it was that *Inspiring Academics* began.

This book reflects and builds on a groundswell of interest in the scholarship of teaching (see, for example, Carnegie Academy for the Scholarship of Teaching and Learning [CASTL]; *International Journal for the Scholarship of Teaching and Learning*). But, to the best of my knowledge, there is no other book like this. It takes up the methodological challenges of autoethnography and moves away from a common pattern in which academic development volumes typically pursue generalizable insights to specific teaching methods and issues. For this volume I sought to steer contributors away from offering teaching tips. Leaving aside the fact that there are already some tremendous books covering that terrain – landmark volumes like Bain's (2004) *What the Best College Teachers Do*, Boice's (2000) *Advice for New Faculty Members: Nihil Nimus*, or McKeachie and Svinicki's (2005) *McKeachie's Teaching Tips: Strategies, Research and Theory for College and University Teachers* (2010), now in its 13th edition – as well as a plethora of journal articles (e.g. lecturing [Revell and Wainwright 2009]; using clickers in large classes [Patry 2009]; simulation as a participatory learning method [Davidson *et al.* 2009]; linking disciplines, language and academic skills [Wrigglesworth and McKeever 2010]), I wanted to find out from proven great teachers not so much the specific practices or teaching tips they might have to offer, but instead how and why they have taken particular approaches to their teaching. I sought captivating and illuminating personal explorations of the 'how and why' of excellent university teaching.

So, as I noted above, an ambition of this book is to present consciously personal, yet scholarly, insights to good teaching. To this end the book makes use of analytic autoethnography to shed light on high-quality university teaching. Whereas ethnography is situated as a means of making sense of the 'Other', with the researcher's viewpoint being one of detachment and high-level conceptual analysis and abstraction, autoethnography has emerged from postcolonial and postmodern sensibilities to centre 'self-awareness about and reporting of one's own experiences and introspections as a primary data source'

(Patton 2002: 86). According to Liamputtong (2009: 334), the 'aim of auto-ethnography is to tell the story of personal . . . experience as a basis for connecting with others so that the others might reflect on their own experiences'. As such it offers a promising approach to advancing teaching practice for, as Biggs observes in his acclaimed volume, *Teaching for Quality Learning at University*, resolution of teaching challenges 'will not be found in learning a whole new bag of teaching tricks, any one of which may or may not be useful for your particular circumstances, but in reflecting on your teaching problems, and deriving your own ways of handling them within your departmental context' (Biggs 2003: 5).

Hayano's (1979) seminal elaboration of autoethnography established it as the study of the cultures of the ethnographer's own people. Since then, it has been extended to include critical writing about oneself as a researcher-practitioner (Reed-Danahay 1997; Boyd 2008) and has found recent use in a variety of professional fields (e.g. vocational psychology [McIlveen 2008], nursing [Foster *et al.* 2006; Wright 2008]), and educational leadership (Walford 2004). While Butz (2010: 139) points out that 'there is no coherent autoethnographic method', key features of analytic ethnography are understood, in brief, to include: (i) complete member researcher status (i.e. the autoethnographer is a full group member, rather than an 'outside' observer); (ii) analytic reflexivity; (iii) narrative visibility of the researcher's self; (iv) dialogue with informants beyond the self; and (v) commitment to theoretical analysis (Anderson 2006). So while the outputs of other qualitative research methods such as interviews and focus groups offer insights to social worlds that have been filtered, edited and moderated by a researcher, autoethnography offers more direct access to participants' experiences and voices and is apposite when contributors are highly literate.

Where a group of autoethnographies is used simultaneously to illuminate different aspects of a topic or to shed different lights on a subject – as is the case in this volume – novel challenges for the editor are evident. In the case of this book, some of my key roles have been to: provide a clear and coherent framework upon which each contributor's autoethnographic reflections build; focus contributors' deliberations within parts of that framework; and, vitally, encourage and support scholars from backgrounds such as pathology, physics and economics, perhaps unaccustomed to producing the first-person scholarly narrative that is typical of autoethnography (Butz 2010: 142), to take up the autoethnographic challenge. Indeed, several of the authors remarked to me how challenging – and liberating – this form of reflective writing proved to be.

The contributors to this book are great university teachers from Australia, Canada, New Zealand, the United Kingdom and the United States who have been determined by rigorous, independent, national peer- and student-scrutiny to be among the world's best. They include recipients of Australian National Teaching Awards, New Zealand National Tertiary Teaching Excellence

Awards, Canadian 3M National Teaching Fellowships, and Senior Fellowships of the United Kingdom's Higher Education Academy.

Reflecting the distribution of awards – and heightening the book's scholarly significance and practical applicability – contributors come from a wide array of discipline backgrounds. These include: political science, cultural anthropology, pathology, chemical engineering and graphic design. And although there is a tendency for major teaching award winners to have the academic seniority that allows them to demonstrate sustained commitment to high-quality teaching practice, I have tried to ensure that scholars from a range of career stages are included in this volume – from those closer to the beginning of their career than to the end as well as those who can draw on several decades of experience in their reflections.

In 22 pithy chapters authors discuss one of five areas that have been identified by the Australian Learning and Teaching Council (ALTC) as framing high-quality university teaching and learning. This scaffold is one that has been accepted and promoted for over a decade and comprises:

1   Approaches to teaching that influence, motivate and inspire students to learn.
2   Developing curricula and resources that reflect a command of the field.
3   Approaches to assessment and feedback that foster independent learning.
4   Respecting and supporting the development of students as individuals.
5   Scholarly activities that influence and enhance learning and teaching.

While other national bodies identify their own criteria for recognizing high-quality learning-and-teaching (see Box 1.1), the Australian framework offers a succinct, precise and well-tested structure that covers a broad range of teaching activity and engagement. And as one would expect, there is some overlap between the type of considerations it raises and those set out in the other jurisdictions.

It is neither my intention to reflect critically on the relative merits of each of these sets of criteria nor to scrutinize the comprehensiveness or inadequacies of the Australian framework for it is not the intent of this book to uncover or explicate 'determinants' of high-quality teaching (notable work of this type has already been undertaken by scholars such as Bain [2004] and Chickering and Gamson [1987]). Instead, I adopted the five-part framework as a ready, rehearsed and reasonably comprehensive means of structuring reflections on the broad spectrum of teaching activity from contributors across a wide range of discipline areas and from multiple national jurisdictions.

Within each of the book's five parts are four or five chapters in which the authors provide analytic and autobiographical insights to the ways in which

---

Box 1.1   Various international criteria used in the identification and promotion of high-quality university teaching

---

Canada
3M National Teaching Fellowships

- Excellence in teaching over a number of years, principally (but not exclusively) at the undergraduate level
- Commitment to the improvement of university teaching with emphasis on contributions beyond the nominee's discipline or profession

New Zealand/Aotearoa
Ako Aotearoa National Centre for Tertiary Teaching Excellence – Tertiary Teaching Excellence Awards

- Design for learning
- Facilitating learning
- Assessing student learning
- Evaluating learning and teaching
- Professional development and leadership

United Kingdom
Professional Standards Framework for teaching and supporting learning in higher education (used in assessing recognition for Fellowships and Senior Fellowships of the Higher Education Academy)

- Areas of activity
    1   Design and planning of learning activities and/or programmes of study
    2   Teaching and/or supporting student learning
    3   Assessment and giving feedback to learners
    4   Developing effective environments and student support and guidance
    5   Integration of scholarship, research and professional activities with teaching and supporting learning
    6   Evaluation of practice and continuing professional development

- Core knowledge
    Knowledge and understanding of:
    1   The subject material
    2   Appropriate methods for teaching and learning in the subject area and at the level of the academic programme
    3   How students learn, both generally and in the subject
    4   The use of appropriate learning technologies
    5   Methods for evaluating the effectiveness of teaching
    6   The implications of quality assurance and enhancement for professional practice

- Professional values
  1 Respect for individual learners
  2 Commitment to incorporating the process and outcomes of relevant research, scholarship and/or professional practice
  3 Commitment to development of learning communities
  4 Commitment to encouraging participation in higher education, acknowledging diversity and promoting equality of opportunity
  5 Commitment to continuing professional development and evaluation of practice

United States
US Professors of the Year Awards Program – Carnegie Foundation for the Advancement of Teaching; Council for the Advancement and Support of Education

- Impact on and involvement with undergraduate students
- A scholarly approach to teaching and learning
- Contributions to undergraduate education in the institution, community and profession
- Support from colleagues and current and former undergraduate students

they have learned about teaching and how they have brought that learning to life personally and in their classes. Although the book's five parts do build on a clear and explicit framework for high-quality teaching, the focus here is on autobiographically focused chapters illuminated to a greater or lesser degree by scholarly work in the field. I asked each author to tell *their own 'how and why' story* about teaching, informed where appropriate by relevant scholarly work. For instance, what were the personal and professional circumstances that led them to emphasize support for the development of students as individuals? How do they offer that support? Why do they engage in scholarly activities that influence learning and teaching?

By virtue of their autobiographical nature, this book's chapters show considerable diversity in style, emphasis and approach. Mirroring the vast range of practices and characteristics that constitute high-quality teaching, authors recount and reflect on the personal and professional circumstances that have made them award-winning teachers. As McIlveen (2008: 5) observes in a recent discussion of autoethnography, no such account has 'rightful purchase on generalizability' but each will have the 'potential to act as a stimulus for profound understanding of a single case and, moreover, act as a stimulus to open new intellectual vistas for the reader . . .'. It is an ambition of this book not only to 'open the doors' of some of the world's great university classes to scholars and students looking for inspiration and understanding, but importantly to provide unique personal insights to how great university teachers have learned their craft.

Although the chapters are intended to offer a valuable, insightful and – hopefully – inspiring resource for postgraduate students and new academic staff commencing university teaching, many of them are likely to be of broader interest to more senior scholars seeking to revitalize their pedagogic, or perhaps more correctly andragogic (adult education – from Knowles *et al.* 2005) practice and understand how other scholars approach that most significant of all university roles – teaching. While I hope this book might be a useful addition for personal and institutional libraries, more importantly I hope it serves as a distinctive and helpful resource for the growing number of university professional development and tertiary teaching certification initiatives being taken up voluntarily or compulsorily by academic staff (see, for discussion, Karjalainen and Nissilä 2008; Rich 2009).

I think it is worth noting that it is not my intention for any parts of this work or indeed for the book itself to be read as a whole, and anyone doing so will quickly observe the diversity I note above. Instead, I imagine chapters being read independently of one another or in small groups, wherever one's mind chooses to go, for it seems to me that it is often in those haphazard and curiosity-driven ramblings that one finds one's own inspiration. Having said this, and as noted above, the book is divided into five principal parts, each dealing with one dimension associated with high-quality teaching. Part 1 explores the contributors' approaches to teaching that influence, motivate and inspire students to learn. This includes, for example, developing classroom and other learning places that are supportive of learning and teaching, stimulating curiosity, encouraging engagement and learning through enthusiastic teaching, and contributing to the development of students' critical thinking skills, analytical skills and scholarly values.

In Part 2 of the book, contributors discuss curriculum and resources development that reflects a command of their field. That the contributors have a real command of their field is signalled by the inclusion of a chapter by Carl Wieman, winner of the Nobel Prize for Physics in 2001 and 2004 Professor of the Year among all doctoral and research universities in the United States. With Wieman, the distinguished contributors to this part offer their views on matters such as linking research and teaching in productive ways, demonstrating current knowledge of the field in the design of curriculum and learning resources, and incorporating the process and outcomes of scholarly practices into teaching.

Part 3 takes as its focus approaches to assessment and feedback that foster independent learning. Here contributors were asked to think about, for example, assessment methods appropriate to different contexts and diverse student needs and the ways in which they use formative and summative assessment strategies and how these are aligned with learning aims.

For the book's fourth part, I asked authors to set out their thoughts and experiences on respecting and supporting the development of students as individuals. How and why, for instance, do they help students from minority and disadvantaged groups participate successfully in their courses? How do they build students' confidence? And how do they guide and advise students? Although the authors have taken quite different paths, several of the chapters in this part reveal teachers grappling with the relationships or tensions between the needs of individual students and classrooms as communities of learners.

In the book's final part four eminent contributors from disciplinary backgrounds including law, geography and computing offer comment on scholarly activities that shape and support learning and teaching. They were each asked to discuss matters such as how and why teaching and learning methods can usefully be shared with colleagues, how to link scholarship, research and professional activities with teaching, and how networks of colleagues might be usefully developed and influenced.

Before concluding this introductory chapter I would like to acknowledge the tremendous work of each contributor. Several told me that writing their chapter for this book was one of the most difficult yet rewarding academic experiences of their career. Some were initially reluctant and then freed by the opportunity to write autobiographically. In every case, however, the contributors have done an enormous service to me, as editor, by writing thoughtful, introspective and scholarly informed chapters that I truly delighted in reading. I do hope you enjoy reading them as much as I did.

References

Anderson, L. (2006) Analytic autoethnography, *Journal of Contemporary Ethnography*, 35(4): 373–95.

Bain, K. (2004) *What the Best College Teachers Do*. Cambridge, MA: Harvard University Press.

Biggs, J.B. (2003) *Teaching for Quality Learning at University*, 2nd edn. Buckingham: Open University Press.

Boice, R. (2000) *Advice for New Faculty Members: Nihil Nimus*. Needham Heights, MA: Allyn & Bacon.

Boyd, D. (2008) Autoethnography as a tool for transformative learning about white privilege, *Journal of Transformative Education*, 6(3): 212–25.

Butz, D. (2010) Authoethnography as sensibility, in D. DeLyser, S. Herbert, S. Aitken, M. Crang and L. McDowell (eds) *The Sage Handbook of Qualitative Geography*. Los Angeles, CA: Sage Publications.

Chickering, A.W. and Gamson, Z.F. (1987) Seven principles for good practice in undergraduate education, *The American Association for Higher Education Bulletin*, March. http://www.aahea.org/bulletins/articles/sevenprinciples1987.htm, accessed 17 March 2010.

Davidson, J.H., Du Preez, L., Gibb, M.W. and Nel, E.N. (2009) It's in the bag! Using simulation as a participatory learning method to understand poverty, *Journal of Geography in Higher Education*, 33(2): 149–68.

Foster, K., McAllister, M. and O'Brien, L. (2006) Extending the boundaries: auto-ethnography as an emergent method for mental health nursing research, *International Journal of Mental Health Nursing*, 15: 44–53.

Hay, I. (2001) Engaging lessons. Classrooms as sites of engagement in activist critical geography, *International Research in Geographical and Environmental Education*, 19(2): 55–60.

Hay, I. (ed.) (2010) *Qualitative Research Methods in Human Geography*, 3rd edn. Toronto: Oxford University Press.

Hay, I., Foote, K. and Healey, M. (2000) From Cheltenham to Honolulu – the purposes and projects of the International Network for Learning and Teaching (INLT) Geography in Higher Education, *Journal of Geography in Higher Education*, 24(2): 253–9.

Hay, I., Bochner, D. and Dungey, C. (2006) *Making the Grade. A Guide to Successful Communication and Study*, 3rd edn. Melbourne: Oxford University Press.

Hayano, D.M. (1979) Auto-ethnography: paradigms, problems and prospects, *Human Organization*, 38(1): 99–104.

Karjalainen, A. and Nissilä, S-P. (2008) *Towards Compulsory Higher Education Teacher Education in Finnish Universities*. Southampton: Network of European Tertiary Level Educators (NETTLE).

Knowles, M., Holton, E.F. III and Swanson, R.A. (2005) *The Adult Learner: The Definitive Classic in Adult Education and Human Resource Development*, 6th edn. Burlington, MA: Elsevier.

Liamputtong, P. (2009) *Qualitative Research Methods*, 3rd edn. Melbourne: Oxford University Press.

McIlveen, P. (2008) Autoethnography as a method for reflexive research and practice in vocational psychology, *Australian Journal of Career Development*, 17(2): 13–20.

McKeachie, W.J. and Svinicki, M. (2010) *McKeachie's Teaching Tips: Strategies, Research and Theory for College and University Teachers*, 13th edn. Boston, MA: Houghton Mifflin.

Palmer, P. (2007) *The Courage to Teach*, 2nd edn. San Francisco, CA: John Wiley and Sons.

Patry, M. (2009) Clickers in large classes: from student perceptions towards an understanding of best practice, *International Journal for the Scholarship of Teaching and Learning*, 3(2): 1–11.

Patton, M.Q. (2002) *Qualitative Research and Evaluation Methods*, 3rd edn. London: Sage Publications.

Reed-Danahay, D.E. (1997) Introduction, in D.E. Reed-Danahy (ed.), *Auto/Ethnography. Rewriting the Self and the Social*. Oxford: Berg.

Revell, A. and Wainwright, E. (2009) What makes lectures 'unmissable'? Insights into teaching excellence and active learning, *Journal of Geography in Higher Education*, 33(2): 209–24.

Rich, S.M. (2009) 'Teaching is something to rise above': perceptions of science academics in a research intensive university towards teaching and teaching qualifications. http://otl.curtin.edu.au/tlf/tlf2009/refereed/rich.html.

Showalter, E. (2003) *Teaching Literature*. Malden, MA: Blackwell.

Walford, G. (2004) Finding the limits: autoethnography and being an Oxford University Proctor, *Qualitative Research*, 4(3): 403–17.

Wrigglesworth, J. and McKeever, M. (2010) Writing history. A genre-based, inter-disciplinary approach linking disciplines, language and academic skills, *Arts and Humanities in Higher Education*, 9(1): 107–27.

Wright, J. (2008) Searching one's self: the autoethnography of a nurse teacher, *Journal of Research in Nursing*, 13(4): 338–47.

PART 1
Approaches to Teaching that Influence, Motivate and Inspire Students to Learn

For Part 1, contributors were asked to set out their reflections on approaches to teaching that influence, motivate and inspire students to learn. As prompts each author was encouraged to consider, for example, 'how and why' they develop classroom and other learning places that are supportive of learning and teaching, 'how and why' they seek to stimulate curiosity, 'how and why' they encourage engagement and learning through enthusiastic teaching, and 'how and why' they contribute to the development of students' critical thinking skills, analytical skills and scholarly values. The accounts they have offered are as fascinating as they are diverse, together pointing to quite different yet highly effective approaches that range from the highly supple (e.g. Kahane, Wesch) to the more directive (e.g. Dahlstrom and Akerlind, Moss).

In Chapter 2, political scientist David Kahane recalls his personal journey which begins, like that of many others including myself, as a teacher wracked by miserable anxiety, seeking to cover up what he did not know through seamless teaching performances. But he moves from there to a mindful state where groundlessness and uncertainty become the very heart of learning and where his growing ease with *not knowing* provides a basis for authentic and joyful learning – his own and that of his students. It struck me as I read this chapter that in his teaching Kahane had brought to life an idea captured so eloquently in James Boyd White's 1989 book on the rhetoric and poetics of law, *Heracles' Bow*:

> When we discover that we have in this world no earth or rock to stand and walk upon but only shifting sea and sky and wind, the mature response is not to lament the loss of fixity but to learn to sail.
>
> (White 1989: 95)

In the next chapter, Mike Wesch – an e-famous cultural anthropologist – recalls the ways in which his wife and an *American Idol* contestant sparked his own shift from an initial fear of teaching. Rather like Kahane, Wesch draws our attention to a shift from focusing on ourselves and our performance (making an impression) to emphasizing students and their learning (also making an impression – but with quite a different emphasis). He recounts his own move from a near single-minded attention to means of delivering high-quality learning content (Friere's [1970] 'banking method' of education) to a more 'loving' and fruitful focus on what students are actually learning and how. Wesch takes us along his path from teaching a 'subject' to teaching new 'subjectivities' – new ways for students to see and make sense of the world. This approach is also taken up to some extent in Chapter 7 of this volume in Boyd and Singer's discussion of their own passage through Alan Skelton's (2005) models of teaching excellence.

The chapter that follows is written by outdoor education specialist – and mountaineer – TA Loeffler. In the kind of extended metaphor she finds helpful in teaching, she writes of the links she sees between mountains and her teaching philosophy. She takes up the matter of 'mindfulness' that David Kahane introduced in Chapter 2, making the point that teaching or learning – or climbing – without mindful engagement may yield unwelcome consequences. She then goes on to describe some of the specific experiential learning practices (including dropping eggs from campus roofs) she emphasizes in her classes, noting the need for classroom community or security as a form of belay for students (and teachers) taking risks. Loeffler's chapter is something of a bridge in this part of the book, connecting the more philosophical emphases of Kahane and Wesch with the more practically oriented discussions of teaching approaches that are offered in Chapters 5 and 6.

Chapter 5 takes a different form from other chapters in this collection, being set out as the transcript of an interview between pathologist–teacher Jane Dahlstrom and education developer Gerlese Åkerlind, with Gerlese prompting Jane to make explicit the principles of her work and the specific teaching practices she adopts. Of her own approaches, Jane asks Gerlese, as an external observer, 'doesn't everybody do that?', and so reveals an intuitive teaching ability that is in practice informed by a range of sources including scholarly work in the field, repeated thoughtful engagements with other pathology teachers, feedback from students, professional development classes, and interactions with her children.

British social work professor Bernard Moss offers the final chapter in this part. Like Loeffler, he is interested in experiential learning and he provides a detailed account of the ways in which he uses a role play exercise to help social work students understand the role of other professionals alongside their own. His colourful and thoughtfully constructed vision of the teacher is like that of a theatrical director, working behind the scenes – and often unnoticed, perhaps until years later – to lead student/actors to their own interpretations of a profession/role.

References

Freire, P. (1970) *Pedagogy of the Oppressed*. New York: Continuum Publishing Company.

Skelton, A. (2005) *Understanding Teaching Excellence in Higher Education: Towards a Critical Approach*. London: Routledge (Taylor & Francis).

White, J.B. (1989) *Heracles' Bow: Essays on the Rhetoric and Poetics of Law*. Madison, WI: University of Wisconsin Press.

2 Mindfulness and presence in teaching and learning

David Kahane

I was miserably anxious starting out as a teacher. There was an exhilaration in sitting or standing at the front of a classroom, but also deep insecurity about my knowledge and competence. I teetered between a sense of inadequacy and (when convinced that I'd given a seamless lecture or facilitated a great discussion) the surging exhilaration of accomplishment.

I embodied, in other words, a vacillation between senses of worthlessness and worth that constituted my normative world as an undergraduate and graduate student. In this world, education is a hierarchy: you begin as a fundamentally inadequate novice and set about stacking up knowledge, skill and accomplishment in order to deserve the esteem of those who survey and evaluate your performance. And we can become the harshest observers of our own performance, reading this harshness into the reactions of our students, peers and teachers.

My teaching, especially starting out, tended to be about covering up what I didn't know, about coming across as accomplished, about performing seamless knowledge in order to stave off the ever-present spectre of humiliation. I taught from a deep-seated sense of lack, and inadvertently modelled for my students that they could overcome their own lack by learning to perform expertise.

The alternative that I experience more often now is a pedagogy of plenty. My anxiety as a teacher is not gone – this jittery pulse is often with me in the classroom. But I am more able to work with it: to embrace groundlessness and uncertainty as the heart of learning. Instead of modelling academic (and teaching) mastery as an escape from lack, I hope that I invite students to recognize that they are already good enough, that their learning can be a way of more fully experiencing themselves and their fundamental adequacy.

My graduate education started with an MA in Political Theory at McGill University and work as a teaching assistant (TA) in ancient political theory. I read voraciously in primary and secondary texts so as to present material skilfully in my TA-led discussion sections, and I was good at it: highly organized, smart, and willing to put in tens of hours preparation for each meeting. (The fifty or so pages of notes I took on Aristotle's *Nicomachean Ethics* supported me through several years of graduate work on that text.) In retrospect, though, this reduction of skilled teaching to content mastery was both subtly unhappy and subtly unskilful. Subtly unhappy because while part of me enjoyed the stressed frenzy of preparation, the sense of accomplishment in presenting a crisp overview of tough material, and the authority with which I could handle student questions, there was always a panic to this, a sense of papering over gaps in my knowledge, gaps that pointed (some visceral part of me believed) to my fundamental inadequacy at the job. And unskilful because it inducted my students into these psychological dynamics in ways that – I suspect, at least – made learning less engaging and nourishing to them. My approach to teaching focused me on the material, and so turned my appreciation away from the mutuality and intersubjectivity that also were part of the scene of teaching. I offered students useful tools and knowledge, but in forms that may have kept them from fully inhabiting and appreciating their learning.

I went off to the University of Cambridge for my PhD, then spent a year as a sessional instructor at McGill before doing a postdoctoral fellowship at Harvard, with my paltry Canadian-dollar fellowship supplemented by a Lectureship in Social Studies. By this time my research (on citizen engagement and deliberation in multicultural societies) and my interest in progressive pedagogy (Paolo Freire, bell hooks) had me interested in the classroom as a potentially democratic and emancipatory space. I also was increasingly aware of my own anxiety and stress as a teacher, and wanted to be able to facilitate learning more effectively. So I worked at being 'present' as a teacher, and at pedagogies to empower diversely situated students. Harvard was a strange place to be exploring these aspirations. More than anywhere else that I have studied or taught, it feeds the hierarchical mentality of lack and accomplishment. Students are fixated on performing well, and those teaching them also scramble to impress, to cover over weakness and ignorance. Not only is 'presence' as a teacher difficult in this setting – one is always reviewing one's performance, scurrying toward the next thing, riddled with uncertainty – but the aspiration to presence can become one more axis of success or failure. I taught well, I think, and pushed students to take responsibility for their learning. But I modelled a relationship to scholarship and learning that treats knowledge as a place of security, and unknowing as dangerous.

In 1997 I moved from Harvard to my current teaching home, the University of Alberta. The UofA is one of the largest universities in Canada; like virtually all Canadian universities, it is publicly funded. The move to UofA helped me come into my own as a teacher. For one thing, it was a tenure-track job, and job security is itself helpful for relaxing into this vocation. For another, Canadian undergraduate programmes draw their students regionally, without the acute hierarchies built into the United States' university system; perhaps as a result, undergraduates tend to be more open to variety and experimentation in teaching, so long as instructors attend perceptibly to students' learning and enjoyment.

My central teaching assignment during the decade I spent in the Department of Philosophy at UofA was a large, co-taught, first-year course, Introduction to Philosophy: Values and Society. When I arrived in the Department, the course was going poorly, delivered to passive and often disengaged students, by a loose sequence of ten faculty members and sessional instructors, with weekly discussion groups led by under-supported teaching assistants. I took charge of this 250-student course (given its large size, it was known as the 'Supersection') and remade it, focusing on building a truly collaborative team of faculty and TAs genuinely curious about the work of teaching.

Core to this work was breaking down hierarchies of expertise between our TAs (graduate students new to teaching) and more experienced faculty. Too often, teaching is presented to novices in ways that perpetuate the dynamics that I experienced in starting out: many new teachers are desperate for the protective mantle of content expertise, and exhilarated when they can perform this. But even when the performance can be pulled off (remarkably hard for a novice), fixation on content cuts teacher off from students, and models for students that uncertainty and unknowing are dangerous, while security lies in command of content.

A key to disrupting this 'pedagogy of lack' in the Supersection was for experienced faculty in the course to model for TAs genuine curiosity about the nuances of teaching. The course had two 50-minute lectures a week and a third period each week when students broke into ten assigned groups, each led by a TA. TAs were paid to come to lectures, and faculty made use of these eyes on their teaching, sharing uncertainties about pedagogical choices, using regular mini-evaluations to explore undergraduate perspectives on their learning, and seeking feedback from TAs in weekly team meetings; while modelling this inquisitiveness about our own teaching came more easily to some faculty than others, it became easier as a culture of collaboration and trust developed within the teaching team. This inquiry into our teaching and learning as faculty licensed TAs to admit their own uncertainties, and to treat these not as tokens of inexperience but as bases for collective learning. Team meetings became proving grounds for pedagogical experiments undertaken in the lecture hall and in TA-led sections, and TAs brought in their failures as well as successes for discussion. We had, from the beginning, encouraged active learning methods in both the large lecture hall and the TA-led sections; but it was the authenticity of learning about our own teaching that built a culture of inquiry able to animate active learning in these other contexts.

Another effect of the team culture of the Supersection was our ability, as instructors and TAs, to learn to be ourselves in our classrooms. Part of the pedagogy of lack, for teachers and students alike, is a sense that we need to cover over fundamental inadequacy. This is certainly true for many new teachers, who seek safety in a brittle emulation of authoritative knowledge of material. Our team meetings, though, and the honesty they allowed about what we didn't know about our teaching, helped us to gain courage to bring more of our own styles and values into our teaching. We could offer a more authentic curiosity in the classroom, and carve out space for our distinctive ways of being. Whereas clinging to competence can make us boring (a cardboard cutout of the 'good instructor'), facilitating learning processes from a place of curiosity and unknowing is more likely to be engaging and charismatic. My own lecturing to the Supersection became more enjoyable and more genuinely mine as I let go of the need to make it seamless, and was willing to be more honestly, goofily myself.

There is of course a social and political context to this: my experience of teaching is inextricably connected to social authority granted me by virtue of gender, race and career stage. Nor is content mastery irrelevant to good pedagogy, which requires knowledge of course material and is enhanced by scholarly depth. I am stressing presence and downplaying content mastery because the culture of the academy so often skews things in the opposite direction. Each teacher needs to navigate this balance for themselves, including in light of the risks and rewards of particular teaching contexts and power relations. And, indeed, part of collective learning within the Supersection was about how our authority and comfort as teachers was inflected by race, gender, age, accent and more.

After four years in its revamped form, the Supersection won both a university and a national award.[1] And at about this time I began mindfulness practices that helped me to clarify the meaning of 'presence' in teaching. I stumbled into a week-long retreat at the Zen Monastery Practice Center in California and started learning basic mindfulness meditation. I connected deeply with this challenging practice of staying with the present-moment experience of my breath, gently releasing the thoughts and sensations and emotions that relentlessly drew me away. There was a connection between this mindfulness practice and many of the things I had been seeking in my teaching: an ability to be present to the nuances of the classroom in each moment, a sense of fundamental adequacy rather than lack, an open, non-judgemental curiosity about my own experience, and skilled ways of supporting others in this kind of learning. At Harvard, my desire to be more present in my teaching was one more frustrated performance; in the Supersection, we somehow created a space for greater presence without aiming at it; and in meditation, I found a rigorous practice for cultivating presence.

I was so struck by the connection between my experience of Zen and my aspirations in teaching that (in addition to taking up meditation through daily practice and a rhythm of retreats) I looked for literatures and communities that explored links between mindfulness, meditation and teaching. A number of

Google searches later, I found the Center for the Contemplative Mind in Society,[2] a US-based organization that ran a summer session for post-secondary educators using meditation in courses ranging from philosophy to physics. I attended three summer sessions, sustained by the values of this community and inspired by its diverse experiments in teaching. These summer sessions gave me the confidence and skills to bring meditation overtly into my own classrooms. Let me provide just a glimpse of the form that this has taken.

I taught three iterations of a third-year course on Obligation, Compassion and Global Justice, where we studied texts from ethics and political philosophy on obligations to strangers while also undertaking contemplative inquiry into our relationship to our own and others' suffering and how this shapes our motivation to help.[3] Each class began with about eight minutes of mindfulness or 'shamatha' meditation: sitting straight in our chairs and training ourselves to stay with our breath, compassionately noticing when our minds got caught up in thoughts and gently coming back. This meditation had a number of effects. First, it brought all of us into the room together: we could calm down, drop the preoccupations we carried in, and focus on the conversations to follow. Second, meditation honed our abilities to actually notice our own experience: it laid the groundwork for articulating our own experience as part of our subject matter. Third, it attached a rigour to how first-person experience entered the course: rather than simply rehashing habitual stories of who we were, we could look and see in new ways. And fourth, it showed how each of us had a plenitude of experience and knowledge relevant to the course: while there were difficult materials and skills to learn over the term, none of us was operating from a place of lack.

I am now piloting another contemplative course, on Mindfulness, Activism, and Citizenship for Democracy. This course, too, stages a dialectic between 'third-person' texts (on deliberative democracy and mindful social activism) and 'first-person' inquiry based on meditative and contemplative practices. There also is a community service learning (CSL) component: each student spends 20 hours working with a dialogue convening or frontline service organization as a counterpoint to classroom dialogues, contemplative techniques, reading and journal writing. A key role of these CSL placements is to provide a context for students to explore their ability to remain present in the face of complexity and difficulty, and to notice what shifts when they can sustain this mindfulness.

Students are energized and inspired by these highly participatory, contemplative courses. The methods and subject matters of the courses speak to students' search for meaning in their lives and educations: they explore themes that matter in an unusually deep way, and share this exploration with fellow students in a context of calm and trust. I have learned several things in teaching these courses. First, while students gain a lot through regularly practising meditation in class, my ability to model and embody mindfulness and compassion is nearly as important. The classroom 'presence' that has preoccupied me through my teaching career is crucial. Second, my ability and that of my students to cultivate presence are mutually reinforcing: practising as a class dramatically increases our individual capacities for mindfulness. Third, meditation encourages acceptance of whatever thoughts, emotions and mental states arise: we notice them and return to the breath. This meditative orientation provides a grounded basis for dealing with strong emotions and energies that arise for each of us in the classroom, including my own anxiety as a teacher. Rather than experiencing this as debilitating, a meditative orientation allows me to recognize the powerful energies underlying 'anxiety' and to channel these into my teaching.

As I have found new ways to bring mindfulness and presence into my teaching, I have deepened my understanding and love for this vocation. I have started to glimpse, with my students, how increasing our ease with not knowing provides a foundation for our most authentic and joyful learning.

Notes

1 The University of Alberta's *Teaching Unit Award* and the Society for Teaching and Learning in Higher Education's *Alan Blizzard Award for Collaborative Projects that Improve Student Learning.*
2 Details of this Center are available at http://www.contemplativemind.org.
3 For more detail see Kahane, D. (2009).

Reference

Kahane, D. (2009) Learning about obligation, compassion and global justice: the place of contemplative pedagogy. *New Directions for Teaching and Learning: Special Issue on Internationalizing the Curriculum in Higher Education.* San Francisco, CA: Jossey-Bass.

3 The art of loving and learning: Erich Fromm and the learning (of) transformation

Michael Wesch

About three years ago I quickly became e-famous for my efforts and experiments with new media and education. A video I produced in my basement in a little farmhouse in Kansas called *The Machine is Us/ing Us* went viral with millions of views on YouTube. Soon after that I worked with 200 students in my Introduction to Cultural Anthropology class at Kansas State University to produce *A Vision of Students Today*, another multi-million viewer viral video hit. In all, videos I have produced on the subjects of technology, culture and education have been viewed over 16 million times, translated into more the 15 languages, and are frequently featured in conferences and film festivals worldwide. As a result, I receive hundreds of requests from all over the world to speak on the uses and implications of new technologies in education. For those of you who hate or fear the idea of technology in the classroom, I am probably 'that guy' that you hate more than anything. I'm 'that guy' that gets invited to your campus to inspire (or 'dupe') your fellow faculty members to use increasingly complex ('distracting') technologies in the classroom or even suggest we rethink or annihilate the classroom altogether ('ugh'). If you are the one sighing just at the thought of my overly enthusiastic techno-babble, then truth be told I probably have more in common with you than with the techno-optimists cheering my every word. I don't travel the world hoping to unveil the latest cure-all save-the-education-of-our-children technology. Of course, I do think that technology can play an important role in education, but my real hope is to open up a conversation about what I consider to be the real secret of great teaching, a force more powerful and disruptive than any technology: love.

My first insight into the transformative possibilities of love came while I was buried and blinded by the fear and anxiety of preparing for my first lecture in front of 400 students and the entire anthropology programme faculty at Kansas State University. This was their idea of a campus interview. Each of the three finalists for the job was invited to give a presentation to the Introduction to Cultural Anthropology class. We were offered 50 minutes to wow the faculty and students and show that we could be effective and engaging teachers.

The winner would be awarded a dream job: a tenure track position at a university that distinguished US newscaster Paul Harvey once fondly called 'the Harvard of the Plains', set in an idyllic small community nestled in the beautiful Flint Hills of Kansas. I was preparing for the performance of a lifetime, the success of which the rest of my life would depend upon, and I was completely frozen in fear.

This is when my wife saved me with an insightful story from a most unlikely source: *American Idol*. Diana Degarmo, a young 16-year-old contestant, was struggling in the singing competition, narrowly escaping elimination in three of the first five weeks. She was clearly very talented, but seemed timid, anxious and self-conscious on stage. At times it was hard to watch her as she awkwardly walked the stage, struggling meekly to find the right pitch. Then, suddenly, everything changed. One week after barely escaping elimination she came out and wowed the judges and the fans. Almost overnight she became a front runner, dazzling fans week after week for the next seven weeks, making it all the way to the finals where she was narrowly defeated by long-time favourite Fantasia Barrino. When asked for the secret of her turnaround success, she offered the sage advice she had received from her hairdresser at that critical moment: 'Love your audience, and your audience will love you back.'

That advice echoes the words of Erich Fromm, as he writes, 'Love is a power which produces love' (1956: 21). Fromm's text is an insightful and scathing critique of the rather superficial modern approach to love which focuses on surfaces, objects and beauty. For Fromm, love is not a feeling, something you 'fall into' or something that comes to you. It is an art, an ability or faculty that one must practise and develop over time.

The story of Diana Degarmo immediately put me at ease, lifted my spirit, and allowed me to see beyond my own egocentric, self-absorbed obsession with my performance. In the words of Fromm, I shifted from a focus on 'being loved' to 'the art of loving'. I became less concerned with the impression I made, and more concerned with creating a great learning experience for everybody in the room.

In simple terms, the idea of loving your audience is a simple shift of focus from yourself and your performance to your students and their learning, but while this may seem like a minor shift, putting these ideas into practice has slowly and completely transformed my teaching. It has changed what I teach, how I teach, and even why I teach. It has me asking what, how and why in new ways, and asking other questions I would have never considered as well.

First it changed what I teach. Like most teachers just starting out, I considered the question of 'what' to teach to be the most important of all. I spent the entire summer before my first semester carefully crafting my syllabus, making sure all of the major topics of the subject were covered thoroughly. I was starting from the assumption that my primary role was to deliver high-quality core content to my students. This assumption is hard to avoid. It is literally written into the walls of the rooms in which we most typically teach large classes such as the one I was teaching. Chairs are fixed, facing the front of the room where the professor takes the stage, often armed with some 786,432 points of light with which to deliver this valuable information. The assumption that teaching is the simple delivery of information carries with it a rather thin philosophy and definition of learning: to learn is simply to acquire information (which Paolo Freire (1970) describes as the 'banking method' of education). The job of the professor is to make sure the information is complete and of high quality, hence my careful attention to the construction of my syllabus.

But loving my students, focusing on them rather than my performance, opened me up to look beyond the content to see what my students were actually learning. I discovered that while they were doing a marvellous job of memorizing my carefully constructed content, they were only rarely making broader connections or asking the types of questions that would take them further into the field. I realized that most of them would soon forget much of what they were memorizing for my tests. But more disheartening than what they were *not* learning was what they *were* learning: that learning is to acquire information, that information is best received from an authoritative source, and that such information is objectively true and therefore beyond dispute and discussion. Most disheartening is that students come to equate such methods as 'real learning' and fail to see that they are often practising much more sophisticated and effective methods of informal learning outside the classroom.

Such an approach to learning is of the lowest sort. Belenky *et al.* (1986) describe four general categories of learning. Those who learn with the assumptions outlined above, approaching learning as if there is an objective truth to be learned which is best learned through an expert, are called 'received knowers'. Eventually, students might rebel against this notion and go to the opposite extreme, believing that there is no truth and that all we have are opinions. They call these students 'subjective knowers'. The subjective approach is a necessary transition to a more complete and active form of learning that they call 'procedural', in which the learner has learned the procedures of the discipline for determining validity and relevance. When the learner begins integrating these procedures into their everyday life, they reach become 'constructed knowers'. Constructed knowers recognize 'that their frame of reference matters and . . . they feel responsible for examining, questioning, and developing the systems that they will use for constructing knowledge' (1986: 139).

After explaining these different approaches to learning to 200 students during the first week of the semester in my Introduction to Cultural Anthropology class, I conducted a survey and found that over 85 per cent of the students reported that they were mostly 'received' learners. Of the remainder, most were 'subjective' learners while only a handful of students reported adhering to procedural or committed approaches to learning.

I began to fear that my focus on content was only reinforcing the 'received' approach to learning. Furthermore, when I looked carefully at my content I realized that my true goal all along had not been for my students to memorize this content, but to fully adopt and understand the perspectives and procedures that led to the discoveries that make up that content. Instead of teaching a 'subject' as a certain body of content, I realized that what I was really hoping to teach was a 'subjectivity' – a new way for them to see, understand and make connections in the world.

Here is the core challenge though: new subjectivities cannot be directly imparted to the student. Adopting a new subjectivity requires an intellectual throw-down in the minds of our students, who must wrestle with their previously taken-for-granted assumptions, perspectives and beliefs. Taking on a new subjectivity is to transform one's self, and it is arguably the most profound and important form of learning. It is what Thomas Szasz was referring to when he noted that 'every act of conscious learning requires a willingness to suffer an injury to one's self-esteem' (1974: 18).

And so loving my students led me not only to question what I was teaching, but also *how* I was teaching. If I was to inspire my students to take on the trials and tribulations of self-transformation, it would not happen through lecturing alone, no matter how good the content.

Instead of content becoming the centre of the course, I started to organize the course around real and relevant problems in the world, the answers to which I myself did not even know. In my anthropology course, a class about 'all people in all times in all places', I work with my students to brainstorm the major challenges now facing our world and work with them to find out how the world came to be this way. With trust and respect for my students, I join them on the quest for answers, becoming a learner right alongside them. Technology can be useful here, as we use wikis, social bookmarking and other tools to collaborate outside the classroom. But more important than the technology is that we became what Parker Palmer calls 'a community of truth'. In Palmer's words, 'the community of truth, far from being linear and static and hierarchical, is circular, interactive, and dynamic' (2007: 1. 1344). In this community, I was no longer the arbiter and source of objective truth. If a truth was to be found, we would be finding and questioning it together on our quest for answers to problems that truly matter to us and to the world.

As Palmer notes, there are many forms of the community of truth; some of them even revolve around what appears to be the traditional lecture format. What sets the community of truth apart is openness to the world, to each other, and to difference. In other words, regardless of the specific stylistic tactics, the foundation of the community of truth, like all communities, is love – not love as a feeling – but love as an act and an art to be continually practised.

Erich Fromm (1956) outlines four basic elements to the art of love, each of which is essential to inspiring and participating in a community of truth. The most obvious element is the one that many people mistake for love itself: caring and concern. But simply caring is not enough. We must also take responsibility, not in the sense of a duty 'imposed on one from the outside' but responsibility in what Fromm (1956: 23) calls its 'true sense . . . an entirely voluntary act; it is my response to the needs of others. The loving person responds.' But if we rely on caring and responding alone we create a coddling infantile relationship that disempowers students and makes them dependent on us. To counter this we must also engage in Fromm's (1956: 23) third component of love: respect. 'Respect is not fear or awe', he notes. 'It denotes the ability to see a person as he/she is, to be aware of the unique individuality.' This immediately calls forth Fromm's (1956: 24) final component, knowledge. Knowledge, in the context of care, responsibility and respect is not simply knowing everything about the person as an object, but 'penetrates to the core . . . It is possible only when I transcend the concern for myself and see the other person in his own terms'.

Embarking on such a deep quest and guiding a community of learners takes more time and energy than any lecture course. You are giving of your life and spirit, but it gives back many times over. As Fromm so eloquently puts it, 'In thus giving of his life, he enriches the other person, he enhances the other's sense of aliveness by enhancing his own sense of aliveness. In giving he cannot help bringing something to life in the other person, and this which is brought to life reflects back to him and they both share in the joy of what they have brought to life' (1956: 20).

Neil Postman and Charles Weingartner (1969) have argued insightfully that we too often ask *what* to teach before *how* we will teach and we almost never ask *why* we teach at all. They suggest that we have it upside down, that we should first ask why, then how, and let the what build naturally from there. Approaching the art of learning through the art of loving forces us to take on yet another question first put into words for me by Parker Palmer (2007): the question of *who*. Who are my students? Who are they struggling to become? Who am I? Who am I struggling to become? How can we connect and collaborate in such a way as to co-create a learning environment that will help us all grow and unfold in our own unique way?

Learning through loving puts the questions of who we are and who we might become squarely at the centre and deepens our notions of learning beyond simple information-gathering, even beyond simple cognitive models, forcing us to consider the whole person and our development. We begin to realize that cognitive development does not happen in the absence of attendant physical, moral, emotional and spiritual developments. And because such developments are transformational of the self, it becomes especially important that we continually practise all aspects of love – caring, responsibility, respect and knowledge – to create an effective learning environment.

The final transformation of my teaching that has come from opening up to love was the realization that love itself has been the ultimate goal all along.

Care, responsibility, respect and knowledge are not only the foundations of love, they are also the foundations and goals of learning, and are themselves the most important things to learn. Through practising care, responsibility, respect and knowledge we open ourselves up to the world and to each other and to otherness itself, to make connections across our differences. That's what learning is – not simple information gathering, but opening up to something other and connecting with it. To learn to love is to learn to learn.

It is this, and not technology, that I see as the truly disruptive innovation occurring in classrooms all over the world. Technology itself often acts as nothing more than a magnifier of our pedagogical assumptions. For over ten years, university teachers have had access to LCD projectors that give them 786,432 points of light on giant screens connected to the internet. The possibilities for the use of such machines are endless, yet they have overwhelmingly been used for little else but PowerPoint presentations that reinforce authoritative pedagogical models and support received knowers. Only by working to create communities of truth around the art of loving do we begin to truly unleash the possibilities of new technologies such as those known widely as social media or 'Web 2.0'. Such technologies are welcome, but not necessary. What matters is that we do not mistakenly equate learning with simple information gathering, and start recognizing both learning and loving as skills, faculties or capacities that we must continually practise, nurture and grow.

References

Belenky, M., Clinchy, B., Goldberger, N. and Tarule, J. (1986) The ways of knowing, in P. Jarvis (ed.) *Adult and Continuing Education: Major Themes in Education*. New York: Routledge.

Freire, P. (1970) *Pedagogy of the Oppressed*. New York: Continuum Publishing Company.

Fromm, E. (1956) *The Art of Loving*. New York: Bantam.

Palmer, P. (2007) *The Courage to Teach. Exploring the Inner Landscape of a Teacher's Life (Kindle edition)*. San Francisco, CA: Jossey-Bass.

Postman, N. and Weingartner, C. (1969) *Teaching as a Subversive Activity*. New York: Delta.

Szasz, T. (1974) *The Second Sin*. New York: Routledge.

4 I teach as the mountains teach me

TA Loeffler

Mountains are my teachers

Metaphors are how I make sense of the world and how I communicate that understanding to others. I also teach using metaphors (Gass 1995; Luckner and Nadler 1997). In recent years, I have been on an intense journey seeking the summits of some of the world's highest peaks. As a result, mountains have become my teachers and they exact deep lessons. In 2006, I climbed Cerro Aconcagua, the highest peak in the Western Hemisphere. Its name means 'Stone Sentinel', signifying its high position over the Andes. In reflecting on that experience, I wrote these words in my blog (Loeffler 2007):

> Hardship. That's life at extreme altitude. Vision. Views from high places. Stark understanding. Rising above. Seeing nothing higher. Seeing in new ways. This is what makes the hardship both bearable and worth it. Seeing and then coming down having seen. Pushing through. Giving up comfort. Working with my mind. Finding small pockets of fun and absurdity and laughter and connection. Seeing the morning light dance circles. Watching the evening sun drain from the hills. Sinking into a rich rhythm of physical exertion and mental stamina. Learning the lessons that come from days and days of outdoor living, the whispers of the stars, and the drone of the wind.

I teach my students like the mountains teach me. With vision. With struggle. Asking them to reach up and out and to reach for an unknown sky. To learn while filled with uncertainty and sometimes with joy and mirth. I ask for mindful engagement always – to climb or teach or learn without focus leads to unwelcome consequences.

Mountains are both solid and moving. They are steady, wise and seemingly unyielding while at the same time they are changing through erosion and time. As a teacher, I seek to provide a solid presence for my students. I am reliable, accessible, and my students come to know they can depend on me both inside and outside the classroom. I also move and change. I reflect on my life experiences and bring change to who and how I am which, in turn, shifts how I teach. I teach differently over time and season, trying continually to improve my ability to facilitate student learning.

Mountains are both demanding and compassionate. The obstacles to their lofty peaks are many and danger lurks for even the most prepared mountaineer. Amid the perils, however, shelter, beauty and meaning can be found. I am a demanding teacher. I have and communicate high expectations for my students. I want them to work hard, engage deeply and explore new ground. This level of expectation can feel dangerous to students as I ask them to learn in ways less familiar to them. I frame courses as journeys of learning and provide opportunities and activities that encourage the development of community within the class (Palmer 2007). I strive to create an atmosphere of kindness, compassion and understanding that provides a belay. This foundation of care and respect offers a safety line, allowing students to take greater emotional and intellectual risks.

Mountains are both journey and destination. They summon us to climb their slopes, explore their canyons and attempt their summits. The summit, despite months of preparation and toil, is never guaranteed though tastes of sweet nectar when reached. If my only goal as a teacher and mountaineer is the summit, I risk cruel failure if I do not reach the highest apex. Instead, if I accept the mountain's invitation to journey and create meaning in each step, success is manifest in every moment. As a teacher, I seek to balance 'the view' and 'the footsteps'. Without the view, my students and I are lost. Without the footsteps, we don't move from where we began. I create a flow in my teaching that seeks the summit, the learning objectives for each course, and that honours the journey, the experiences and the learning along the way to it.

Mountains are both mirror and void. The brilliant white flanks reflect the blazing sun, magnifying its power to illuminate. The dark recesses of crevasses absorb sound and light, leaving a quiet potential space. As a teacher, I offer students the paradoxes of light and dark, of reflection and absorption, of heights and depths. I offer my entire self by sharing my life process in my blog (Loeffler 2009). I allow students to see me as fully human, fully fallible, fully engaged. I actively facilitate reflective processing of experience in my classes. I hold up a metaphorical mirror that allows students to glimpse themselves in new or different ways. I also become a sounding board who can listen and absorb their pain, confusion or loss.

Richard Bach (1977), in *Illusions*, said, 'I teach best what I most need to learn.' It was a sentence that stopped me cold when I first read it as a 20-year-old undergraduate and has been my constant companion throughout my teaching career. In recent years, mountains have taught me so much and so, in turn, I seek to teach like the mountain, sharing both the high summits and deep valleys with students in my classroom.

Bringing mountains to class

In the previous section, I described my teaching philosophy using the metaphor of a mountain. I used images and experience of mountaineering to signify both the individual parts of my philosophy and how they come together to form an integrative whole. This section demonstrates how I put my philosophy into practice through the description of some of my teaching strategies. I put my foundational beliefs about teaching and learning into practice by creating an experiential, supportive and contextual framework for students' learning (Martin *et al.* 2004).

I integrate active learning experiences into every course I teach. Often these experiences require group problem solving and sometimes they involve moving off campus for a field trip. I offer field trips to local sites to provide a real-world context and structure for what the students are learning (Millan 1995). Each field trip requires students to hike around the site and apply course concepts to what they are observing. Through discussion and worksheets, I lead students in a Socratic discovery of how what they are seeing and experiencing relates to the theories we cover in the classroom. Additionally, the field trips provide the class with many opportunities for informal socializing, cooperation and physical challenge – all of which contribute to the development of a robust learning community (McKiernan 1995).

I have a love of high places. One summer, I was almost arrested by Campus Enforcement and Patrol. I was poised on the edge of the roof of the Physical Education building when a campus patrol officer passed by. He peered up, startled, noted that I was not wearing proper safety equipment, and insisted that I come down from my high perch.

> 'But I have only three more eggs to drop', I protested. He insisted on my descent a little more forcefully and I climbed back through the window.
>
> 'Just what were you doing on the roof?' he asked with a perplexed look on his face.
>
> 'I was teaching a problem-solving model to my HKR 3555 Outdoor Recreation Management Class', I answered confidently. He turned and strode back to his patrol car.

I know what you are thinking: 'What do eggs, roofs, mountains and problem solving have in common?' I will explain.

As an experiential educator, having students learn through direct experience is an essential component of my teaching philosophy (Warren *et al.* 2008). I try to incorporate experiential learning into every class I teach. John Dewey (1938: 79), considered by many to be the father of experiential education, declared. 'Growth depends on the presence of a difficulty to be overcome by the exercise of intelligence.' This difficulty can be physical, emotional, social, intellectual or a combination of all. I am constantly creating such difficulties for my students to surmount.

I use whole-class problem-solving experiences, case studies, real-life narratives, skill challenges and large-scale projects to challenge and impel my students to grow (Beard and Wilson 2006). The subject matter of any class must never be divorced from the context in which it occurs. The big picture is important. My classroom is a place for both safety and challenge. Racism, classism, ableism, heterosexism and other oppressions have no place in my classroom. I provide opportunities for all students to participate in class in whatever way they are able. I challenge students to critically examine the world and their many roles in it.

Back to the eggs and the roof. I use this activity, what I call the 'egg drop', to bring an outdoor recreation management problem-solving model to life. The activity allows students to solve a complex problem and receive almost instantaneous feedback. I start the class with a brief introduction to the model of problem solving that I want the students to learn. Then, I divide the class into small groups and introduce them to their experiential task. Using only 25 plastic straws and 3 metres of masking tape, they must protect the egg from breaking when it falls 3 metres (about ten feet) onto concrete; a task that initially appears impossible and that requires considerable problem-solving skills.

I put the problem-solving model on the overhead projector and ask that the groups follow it step by step and document what they do every step of the way. I often frame the limited resources available for solving the problem as indicative of most management situations today – having to do too much with too little. I give them a time limit and they eagerly begin to work. As the end of the allotted time nears, the groups work frantically to complete their designs. The students are actively engaged and entirely on-task during the entire experience – there is an air of intense concentration in the room.

In order to make the egg dropping a big event, I usually draw a large target on the ground and find a high place from which to let go the eggs. I create a high-energy environment including drum rolls and cheers to enliven the drop zone. Students wait with anticipation for immediate feedback about the effectiveness of their egg-protection design. Cheers of success or groans of disappointment erupt as each egg hits the pavement. Most often, successful designs are dropped from higher and higher heights until all eggs have been cracked. We then clean up and head back to the classroom to debrief and reflect on the experience.

Jernstedt (1980) studied active learning in the university environment and found that students who used information they were trying to learn to solve problems tended to learn more effectively than students who passively read, memorized or absorbed the material. I find a similar pattern in my classroom every spring semester. Of all the questions on the HKR 3555 final examination, students always write excellent answers to the question related to problem solving. Performance on topics that I cover using only traditional teaching methods is not nearly as strong.

Reflection is a critical component of the experiential learning cycle but is sometimes left out or short changed because of a lack of time. To help students reflect on the egg drop experience, I often use the 'what' model. I start by asking the students, 'What just happened?' This starts the discussion on a very concrete level and leads easily to student involvement in the dialogue. Following this, the next question I ask is, 'So what?' This question moves the discussion to a more abstract level and requires that the students generalize and evaluate the learning that occurred during the experience. Finally, the last question I ask is, 'Now what?' This question leads to an application of the experiential learning to the next 'difficulty' to be encountered and also transfers the experience back to the curricular or theoretical component of the class (Carver 2008).

As reflection is an integral part of the experiential learning cycle (Kolb 1984), I continually ask the students to reflect on their learning throughout each class, course and semester. Using their comments as a foundation, I, too, engage in a reflective process where I evaluate both the effectiveness of my teaching and the effectiveness of the course structure and delivery. At the end of each class, I sit quietly and take myself through the 'Three Ws' (What, So What, Now What) as well. Sometimes I undertake this reflection within my mind, sometimes in writing, and sometimes with colleagues over coffee.

At the completion of each course, I write 'Notes to Myself' to formally hold the reflective mirror up to my teaching. Notes captures my thoughts and feelings about a course offering and inform my planning for the next time I teach the course. I assess which parts of the course I hope to replicate, which parts I would like to let go, and which parts of the learning experience moved the students to greater heights of understanding. Ideally, through this reflective process, I improve both my teaching effectiveness and the students' learning because each course I teach results in a different landscape and topography that develops from the shared interactions and experiences within our learning community (Palmer 2007).

Finally, I believe it is important for me to place myself in the student role frequently for several reasons. By being a lifelong learner, I am continuously having new experiences that enrich the examples I am able to give in class. I am learning and staying fresh. I can observe the teaching styles of others and integrate what works well into my classroom. I can notice the influence and power of the teacher's role and remember how it feels to be under that power (Tyson and Asmus 2008). I can feel scared and nervous as I push myself close to and over my perceived limits. I can stretch in the ways that I ask my students to stretch. Teaching and learning are points on the same continuum and I believe it is critical to move along all points of this continuum. With this in mind, it is time to close this chapter, head outside, and seek the learning of the hills as described by Peter Severinus in 1571 (cited in Sheppard 2009):

> Go my children, burn your books,
> Buy yourselves stout shoes.
> Get away to the mountains, the deserts
> And the deepest recesses of the earth.
> In this way and no other will you gain
> A true knowledge of things and
> Of their properties.

References

Bach, R. (1977) *Illusions: Adventures of a Reluctant Messiah*. New York: Dell Publishing.

Beard, C. and Wilson, J. (2006) *Experiential learning: a best practice handbook for educators and trainers*. http://qe2aproxy.mun.ca/login?url=http://site.ebrary.com/lib/memorial/Doc?id=10137816, accessed 29 June 2009.

Carver, R. (2008) Theory for practice: a framework for thinking about experiential education, in K. Warren, D. Mitten and TA Loeffler (eds) *Theory and Practice of Experiential Education*. Boulder, CO: Association of Experiential Education.

Dewey, J. (1938) *Experience and Education*. New York: Macmillan.

Gass, M. (1995) *Book of Metaphors: Volume 2*. Dubuque, IA: Kendall Hunt Publishing.

Jernstedt, G.C. (1980) Experiential components in academic courses, *Journal of Experiential Education*, 3(2): 9–11.

Kolb, D. (1984) *Experiential Learning: Experience as the Source of Learning and Development*. Englewood Cliffs, NJ: Prentice-Hall.

Loeffler, TA (2007) *Happy New Year*, 4 January 2007. TA Loeffler: Blog. http://www.taloeffler.com/aconcagua/accountentries.asp#1/4/2007, accessed 30 June 2009.

Loeffler, TA (2009) *Big Blue Birthday*, 27 June 2009. TA Loeffler: Blog. http://www.taloeffler.com/newHeights/journalentries.asp#6/27/2009, accessed 30 June 2009.

Luckner, J. and Nadler, R. (1997) *Processing the Experience: Strategies to Enhance and Generalize Learning*. Dubuque, IA: Kendall Hunt Publishing.

McKiernan, R. (1995) The influence of expeditionary learning in Outward Bound and college, in B. Horwood (ed.) *Experience and the Curriculum*. Dubuque, IA: Kendall Hunt Publishing.

Martin, A., Franc, D. and Zounkova, D. (2004) *Outdoor and Experiential Learning: An Holistic and Creative Approach to Programme Design*. Aldershot: Gower Publishing Limited.

Millan, D. A. (1995) Field trips: maximizing the experience, in B. Horwood (ed.) *Experience and the Curriculum*. Dubuque, IA: Kendall Hunt Publishing.

Palmer, P. J. (2007) *The Courage to Teach: Exploring the Inner Landscape of a Teacher's Life – 10th Anniversary Edition*. San Francisco, CA: Jossey-Bass.

Sheppard, P. (2009) Sense of place course outline. http://www.ltrr.arizona.edu/~sheppard/sop/, accessed 30 June 2009.

Tyson, L. and Asmus, K. (2008) Deepening the paradigm of choice and power in experiential education, in K. Warren, D. Mitten and TA Loeffler (eds) *Theory and Practice of Experiential Education*. (pp. 262–81). Boulder, CO: Association of Experiential Education.

Warren, K., Mitten, D. and Loeffler, TA (eds) (2008) *Theory and Practice of Experiential Education*. Boulder, CO: Association of Experiential Education.

5 The what, why and how of inspiring learning

Jane Dahlstrom and Gerlese Åkerlind

Introduction

Being an inspiring teacher and being able to articulate what it is that makes one inspiring do not necessarily go hand in hand. In this chapter, Jane (an award winning teacher) articulates her practice and some educational principles underlying that practice to Gerlese (an education developer who helped her prepare her award application) with the aim of providing some practical insights for postgraduate students and teachers.

Inspiring students to want to learn more

Gerlese: You've been asked in this book to address approaches that influence, motivate and inspire students to learn. So, I was wondering which of those terms has greatest resonance for you?

Jane: I think inspiring students. My own experience as a student showed me I learnt best when my teacher was enthusiastic and was able to teach in such a way that it really inspired me to want to learn more. So, I think my own experience as a student coloured what I thought I would like to do as a teacher, which is to encourage students to want to learn more and really devour my passion, which is 'pathology'.

Gerlese: I like the word 'devour'. It creates a sense of hunger. How does this relate to inspiring students?

Jane: Well, like hunger, knowledge is a strong desire. By bringing knowledge to life, I want to make my students hungry to learn. If a student can understand the basic concepts of pathology it gives them a really good base from which they can then launch other learning and understand medicine better. If students don't engage with the topic, if it doesn't come to life for them, they will be left with huge gaps in their learning as they progress through medical school to become doctors.

Gerlese: So, how do you go about inspiring students to learn?

Jane: My experience shows that students learn in different ways. So, I need to *mix up the kind of modalities* in which students learn. The mix includes straightforward lectures, with or without PowerPoint slides, small group tutorials in a question-and-answer format with specimens and models, larger group sessions with microscopes and laminated images, clinical scenarios and computer-assisted learning. This way I *produce a variety of tools from which students can learn*, hoping that those who are better at visual things will respond to visual tools and those that are better at oral, to verbal tools, and so on.

    Then I guess I try to make my objectives very clear and always talk to them about the *relevance of what they are learning for their future as a doctor*. They go into medicine to become doctors. So, from week one, when I'm teaching them histology, which I can tell you can be pretty 'dry', I explain to them that the reason for learning histology (the study of normal tissues) is to better understand abnormal tissues (pathology). So, when I'm talking about normal tissue, I then talk about disease in that tissue. I'll often refer to a media celebrity who has that syndrome or disease, because if they *know someone they can identify with* who has that particular problem, it makes it come alive, makes it more relevant. Like if you take atherosclerosis, which causes heart disease, I give them a picture, a big colour picture of this over-weight middle-aged man holding a cigar. He's got a rather red and ruddy face, a big hat and all these oilfields out the back. And I say to them, well let's think about the risk factors for coronary artery disease. Let's see if we can work out the risk factors from the picture. So, by *making it a bit more interesting and applying knowledge to a 'problem'* I hope that that inspires them to continue to want to read more. Lectures only give students a 'taste' or foundations of the topic. It's really up to students to go and revise and build on the formal teaching we provide to make themselves better doctors.

Sources of teaching insights and strategies

Gerlese: How did you come up with the idea of using pictures, and some of your other ideas to inspire students? Where did they come from?

Jane: As doctors we have to do a lot of continuing professional development. We go and hear a lot of people talk, and in the last few years I've shifted away from actually listening to lecture content – maybe that's a bad thing – to *looking at the styles of delivery*, and seeing what I like or I don't like about what speakers do. Other ideas, like the visual cue for athero-sclerosis, have come from my colleagues, teaching into the programme.

I'm also *constantly modifying my programme to try to inspire student learning.* Last year the answers in the oral exam showed the students did not know fundamentals of deep vein thrombosis (DVT). Student feedback also indicated that they didn't really understand some core concepts. I thought, well this has obviously not worked, this learning, so let's look at how we taught it. They only had lectures. So, what we did was to introduce a scenario based around a woman who had just been overseas and developed calf pain. We used an interactive small group teaching approach as past student feedback indicated most students learnt well with this approach for other difficult topics. The student feedback has been very positive but the exam results will also be a guide.

Specialist doctors have often told me pathology is a 'black box' to them. This motivated me to ensure every student spent time in our department seeing the 'nut and bolts' of what we do. They are asked to follow a patient and write a report on how the pathology results influenced patient management. I also secretly hope this may inspire some students to want to be pathologists!

Gerlese: When you say that students didn't really understand, how are you finding out?

Jane: I have *a complex system of feedback*. So, in Years 1 and 2 we get feedback on every lecture, practical or tutorial. Once a week during their problem-based learning tutorial students write an online review of their reflections on the teaching week. That goes to the University's Medical Education Unit and then, deidentified, back to the teacher. In Years 3 and 4 we give the students a series of approximately seven statements for every topic covered and ask then to rank them from awful (1) to great (5). The statements include: 'I have a better understanding of the approach to the diagnosis of patients with the conditions discussed in the clinicopathological correlation (CPC) session'; 'The teaching style was appropriate for the topic'; 'The presentation of the material at the CPC sessions was interesting and informative'. We also ask open questions, like 'What are the three things that you liked, the three things you didn't like, and what would you like to see improved?'. The other kind of feedback we use is the 'muddiest' moment. The students write on paper at the end of the practical or lecture if there any concepts they had problems with. Then, the next time we meet for a teaching session I do a five minute reply to the issues raised.

If I want to get instant feedback I use clickers[1] – where you give a multiple-choice question and students click in their responses or just raise their hands. I lecture for, say, 20 minutes, and then recap with questions. I found this to be really effective at gauging whether the students are understanding what I'm saying or whether I need to recap something or revisit it in another way. I also run interactive sessions, where different experts come together to enable discussion on a topic. I have a roaming microphone that passes from student to student. The student who holds the microphone gets asked a question by an expert – this keeps the students engaged with the topic and makes sure they don't fall asleep! The expert then summarizes the key learning topics with a few review slides.

I listen to my children too with what they're doing. For instance, I was involved in designing an online interactive programme on histology with the help of a medical student a few years ago. I know my thoughts were influenced by an online maths game I saw my school-aged son playing where a big tick or explosions happen when you got the correct answer. This type of positive reinforcement seems to encourage learning at any age. We all like to be told we are doing well at something.

Gerlese: It sounds as if you're always keeping your eyes open for new teaching possibilities.

Jane: Yes. I also think I've learnt some of these concepts through my Graduate Certificate in Higher Education. I initially enrolled in the Grad Cert as I wanted to be a better teacher and thought if I understood the theory of education better this might help. *Doing my Graduate Certificate* helped me understand the importance of aligning my learning objectives with my assessments, and the different ways students learn.

Gerlese: Does anything else stand out from the Grad Cert? What about the literature you were introduced to?

Jane: I remember the two texts that we had, by Ramsden (2003) and Rowland (2000). They helped my thinking at the time, but in truth, there hasn't been any particular experience that's really moulded how I've ended up constructing the curriculum. I'm sure it's all come from different places. I guess what I'm trying to say is that a lot of these ideas probably just seemed to be sensible to me. So, I thought I'd give them a go.

Gerlese: One of the first statements you made was that students learn in different ways. How did you come to realize that?

Jane: From *the kinds of questions that the students would ask me*, and the kind of feedback I was getting on the teaching I was doing. For example, with the interactive sessions with the microphone that I mentioned, some students thought that they were the best sessions. Others said they found them really frightening and they got turned off. Some say they absolutely love working with specimens in 'hands on' sessions, and others say that they would prefer PowerPoint presentations. So I guess the way I've learnt that they're different is by *the spectrum of feedback* that I've had over the years.

Also as a member of the Australian Medical Council assessment team of medical schools I get to *see different pathology programmes.* From interviews with staff and students from these schools it is obvious some students do not enjoy their pathology because of the way it is taught and yet others are inspired to learn.

Working with other teachers

Gerlese: I gather that you have responsibility for the design of the whole four years of the anatomical pathology programme?

Jane: To begin with, I basically did all the teaching. Now, more of the pathologists in our region have become engaged in the course, which has been great. Just as there is more than one right way to treat a disease, I'm sure there are many right ways to teach, so having different teaching styles is good. What I usually do, however, is to get new teachers to come along and see how I teach as most do not feel confident they can teach undergraduates. *I provide a very structured handbook* to the teachers with learning objectives, key questions to cover, answers to those questions and online resource material. The students are given the same learning objective and resource material. This enables me to standardize the teaching across the programme, and ensure core material is covered regardless of the teacher. As the curriculum is mapped across four years it is important each learning experience is a positive one as they build on each other. I also *offer the people who teach into the programme feedback* from the evaluation system we've already got set up. It's done in such a way that if they don't want feedback they don't get it, and if they do want it, I give it to them. Nearly everyone wants feedback. I have found I need to counsel staff on occasions because sometimes the feedback is not all positive. This forms the basis for *talking about what things maybe we could do better.*

Gerlese: I'd like to start winding up, but there's another detail I'd like to check on first. How did you come to develop such a strong focus on getting feedback and on all those evaluation techniques you're using?

Jane: I think because I was developing the curriculum fresh, I needed to develop some processes to work out whether it was working. So, I thought this was the most effective way of working that out.

I should have mentioned I actually also *gather feedback from each of my teachers.* We have a meeting, or email discussion, about four times a year to look in a structured way at what's working and what's not working. On a more functional kind of level, I also have a meeting every two weeks with my staff for half an hour to deal with any immediate problems such as timetabling, specimen collections, and student and staff issues related to the course. It is equally important to keep the staff interested and engaged in the course as it is the students. I found that the feedback from staff is as important as the feedback from students.

Maintaining enthusiasm for teaching

Gerlese: You've talked about keeping students engaged, interactive, things being relevant and the significance of enthusiasm. What about for you? Obviously you're not just enthusiastic about your subject, but you're enthusiastic about teaching. How do you maintain that enthusiasm?

Jane: I just think I'm very fortunate to have the opportunity to be able to share the knowledge that I have with young minds, hoping that they will feel as passionate as I do about such an interesting area of medicine which pervades all that they're going to do. I don't think it's any more complicated than that at the moment.

I guess I'm fortunate because it's not all that I do, because I spend a significant amount of my time still reporting surgical pathology, and I'm involved in a number of research projects. My research enhances my teaching and the students appreciate that some of my understanding of possible new treatments comes from my research interests. So, it's the mix and the variety of what I do that I think just makes it an enjoyable experience.

Gerlese: Okay. Well, I think this is a good point to stop.

Jane: But first I wanted to ask what you see in my teaching, what stands out from your perspective, as an educational specialist.

Gerlese: One of the things that strikes me is the way that *being a teacher is integrated into your life*, the way that you see implications for teaching in so many areas of your life, whether as a doctor, patient or parent. So, you don't treat it as a separate activity.

Also, you really try to *imagine learning from the students' perspective*, and envision the impact of what you do on students – while acknowledging that there can never be a uniform impact because each student is different.

Jane: But isn't that what teaching is? Doesn't everybody do that?

Gerlese: Absolutely not. Many teachers are only seeing teaching from their own perspective, as a teacher, not the students'. Students' responses to their teaching are taken for granted and not investigated or thought about in the way you do.

This relates to the third thing that strikes me about your teaching: that is, the effort you put into *getting feedback on the impact of your teaching* – from students, other teachers, exam results. This is far more comprehensive than I'm used to seeing, and makes you very unusual as a teacher.

Jane: Thanks Gerlese. I hope those who read what we have discussed will find it useful in some way. Articulating what one does, I think, helps one's own teaching.

Note

1 Also called electronic keypads, and 'personal audience response' technology.

References

Ramsden, P. (2003) *Learning to Teach in Higher Education*, 2nd edn. London and New York: Routledge Falmer.

Rowland, S. (2000) *The Enquiring University Teacher*. Buckingham: Society for Research into Higher Education and Open University Press.

6   Your skin or mine? A living drama in interprofessional education

Bernard Moss

The audience rose to its feet to give the cast a standing ovation. It had been a magnificent performance. The actors had put the play across with imagination, creative power and energy. The applause was well deserved.

At the back of the theatre the director joined in the standing ovation, unnoticed, unacknowledged, but bursting with a quiet pride in a job well done. All the hours spent in rehearsals had been well worth it. And now, mission accomplished, it was time to slip away quietly. Another task beckoned.

Programme notes: about the (role) play

The 'play' is set in a training suite at Staffordshire University UK in the present time. The cast is a group of 20 first-year social work students. There is no scenery, no audience, only a set of tables and chairs that are easily movable. There is no set script that the 'actors' have learned: on the contrary, as the storyline develops, they will all take on different roles and interpret them as they see fit. It is experiential learning at its most risky and at its very best, and it tackles a key theme of interprofessional education, which seeks to ensure that students fully understand the role of other professionals alongside their own (Barr 2002).

Director's notes: the challenge of being a pedagogic director

Sometimes it is stories, images and pictures that have the greatest power. For all the importance of pedagogic theory to inform and underpin educational practice, for all the undeniable benefits of research and deep scholarship without which lively teaching would surely wither and die, in the end when we think about our own education it is particular teachers who spring most quickly to mind. We remember vividly the kindly encouragements, the inspirational opening of the windows of our imagination and the awakenings of our intellectual thirst. More than that we remember the personality of our teachers, with all the endearing quirks many of them displayed, who helped to shape our lives and stimulate our vision. At the time we probably never thanked them – not properly anyway; somehow we felt awkward at the time, not knowing what to say, and probably not realizing the full implications of what had been quickened within us. But later on, perhaps many years later, we look back and hope that they will be proud of what we in our turn have achieved, and what we have done to nurture the vision first awakened by their teaching skills. Each of us stands on our particular stage, enjoying life's accolades when they come, while in the background our teachers have slipped away quietly, job done.

In telling my own story, the image and picture of the theatrical director has always featured strongly. Many of my quirks are indeed theatrical: in my experiential approach to teaching I wander round; I sometimes wave my arms around, and seek in all manner of ways to engage with my students. They get used to picking up my specs for me when in a moment of over-eager emphasis and expansive gestures I knock them from my face into the first row. But more importantly, the image of the director has particular resonance for my approach to teaching, because directors have to work closely with the actors to gain their confidence and respect; they have to get inside the actor's skin to help them become what they need to be, and to make the journey towards a complete performance. They need to know when to be patient and to cajole; when to rebuke and when to let well alone; when to praise and when to show disappointment. They need to help the actors be true to the letter of the script but also to have the courage and imagination to enter into the spirit of the words, and to own them through their own interpretation. They have to be humble enough to let go and stand back, but strong and assertive enough to keep people on track and not to lose focus. And for most of the time they need to be sufficiently self-aware and confident enough in their calling to let the accolades fall to others as they achieve their well-deserved success. Their reward lies precisely in the success of those whom they have taught to do well.

But not all plays and shows are instant 'hits' – indeed, even in the West End or on Broadway, some shows quickly fold and are box office disasters. However badly the actors may feel about such failures, the director will feel it even more acutely, for upon no one else's shoulders does the ultimate responsibility lie for bringing a play or a show to life, and for giving it an immediate audience appeal. Being a director can be *a tails you win, heads I lose* occupation: when all goes well the actors receive the praise; when it 'flops' then it is all the director's fault.

And so it can feel as a teacher. We burst with pride when our students gain first class honours degrees, or achieve their full potential, sometimes against considerable odds or at great personal sacrifice. But when they underachieve, or perhaps fall by the wayside, we worry and go round and round in our minds wondering what more we could have done to help them become better motivated, to engage them more effectively, and to help them achieve great things. And over our shoulder the 'management' looks ever critically at the outcomes of our endeavours, and how they will affect academic 'league tables' and student recruitment. In this kind of environment, teacher stress, with subsequent burn-out, is an ever-present spectre, perhaps especially for those dedicated colleagues who seek to go 'the extra mile'.

Programme notes: about the 'play'

This 'play' was at one level 'directed' by me. I created the scenarios and the storylines that enabled the students to explore some of the challenges and complexities of interprofessional education. Each group of students who enacted this 'play' brought to their story their own unique style and interpretation. As each scene in the story was introduced, students spontaneously enacted the various roles allocated to them to bring the story to life. Those who did not have a 'solo' role to play were soon involved in small 'crowd scenes' whose opinions and reactions to the unfolding drama were 'drawn out' by the director. It was important pedagogically that no one was a spectator: everyone had a role at every point in every session.

This pedagogic production is startling and innovative in its approach to student learning. Over a period of weeks it explores issues that are of fundamental importance to students training to become professional 'people-workers': in this case, social workers. But its relevance as an experiential approach to learning and teaching is easily transferable to other disciplines (Kolb and Kolb 2005). The 'play' tackles the huge themes of interprofessional education, and how to help students begin to 'get inside the skins' of their own profession and that of others. Importantly, it also helps them at least to begin a journey of discovery into the lives of people who use services; who sometimes daily have to face the discomfort and often the embarrassment of asking for help, or having to deal with the unavoidable intrusion of professional people. It is one thing to read about this – it is another thing altogether to begin to glimpse and feel what it must be like, even though in the classroom context the complete reality can never be portrayed or experienced fully.

Synopsis of the play

The director introduces the 'story' of two young 17-year-old people (D and M) who meet, and fall in love, while at college. M's unexpected pregnancy throws their career plans into turmoil and brings their relationship with their parents to breaking point. D and M stay together, and in due course D goes to the local university to study to be a teacher. Eventually they move out of the area with their young son (P) to enable D to take up a teaching post as a newly qualified teacher. Several years later a second child arrives, but M becomes increasingly depressed and socially isolated and their relationship becomes strained. They decide to move once again for a fresh start thanks to D's promotion to a new school. Here D meets another new member of staff (T) whose own story is one of personal difficulties including a disabling accident to her husband. They form a relationship and decide to set up home together with the two young teenage sons (P and S) they each bring from their former relationships. This family upheaval has a profound impact upon the two teenagers, whose behaviour at school deteriorates; they begin to get into trouble by stealing from the local shops, and eventually are caught breaking into cars. They are brought before the local youth court for sentencing. Throughout this entire period M has been struggling to look after her young daughter as well as her parents who are becoming increasingly frail and vulnerable, a situation that reaches crisis point when her mother has to go into hospital after falling in the garden and breaking her leg. The play ends in the youth court, where the magistrates consider what to do with the two young people, and what sentence to pass upon them.

The curtain rises

The first scene brings the two young people D and M together, with the director encouraging them to get into role and to explore what their characters are really like. They hear from their parents and friends; from fellow students and tutors at the college – all these roles are played out by students, encouraged by the director. Everyone is given a role to play.

As the story unfolds, new characters are added, and at key moments the actors must interact with each other in role. They explore what it is like to be the upset parents with a pregnant daughter, or to be caught up in the dilemmas of whether or not to keep their unborn child. Members of the cast play the role of friends, neighbours, college tutors, all of whom have opinions about what is happening. The pace of the 'play' quickens as the director moves the cast into each new scene with different issues to explore, new roles to interpret, and new dilemmas to wrestle with.

Within a very short space of time the 'play' has become 'real' to the 'actors', all of whom have quickly had to take on one role or more, and to react spontaneously to the drama of which they now feel part.

It is of crucial importance that the director knows the students and has built up a level of trust with them before the role play begins. Some of the issues highlighted in the play may be real to the students in their own lives, and the director (tutor) needs to know when to 'press the pause button' and to explore in the relatively safe environment of the classroom how students' personal lives can impact upon their professional practice. This will be an important issue for them to explore throughout their professional careers, and this role play scenario provides a carefully structured opportunity for such issues to be considered.

As the story reaches its climax, the range of roles that students will be expected to fulfil includes the principal characters outlined in the synopsis, as well as social workers, teachers, youth workers, doctors, police officers, hospital staff and occupational therapists. Finally, in a change of venue, the court scene is enacted in the university's mock court room, where the 'actors' take on the roles of court clerk, Crown Prosecution Service, defence solicitors, probation officers, 'gowned' usher and, most popular of all, the magistrates with the power to bring social workers into the box to answer questions about the two young people appearing before them. The play ends as sentence is passed.

Throughout the court room scene the director has been standing to one side, as the 'actors' play out the final moments of the drama they have themselves created so powerfully. At the end he leads the applause, and listens to the feedback from the 'actors' as they reflect on the lessons they have learned from being inside other people's 'skins', however briefly.

In the bar afterwards

The director and the 'actors' have the opportunity after the 'play' to reflect on their learning. In reality the 'play' stretched over several weeks, with the story developing in a series of two-hour 'acts'. Opportunities for learning about certain aspects of the story were interwoven with the actual drama. At times a range of scenes was played out simultaneously as some key themes were explored by different sets of 'actors'. Key moments included an interprofessional case conference which explored the different aspects of the story and its impact upon the principals involved. Preparation time was allocated for an introduction to court room skills and for the 'actors' who were taking on professional courtroom roles to prepare what they needed to do and to say. And throughout the 'play' there were pauses to reflect on their learning and what it felt like trying to live in someone else's skin, be that another professional or someone who was on the receiving end of a range of professional services.

The mood in the bar afterwards was full of enthusiasm; the 'actors' felt the real 'buzz' of experiential learning, especially as all of them had felt nervous and anxious at the outset about what they were letting themselves in for. Everyone needed to take the risk implicit in all experiential learning, without which the whole enterprise would founder. Student evaluation and feedback suggested that the greater their investment in the role play, the deeper was their learning.

But there was a note of realism too. Some students had missed some of the sessions, and this made it difficult for them to 'catch up' and difficult for the group story to demonstrate genuine progression. Not all students remembered 'the story so far'; some students entered into certain aspects of the story more vigorously than others, making it difficult for the director, who was running three separate groups each week, to keep on top of the individual character and 'feel' of each group's interpretation and its development. Unavoidable absenteeism sometimes led to difficult casting decisions for some sessions, which required the director to take some time to bring everyone 'up to speed' with the story so far. In spite of careful initial planning, the three groups did not always have equal numbers each week, thereby requiring the director quickly to invent new roles for some sessions, or to reduce roles for others, depending on the numbers present and the point reached in the overall story. It is important therefore for the director to have thought through in advance of each session how to respond to such eventualities, by having relevant additional roles to introduce, or deciding which roles could be safely omitted without undermining the core story line.

In its early days the 'role play' scenario was introduced as an exercise in experiential learning about interprofessional education without any summative assessment. More recently, however, a different scenario has been developed with a summative assessment task requiring students to write reflectively on the social work assessment and intervention aspects of the role play.

Clearly the role of the director is crucial. Without a clear understanding of the key themes needing to be explored, a willingness to take risks, and a capacity to enable the students to take part and to enjoy the learning opportunities, such pedagogical experiments would fail quickly. The director has to be able to live the 'play' as each group develops it, to respect how the 'actors' choose to interpret their roles, and to have the confidence and imagination to 'go with the flow' of the play and to draw out appropriate learning points for the students.

In short, the director has to model good, reflective, pedagogic practice, underpinned by the conviction that what is being attempted will make a significant difference to the quality of the students' eventual professional practice. The real impact of this approach needs further research, although anecdotal feedback from students now in professional practice indicates that enhanced interprofessional sensitivity gained from this role play has played a significant part in their new careers. They have in fact discovered what Thompson and Thompson (2008: 15), in their discussion of reflective practice based upon Schon's (1989) notion of professional artistry, describe as the ability to cut the cloth of their professional knowledge base 'to create appropriate solutions to fit the requirements of the specific practice situation'. A similar professional artistry is also the hallmark of a great teacher.

What the papers said

See it for yourself on http://www.bernardmoss.org.uk – this contains video footage of the role play taking place. Students have given their permission for their work to be made public.

Explore ways of using it in your own teaching by looking at the Staffordshire University Learning and Teaching DVD *Using Large-group Role Play in Higher Education* by Bernard Moss. Available from the Academic Development Institute, Staffordshire University, or from the author.

Read more about it in Moss, B. (2000) The use of large group role play techniques in social work education, *Social Work Education*, 19 (5): 471–83.

> It was inspirational – one of the best parts of my course – I learned so much from doing it.
>
> (Student feedback)

References

Barr, H. (2002) *Interprofessional Education: Today, Yesterday and Tomorrow. A Review Commissioned by the UK Centre for the Advancement of Interprofessional Education (CAIPE).* London: CAIPE.

Kolb, A.Y. and Kolb, D.A. (2005) Learning styles and learning spaces: enhancing experiential learning in higher education, *Academy of Management Learning and Education*, 4 (2): 193–212.

Schon, D.A. (1989) *The Reflective Practitioner: How Professionals Think in Action.* New York: Basic Books.

Thompson, S. and Thompson, N. (2008) *The Critically Reflective Practitioner.* Basingstoke: Palgrave Macmillan.

PART 2
Developing Curricula and Resources that Reflect a Command of the Field

In this, Part 2 of the book, contributors discuss curriculum and resources development that reflects a command of their field. Contributors are a particularly distinguished group, sharing between them, for example, a Nobel Prize, premier national teaching awards and institutional awards for creative scholarship, and senior university and national leadership roles. Together, these scholars offer their quite different and sometimes provocative views on matters such as linking research and teaching in productive ways, demonstrating current knowledge of the field in the design of curriculum and learning resources, and incorporating the process and outcomes of scholarly practices into teaching.

Anthropologist Donna Boyd and biologist Fred Singer revisit the theme of personal transformation that was introduced in Part 1, on this occasion setting out their shared career journeys through Alan Skelton's (2005) very helpful four models of understanding teaching excellence. They emphasize the importance of observing and learning from colleagues' teaching, gaining insights to different philosophies, styles and methods. Within their chapter they examine links between their understandings of teaching excellence and curriculum design. Then, as 'committed relativists', they conclude, among other things, that there is no single best way to teach. In their view each of Skelton's models has some validity, depending on the particularities of the learning-and-teaching context.

This contention is contradicted to some extent in Chapter 8 by Carl Wieman (I did warn that this book shows considerable diversity of style and opinion!) who, pointing to 15 years of his own research on learning and drawing from the work of scholars such as Bansford *et al.* (2000), Mayer (2003) and Ericsson (2006), argues that good learning will result – irrespective of student age, ethnicity or background – if some basic principles of good teaching are put into practice. Working through the detailed example of an Introduction to Modern Physics course, he makes the case that learning is not some magic spark between student and teacher. Instead, it requires the correct application of principles known to result in effective learning, taking some account of students' prior knowledge and subject experience.

In Chapter 9, Rhona Free reflects frankly and thoughtfully on the ways she uncovered and made use of scholarly work on curriculum design and teaching practice in her career teaching economics. Prompted by early classes where there was a clear disjuncture between her own enthusiasm for the subject material and that felt by students, she began to develop a deeply scholarly approach to teaching, first seeking help from colleagues (some of it less than useful) and then from published work on teaching practice. She recalls taking particular comfort in Weimer's (1990: 7) argument that great teachers are made, not born, and goes on to discuss the ways in which her command of economics was complemented by her growing concern for teaching, and heightened capabilities as a teacher.

Following his shock introduction to teaching engineering in an Argentine university – in Spanish – Chapter 10 author and native English speaker Ian Cameron recalls the different experiences over his career that have allowed him to link teaching and research in productive ways. For instance, he discusses ways in which he has successfully connected aspects of his research on process systems engineering to educational environments and how this connection led him to work on engineering education pathways, aligning outcomes-based subject design with assessment. Among Ian's observations about the links between his engineering research and teaching are the centrality to both fields of relationships, realism and relevance (R^3) to which he has more recently added places, people and processes (P^3).

References

Bransford, J., Brown, A. and Cocking, R. (2000) *How People Learn: Brain, Mind, Experience, and School*, expanded edition. Washington, DC: National Academy Press.

Ericsson, K.A. (2006) The influence of experience and deliberate practice on the development of superior expert performance, in K.A. Ericsson, N. Charness, P. Feltovich and R. Hoffman (eds) *The Cambridge Handbook of Expertise and Expert Performance*. New York: Cambridge University Press.

Mayer, R. (2003) *Learning and Instruction*. Upper Saddle River, NJ: Merrill Prentice Hall.

Skelton, A. (2005) *Understanding Teaching Excellence in Higher Education: Towards a Critical Approach*. London: Routledge (Taylor & Francis).

Weimer, M. (1990) *Improving College Teaching*. San Francisco, CA: Jossey-Bass.

7 The meaning and evolution of teaching excellence: a 'radical' case study from Radford University, Virginia

Donna C. Boyd and Fred Singer

> It is important that people take responsibility for their views on teaching excellence and recognize that their own understanding is provisional and subject to change.
>
> (Skelton 2005: 174)

What is 'teaching excellence'? Is it based on expert knowledge of a subject, understanding our students and their needs, deft use of technology, communication (or acting) skills, or some combination of all of these? Is it truly defined by outstanding teaching awards? Alan Skelton (2005) asks these questions in his book *Understanding Teaching Excellence in Higher Education*. In this volume, Skelton presents four models for understanding teaching excellence: traditional, performative, psychologized and critical. In this chapter, we explore each of these approaches as experienced first-hand in our own teaching and in so doing create our own understanding of the meaning of teaching excellence, how it has affected the curricula we have designed, and how our interpretation of it has changed over our 20+ year teaching careers.

Skelton's four models

1 Traditional model

The standard (and historically precedent) approach to teaching uses the traditional lecture format. Both of us are products of large research universities where we learned to teach based on the prevailing paradigm of the day: carefully conceived and crafted lectures with a small amount of student interaction built in to break up the monotony. In this paradigm, teaching excellence is defined through the differential ability to present engaging and thoughtful recitations. Though early in our teaching careers we were comfortable giving lectures, we also recognized that we were not getting through to all of our students, so we began a search for more meaningful approaches.

2 Performative model

Teaching excellence in this model is based on performance measures as well as a focus on marketability and productivity of academic programmes. In this business-like approach, teaching excellence may be externally defined through conformity to state or university productivity standards. Early in our teaching careers (before tenure), design of curricula was undeniably tethered, even perhaps on a subconscious level, to these performance statistics (i.e. exam scores, teaching evaluations). For example, a significant portion of our salary (in terms of merit pay) is determined by how students answer the following question: 'Overall, how would you evaluate the effectiveness of your instructor?'

3 Psychologized model

This model of teaching excellence draws on cognitive psychology in the creation of a meaningful interpersonal and individualized relationship between professor and student. This relationship examines each student's individual needs and allows students to 'actively construct meaning in the light of their existing knowledge and experiences' (Skelton 2005: 32). Students are encouraged to take responsibility for their own cognitive development by reflecting on the quality of their learning experience. For the professor, teaching excellence is also internally constructed through extensive, continuous reflection.

4 Critical model

A critical model for understanding and promoting teaching excellence focuses on a teacher's ability to provide access to knowledge which can liberate and empower students. Skelton (2005: 33) describes the role of a teacher as a:

> critical or transformative intellectual who disturbs the student's current epistemological understandings and interpretations of reality by offering new insights and theories. This involves creating teaching and learning situations which question 'common-sense' ways of thinking and behaving, leading to new forms of consciousness and ideas for effecting social and political change. Empowerment through participation is also central to critical understandings of teaching excellence. In order for students to act confidently with critical intent in their future lives, participatory forms of engagement in teaching and learning situations are required. This may involve

greater reciprocity between teacher and taught than is commonly the case.

Still assistant professors, and still searching for more meaningful teaching outcomes, our breakthrough was an opportunity in 1993 to collaborate with two senior colleagues at Radford University, Dr Charles Kugler in biology and Dr Rich Murphy in English, to develop a two-semester, interdisciplinary experimental general education course entitled Science, Social Science, and the Humanities. In a radical departure from previous courses, we were given complete freedom to merge three disciplines intellectually and structurally. It was through this course that we experienced Skelton's critical and psychologized approaches to teaching excellence.

Science, social science and the humanities – a radical experiment

Our interdisciplinary course experimented with Skelton's last two models in many ways. First, as part of our self-education, we had wide-ranging philosophical discussions on teaching goals and approaches for attaining these goals one year prior to teaching the course. These discussions continued during the year it was taught, as a significant amount of time was spent collectively revising the goals and methods of the course on the basis of our reflections about our previous day's teaching experiences. All four professors and 48 students experienced total immersion in this teaching experiment – meeting together in the classroom for eight and a half hours per week plus many additional hours for laboratory and group project work. We developed meaningful, but still professional, interpersonal relationships with each other. Most significant in our growth as professional teachers was the long-term observation of each other's teaching over the course of the year – including four quite different teaching styles, philosophies and methods. This often led to stimulating discussions inside and outside the classroom, which became a learning experience in itself for us and our students. Subjecting our teaching approaches to constant evaluation and review was, admittedly, an intimidating experience for each of us, but ultimately it was one of the most rewarding aspects of the course, liberating us to experiment with alternative teaching methods outside our comfort zone.

In terms of curriculum development, the four general goals for our students were:

1   to learn basic concepts and methods in science and social science;
2   to solve problems as part of a research group;
3   to think creatively and critically; and

4   to read carefully, with confidence and pleasure, and to formulate and communicate ideas effectively in writing and speaking.

Our units for the first semester were:

1   What does it mean to be 'human'?
2   Rhetoric – how is rhetoric used to represent and misrepresent knowledge?
3   Evolution of animal and human behaviour.

The second semester addressed the question 'What is truth?' using the field of ecology as its thematic context. Each unit was analysed through a truly inter-disciplinary view as we (biology, anthropology and English professors) struggled to explore commonalities and discontinuities across our disciplines. Our approaches ultimately converged on four important themes, which reflect Skelton's third and fourth models.

Theme 1: Students learn best when they can see a purpose to the knowledge

As part of each unit, students were expected to develop and implement group projects that addressed questions of importance to them. They were required to present the results of their investigations to an appropriate and real audience. One group addressed the humanity of Neandertal society and presented their findings to a high school biology class. A second group wrote an article to the local newspaper on when life begins as part of the abortion discussion. There were projects on using non-human animals versus humans for research purposes, on dehumanization of African slaves, and many others. By allowing students to ask and develop their own questions, we found they engaged fully with their work. By requiring students to present their findings to a relevant audience, they received extra motivation to perform to a high level.

Theme 2: Students learn best as partners in learning

The confidence to ask meaningful discipline-specific questions, and the skills to answer them, do not develop quickly. While there is some carryover in skills and applications from one project to the next, it is equally true that each assignment has unique problems that must be negotiated. Consequently, students must continually practise the art of asking questions and developing methods to answer them.

Students developed all of their projects in small groups, and were required to change group membership for all four of their major projects. All of the projects that they designed went through a rigorous peer-review process, which served several functions. It identified problems with student proposals, gave students opportunities to evaluate ideas critically, and made them more critical and reflective of their own work.

Theme 3: Critical thinking must be taught explicitly, but in the context of course content

Most of our students were freshmen (i.e. first-year) education majors, so we decided to engage them in learning theory. First we had to learn about it ourselves. After reading William Perry's (1970) *Forms of Intellectual and Ethical Development in the College Years*, we decided to introduce students to the distinction between different stages of intellectual development: dualism (thinking in terms of right versus wrong, true versus false), multiplism (all viewpoints are equally valid), and committed relativism (truth is contextual and dependent on the observer's informed evaluation of evidence). Students were expected to use Perry's stages of development as a framework for reflecting on their own thinking. The first exam for the second semester required students to apply this understanding:

> Write a personal essay on some contentious or debated issue in our society that is important to you. In this essay we want you to do metathinking ... that illustrates the three general categories of thinking that we have discussed this semester (dualism, multiplism, and committed relativism) in a way that shows understanding of them.

We very clearly identified ourselves as partners with students on the path to committed relativism and spent considerable time modelling the process of critical thinking for our students. We expressed this perspective through numerous in-class debates, discussions and dialogues about virtually every topic in the course – both with each other and with our students. It soon became clear to our students that dualistic answers to scientific questions are often simplistic and that the process of evaluating truths based on contextual evidence is an ongoing one, for students and professors alike.

We discovered in our unit on 'What is truth?' that most of our students had little experience with evaluating evidence. To prepare them, we constructed 'Guides to evaluating information', which showed students how to examine sources and evidence, evaluate conclusions and recognize unstated assumptions. For example, under 'examine the evidence', we encouraged students to recognize appeals to authority and to majority opinion, to note sample sizes and recognize anecdotal evidence. We gave students papers and reports that were deficient in these regards, and required them to identify the problems. In many cases, these exercises created disequilibrium in the classroom by challenging students' *a priori* assumptions about the world around them.

Critical thinking skills are best learned in the context of course content. Students learned about DNA structure from reading Watson's classic, *The Double Helix* (Watson 1968). In addition to learning about the process of discovery, the students also criticized the book as a work of literature. In the process, they identified rhetorical tools used by Watson to denigrate Rosalind Franklin's contributions and to validate his own truth claims.

Theme 4: Knowledge builds on previous knowledge, but the construction process is very messy

To teach our students about the evolution of knowledge, we required them to read and discuss several classics of discovery including *In the Shadow of Man* (Goodall 1968), *The Double Helix* (Watson 1968), *Yanomamo: The Fierce People* (Chagnon 1992) and *Ravens in Winter* (Heinrich 1989). Students were amazed at how hard these researchers worked, and were engaged by their intellectual breakthroughs. However, as the course developed, we became concerned that students were missing an important point in these assigned readings: that the construction of knowledge is very non-linear, and runs into many blind alleys. We wanted them to experience the complexities of a research programme on their own, and to be able to distinguish clearly between the three research projects they had completed during the first semester and a real and substantial research programme.

Accordingly, six weeks of the second semester were devoted exclusively to designing and implementing a research programme addressing some issue in ecology. We outlined a research programme as a seven-part process:

1   coming up with the idea;
2   preparing a literature review;
3   framing the questions or hypotheses clearly;
4   writing a proposal for a pilot study;
5   doing the pilot study;
6   refining the project based on the pilot study and trying again; and
7   branching into new related questions.

We emphasized the non-linearity of this more true-to-life approach – that students might need to go back to stage 2 or 3 after their pilot study, which made them extremely unhappy. To keep their spirits up, and their minds focused, we reminded our students of how researchers they had just read about stumbled down many blind alleys on the path to discovery.

Of course, an important step in any research programme is publishing the results. Given that our students were freshmen, we did not ask them to submit their papers to scholarly journals, but instead compiled their reports into a book entitled *The Hidden World Around Us: Science, Social Science and*

Humanities. They each received a copy of the book, and one resides in Radford University's library.

This course was very expensive (in terms of labour and time investment) to teach and was therefore not repeated. But the course and the four themes derived from it contributed significantly to how we define ourselves as teachers today. We've spent the past 15 years of our teaching careers sifting through these experiences and applying our insights to courses constrained by more conventional structures and a changing student body.

The evolution of our ideas about teaching excellence: post-radical class

Although opportunities for interdisciplinary collaboration like the one described above have waned, we maintain our focus on intensively immersive, personally meaningful and relevant teaching experiences in our individual courses. Many of these have been research-based teaching experiences. For example, the introductory course for biology majors is Ecology and Adaptation. To begin developing observational and questioning skills, students in their first laboratory visit a natural setting, and are required to spend about 75 minutes observing the natural world (without mobile phones) describing what they see, and compiling 50 ecological questions based on their observations. We then gather, and each student shares one question and describes how this question could be investigated. Students collectively choose one question which becomes the research problem we address in the next laboratory period. From this initial experience, students learn quickly that they are partners in learning, that they can ask meaningful questions, but that some questions are better than others. In more advanced courses, students experience more demanding iterations of the same basic process.

Both Human Osteology and Forensic Anthropology use a traditional lecture approach to teach the basic structure of human anatomy, reinforced by many hours of hands-on, personal mentoring in the laboratory. An outgrowth of the 'radical' class is the requirement for original research projects which ask students to explore questions revolving around the scientific study of human remains, formulate a research design to address these questions, and collect metric and morphological data from the remains to investigate the questions. Through involvement in these projects, students begin the process of thinking like a human osteologist or forensic anthropologist, about research questions important to the discipline, why they are important, and how they are interrelated to other questions and concepts within and outside the discipline. It is here that students are transformed from amateurs into professionals and perceive their opportunity to engage in original research, contribute meaningfully to these disciplines (and science in general), and apply this research to understanding human problems.

Both of the previous examples demonstrate how we help transform students into independent thinkers and questioners. However, we agree that there is no single, best way to teach and no all-inclusive model for what constitutes teaching excellence. On the basis of our personal journeys through Skelton's (2005) four models for understanding teaching excellence, we argue (in the committed relativist tradition) that *all* hold the capacity to be valid. For example, both of us use traditional lecture format extensively. Teaching excellence is temporally and spatially contingent and must be personally constructed and deconstructed based on a lifelong process of self-conscious, thoughtful reflection and interaction with our students – mirroring precisely the same 'critical thinking' process we expect from those we teach. Through this process, we have the power to transform our students, as we, ourselves, are transformed. When achieved, this goal defines, for us, the ultimate 'radical' teaching experience.

Acknowledgements

We thank Chuck Kugler and Rich Murphy for making us better and more thoughtful teachers and Steve Pontius, former Dean of the former College of Arts and Sciences, for supporting the 'radical' class.

References

Chagnon, N. (1992) *Yanomamo: The Fierce People*, 4th edn. Fort Worth, TX: Harcourt Brace.
Goodall, J. (1968) *In the Shadow of Man*. Washington, DC: National Geographic Society.
Heinrich, B. (1989) *Ravens in Winter*. New York: Simon and Schuster.
Perry, W. G. Jr (1970) *Forms of Intellectual and Ethical Development in the College Years*. New York: Holt, Rinehart and Winston.
Skelton, A. (2005) *Understanding Teaching Excellence in Higher Education: Towards a Critical Approach*. London: Routledge (Taylor & Francis).
Watson, J.D. (1968) *The Double Helix*. New York: Penguin Books.

8 No magic needed. Designing instruction for learning – a case study

Carl Wieman

Over the past 15 years I have studied the research on learning extensively, with particular interest in the learning of science. I have also regularly tested the application of this research in my own introductory physics courses. I have become convinced that learning is not some magic spark that takes place between the student and the teacher in the classroom. Rather it is a process that can be well characterized and understood in terms of basic principles. If the educational experience is designed according to these principles, good learning will result irrespective of age, ethnicity, student background or any other factors. The proper implementation of these principles for any given student, however, will depend on their prior knowledge and background. Put differently, good teaching is simply putting into practice those principles that are known to result in effective learning. I have written elsewhere about some of the research supporting this idea (Wieman and Perkins 2005; Wieman 2007b). Here I will discuss an example where I systematically applied these ideas to transform a course that had consistently produced small amounts of learning and large amounts of dissatisfaction.

The course was Introduction to Modern Physics, a third semester course with an enrolment of 180 students at the University of Colorado for students pursuing degrees in engineering disciplines. The transformation was carried out in collaboration with another instructor under my direction (Katherine Perkins) and a postdoctoral scholar (Sarah McKagan). Subsequent instructors have used our approach and materials with continued good results.[1]

Assessment

The first step was to establish the learning goals (sometimes called 'objectives') for the course and decide how to measure how well these were achieved. To assess results we first created and validated a multiple choice test to measure learning of concepts of quantum mechanics (QM). This test (the Quantum

Mechanics Concept Survey [QMCS]) (McKagan and Wieman 2005) covered important concepts taught in a variety of QM courses. By giving the test in the course the semester before the course was transformed, as well as in the comparable course for physics majors, I was able to compare learning in the transformed course with learning in those courses.

Other learning goals, such as ability to do various types of quantitative calculations, justify the fundamental ideas of QM and use quantum mechanical concepts to explain and predict behaviour of real world phenomena, were assessed through exams and homework problems. We also collected regular reports from the Teaching Assistants (TAs) on student thinking (interest, confusion, understanding . . .), and gave students a standard survey of student perceptions about physics and how it is learned (Adams *et al.* 2006). Finally we conducted two surveys during the term that asked students their views about the specific elements of the course and how they felt those affected their learning and enjoyment of the class.

Pedagogical design

Much of the research on effective teaching practices (Bransford *et al.* 2000; Mayer 2003; Ericsson 2006, and references therein) can be summarized as follows:

1 address prior knowledge and experiences of the learners;
2 motivate students;
3 provide authentic ongoing practice of expert thinking with effective feedback; and
4 address the limitations on working memory in classroom activities.

1 Address learners' prior knowledge and experiences

Students' prior knowledge and experiences affected all aspects of the design and implementation of the course. To know incoming students' thinking better we looked at the majors and grade levels of the students in the course and the results of surveys and exams from previous years. We interviewed previous instructors, read the research literature on the learning of QM, and gave the QMCS test to students who had taken this course in previous terms. Last, and most usefully, before the course was transformed, McKagan met/ observed a number of the students weekly on an informal basis, usually in the context of homework help sessions. These sessions, where students met to work collaboratively on homework, provided large amounts of input on student thinking, revealing many difficulties and confusions about specific topics as well as the profound difficulties most students were having in understanding the purpose, motivation and structure of the course.

Among other things, we learned that, unbeknown to the instructors, most students had a gap in their knowledge of potential energy curves that instructors had not realized; this neglected gap meant that students had little hope of understanding a large fraction of the material presented.

We designed the course to address this prior thinking, both from a cognitive perspective, making the material easier to learn by providing a coherent intellectual framework that built appropriately on students' incoming knowledge base, and from an affective and motivational perspective, making it desirable to learn.

2 Motivation

Motivation is an essential element of learning – learning takes extended strenuous effort and will not happen unless the learner sees a reason to expend that effort. Research on motivation (Mayer 2003: Chapter 14 and references therein) and my own surveys of students indicate three important motivating factors that should be addressed in every course: a sense as to why the subject is relevant and/or interesting; a sense the learner can master the material and how to achieve that mastery; and a sense of achievement – they see progress in their learning.

With these in mind, I eliminated all material that was impossible to justify to the students as relevant or useful to them based on anything they had previously experienced or would likely encounter in the future. It was sobering to realize that this was nearly half of the traditional material.

Motivational concerns led to the establishment of two broad educational goals: understand the quantum mechanical origins of basic chemical and material properties of matter, and understand the role that QM plays in a number of modern technologies and in explaining phenomena encountered in everyday life. I searched for real world examples of the basic ideas of QM to present in the course and found a surprisingly large number. Traditionally, QM is quite abstract, with students seldom seeing these sorts of applications. I also decided to frame the introduction of the ideas of QM in terms of a new model for understanding nature, a model that emerged as the solution to the puzzle of observations that could not be explained using prior models of physics.

Our data showed that students had a great deal of trouble visualizing the QM phenomena being discussed. This lack of a visual model both hindered their learning and led to demotivating frustration – an example of how cognitive and motivational issues are often coupled. In response, we developed a number of interactive simulations (McKagan *et al.* 2008b) that allowed students to engage with the material in a more rewarding way and greatly helped them develop visual models.

To get student buy-in to the instructional methods being used, on the first day and in later follow-up sessions, we explained to the students why the class was being organized and run quite differently from their previous science courses. This included a discussion of research on learning as given in the references listed above and how the approaches to be used are held to result in better learning. Most students embraced the teaching methods used, and the opposition of those who did not was greatly muted, because they recognized there was a solid research justification for the approach, even though it may have seemed strange and unpleasant to them.

3 Explicit practice of expert thinking with useful feedback

I first identified in my own mind exactly what I thought it meant to think like a physicist about the specific topics in the course. Then we designed activities and tasks that would provide students with practice in this thinking. I began with modelling the thinking and providing practice in the classroom, and then the homework built on and extended this practice, and the exams reinforced it. Some general features of the questions students had to answer in class and on homework were that they:

- had explicit connections to familiar phenomena. Connecting with students' experiences both provides them with a context that enhances their learning and increases interest;
- required explicit sense-making and reasoning;
- had explicit focus on developing a conceptual understanding and then applying the concepts to solving problems;
- used analogies, illustrations and the simulations to help students develop mental models.

4 Address the limitations on working memory in classroom activities

Recognition of the limits on working memory guided the design of every class, setting constraints on the number of topics, terminology, extent of pre-class reading and use of drawings, animations and analogies to reduce cognitive load. PowerPoint slides were used to facilitate this, and they allowed easy reuse and refinement in subsequent semesters. Many of these slides are still being used by different instructors in this and related classes five years later.

Lectures

Class time was used as an opportunity for students to engage with the material and practise expert thinking, with me as instructor serving as a cognitive coach and their peers providing more individualized feedback on specific points.

To provide time for this, transmission of factual material and mathematical derivations, which traditionally took up a large fraction of the class time, were transferred out of class. Students got the factual material by reading the textbook before class, with brief graded clicker (personal response system) quizzes to ensure they did so. Pointless derivations were eliminated and most of the important derivations were moved to the homework, where they were made part of solving an actual physics problem, rather than just an abstract exercise.

We had students use clickers to answer questions during class.[2] Students were assigned to seats and 'discussion-consensus groups' made up of three to four students in adjacent seats on the first day. They were told of the proven value of peer discussion (Mazur 1997; Hake 1998) and how this is facilitated by the assigned groups.

'Lectures' were designed around specific learning goals and a set of challenging conceptual clicker questions that embodied these goals. Typically I had students think about a question individually and then discuss it within their groups before answering. It was invaluable for me to listen in on these discussions 'to see into the students' brains' as it were, to know which things the students understood and which things were causing difficulties. In many cases those difficulties were things I had not anticipated, such as misinterpreting an image or data curve, and could be easily dealt with by directly discussing them. Frequently, in the follow-up to the clicker question, I called on students to explain why a possible answer might be correct or incorrect, before the answer was revealed. I always gave a recap of what the correct answer was and why. I used to skip this when a large fraction of the class got the questions correct, but surveys indicated that even when students got an answer correct, they were seldom sure of their answer and wanted a recap. On more challenging questions, particularly when related to a demonstration using one of the interactive simulations, there were invariably many follow-up questions from students. A single clicker question could often generate 10–15 minutes of questions and follow-up discussion where students would clarify the ideas, explore them in greater depth, and test them in new contexts.

A problem unique to this class was dealing with the large number and depth of the student questions from many different students. The use of assigned groups and assigned discussions, followed by calling on students to 'give the reasons (or answers) your group came up with' and actively soliciting student reasoning and discussion, dramatically lowers the social and cultural barriers to students speaking up in class, and thereby promotes far more student comments and questions from a far larger cross-section of the class than is typically seen in lecture classes. I practised detecting when clarification was sufficient, and then looking for (and occasionally subtly prompting) questions that would lead into the next topic I had planned to cover. My most successful classes were those that covered the prepared material but appeared to be largely driven by student questions. This meant that the students were, with support, reasoning through the body of material as physicists. I also found students asking unusually deep questions, sufficiently deep in many cases that I had to defer responding until after researching the topic. I have come to see many highly substantive questions in class as desirable indicators that students are behaving as 'expert learners' (Adams *et al.* 2008: 1).

Homework

Recognizing the well-established value of homework for supporting learning, we put much effort into the creation of the homework problems. Because of resource constraints, we necessarily used a computer grading system that allowed a variety of quantitative and multiple choice answers, including ticking 'all that apply' out of a long list of possible items. This is the most useful format that I have found for having computer graded homework assignments that have a critical thinking component, particularly involving conceptual reasoning. We also had students do three long answer problems weekly involving extensive calculations and explanations. Graders would randomly choose one of the three to assess in detail. We regularly asked students how much time they had spent on the homework for the week and adjusted accordingly to ensure it was four to six hours per week. This achieved as much learning as possible, without being an excessive burden.

The homework required students to provide scientific arguments, explain the reasoning behind their method of solving a problem, or the logic of the answer. Problems were ideally connected to the real world and framed in a context where it was evident that there was a reason someone would want to know the answer, rather than being abstract exercises. The problem sets were challenging to complete, but the difficulty also stimulated the students to work collaboratively; this collaboration was strongly encouraged. An absolute grading scale was used rather than a curve, because a curve discourages educationally valuable student collaborations.

My experience is that students get valuable feedback from each other and spend less time on unproductive struggling when working collaboratively. Such social interactions also develop the important skills of critically analysing scientific arguments of others and evaluating their own understanding ('meta-cognitive skills'). We saw little indication of students merely copying others' work and turning it in without participating, and we overheard conversations in which students were actively arguing against such practices by their fellow students. This was likely due to the combination of homework problems being of obvious utility, being very explicitly matched to the learning goals for the course and the exam questions, and the fact that a significant part of every assignment involved writing explanations of reasoning in the student's own words. On the end of term survey, students rated the homework as a very important contribution to their learning.

Grading

I try to reward students appropriately for everything that contributes to their learning. Thus I weighted homework relatively heavily, but the exams still counted significantly and were carefully aligned with the homework to make it clear that mastering the homework problems supported exam performance. I also assigned a small number of points to other worthwhile activities such as reading the textbook before class, reviewing past homework and answering clicker questions. A question that we have on every assignment is 'Pick one question from last week's homework that you got wrong, and explain your error.' Students tell us that this going back and reviewing their answers and figuring out what they did right or wrong is valuable to their learning, as is reading the textbook before class, but they also tell (and show) us that they will only do these things if it affects their grade: priority is always given to graded items in this or other classes.

Results and conclusion

Although all our assessments indicated the first offering of this course was much more successful than its previous incarnations, there were obvious opportunities for improvements. The extensive assessment made it quite easy to make adjustments, and the second and third iterations required relatively little work and were highly successful. Student satisfaction and results on the QMCS conceptual test were dramatically higher and have remained high with subsequent instructors, with the latter largely tracking the fidelity with which they use our materials and pedagogical design. I have subsequently used this design and most of the materials to teach a similar course at the University of British Columbia with even better results.

Notes

1   To reduce this chapter's length and physics content, a number of technical details of the transformed course have been omitted here, but are readily available elsewhere (Wieman 2007a). Research publications on the learning of quantum mechanics (QM) emerging from this work include McKagan *et al.* (2008a, 2008b, 2008c, 2009).
2   I have detailed elsewhere the psychological and cognitive benefits to learning provided by effective use of clickers and the best way to use clickers (Wieman and SEI Staff 2009).

References

Adams, W.K., Perkins, K.K., Podolefsky, N.S., Dubson, M., Finkelstein, N.E. and Wieman, C.E. (2006) A new instrument for measuring student beliefs about physics and learning physics: the Colorado Learning Attitudes about Science Survey, *Physical Review Special Topics – Physics Education Research*, 2: 010101. Also http://www.colorado.edu/sei/class/.

Adams, W.K., Wieman, C.E. and Schwartz, D. (2008) University of Colorado Science Education Initiative, and University of British Columbia Carl Wieman Science Education Initiative, *Teaching Expert Thinking*. Available from: http://www.cwsei.ubc.ca/resources/files/Teaching_Expert_Thinking.pdf.

Bransford, J., Brown, A. and Cocking, R. (2000) *How People Learn: Brain, Mind, Experience, and School*, expanded edition. Washington, DC: National Academy Press.

Ericsson, K.A. (2006) The influence of experience and deliberate practice on the development of superior expert performance, in K.A. Ericsson, N. Charness, P. Feltovich and R. Hoffman (eds) *The Cambridge Handbook of Expertise and Expert Performance*. New York: Cambridge University Press.

Hake, R. (1998) Interactive-engagement versus traditional methods: a six-thousand-student survey of mechanics test data for introductory physics courses, *The American Journal of Physics*, 66: 64–74.

McKagan, S.B. and Wieman, C.E. (2005) Exploring student understanding of energy through the Quantum-Mechanics Conceptual Survey, *Physics Education Research Conference Proceedings*, 818: 65–8.

McKagan, S.B., Perkins, K.K. and Wieman, C.E. (2008a) A deeper look at student learning of quantum mechanics: the case of tunnelling, *Physics Review Special Topics – Physics Education Research*, 4: 020103.

McKagan, S.B., Perkins, K.K., Dubson, M., Malley, C., Reid, S., LeMaster, R. and Wieman, C.E. (2008b) Developing and researching PhET simulations for teaching quantum mechanics, *American Journal of Physics*, 76: 406–17.

McKagan, S.B., Perkins, K.K. and Wieman, C.E. (2008c) Why we should teach the Bohr model and how to teach it effectively, *Physical Review Special Topics – Physics Education Research*, 4: 010103.

McKagan, S.B., Handley, W., Perkins, K.K. and Wieman, C.E. (2009) A research-based curriculum for teaching the photoelectric effect, *American Journal of Physics*, 77: 87–94.

Mayer, R. (2003) *Learning and Instruction*. Upper Saddle River, NJ: Merrill Prentice-Hall.

Mazur, E. (1997) *Peer Instruction: A User's Manual*. Upper Saddle River, NJ: Merrill Prentice-Hall.

Wieman, C.E. (2007a) Course transformation case study. Mimeo. http://www.cwsei.ubc.ca/resources/files/Course_transformation_case_study.pdf, accessed 30 March 2010.

Wieman, C.E. (2007b) Why not try a scientific approach to science education? *Change Magazine*, 39: 9–15.

Wieman, C.E. and Perkins, K.K. (2005) Transforming Physics Education, *Physics Today*, 58: 36–41.

Wieman, C. and SEI Staff (2009) *Clicker Resource Guide – An Instructor's Guide to the Effective Use of Personal Response Systems (Clickers) in Teaching.* http://www.cwsei.ubc.ca/resources/files/Clicker_guide_CWSEI_CU-SEI.pdf, accessed 30 March 2010.

9 On scholarly teaching – a personal account

Rhona Free

After only a few semesters in the classroom there were signs that my teaching had to change. While I thought my lectures were full of exciting *voila!* moments, students just seemed relieved when I stopped talking. Their lack of enthusiasm and the minimal time their grades suggested they had allocated to the course were discouraging, especially since I spent hours and hours preparing for each class. And I dreaded the weeks when assignments were due. Reading 160 papers on the same topic was torturous. Guided by theory and evidence about effective teaching practices I have made changes over the last 25 years that have improved my teaching and made classes more rewarding and interesting for me and, I hope, for students.

My initial response to students' apparent lack of enthusiasm about my lectures was to use coloured chalk (this was before whiteboards or PowerPoint), a method recommended by a colleague to liven up the classroom and help students understand the graphs in economics. Of course, this was as helpful as talking louder in English to someone who speaks only Spanish. It's even more embarrassing to admit that, for the second problem, I simply replaced writing assignments with multiple choice tests. Surprisingly, student evaluations of my teaching didn't suffer from these changes, but they didn't improve either; nor did students' grades.

The failure of these half-hearted and uninformed changes eventually led me to an approach that Hutchings and Shulman (1999) refer to as 'scholarly teaching'. I realized that I should tackle my teaching problems the way I would a research problem, starting with a review of the literature. Somewhat to my surprise, I found that there were lots of resources of improving college teaching and that our library had some. I read McKeachie *et al.* (1986) first. It starts with a clear framework: good teaching depends upon at least three kinds of knowledge – knowledge of the subject matter, knowledge of the students, knowledge of teaching strategies (McKeachie *et al.* 1986: 2). While I was pretty confident about the subject matter, I hadn't given much thought to either students or teaching methods – I just copied the style of some graduate school professors whom I admired. It was fortunate for me that McKeachie was the first book I came across. A philosophical tome would not have held nearly as much sway for me as this book's succinct explanations of what research has shown is effective in improving student motivation and learning. The key point I gleaned from the book was that I needed to shift my focus from what I was teaching to what my students were learning. The book not only provided a rationale for doing this, it provided strategies.[1]

At about this time I happened to go to a presentation by a colleague in the Education Department about authentic assessment – evaluating students' learning based on performance in discipline-appropriate tasks that might be encountered outside the classroom instead of on multiple choice tests or simple information-recall exercises. Wiggins (1990) states:

> Assessment is authentic when we directly examine student perform-ance on worthy intellectual tasks. Traditional assessment, by contrast, relies on indirect or proxy 'items' – efficient, simplistic substitutes from which we think valid inferences can be made about the student's performance at those valued challenges.

I was intrigued by the potential for creating assignments that would measure student learning better, be more useful to students in preparing for their careers, and also be more interesting for me to grade.

Just after this, in 1987, Chickering and Gamson's *Seven Principles for Good Practice in Undergraduate Education* was published. Their principles, which are set out in Box 9.1, became important guides as I shifted my focus to learning outcomes and authentic assessment. They helped me to hone in on how I should change what I did in the classroom and how I would assess student learning.

Box 9.1 Chickering and Gamson's seven principles for good practice in undergraduate education

Good practice in undergraduate education:

1   encourages contact between students and faculty;
2   develops reciprocity and cooperation among students;
3   uses active learning techniques;
4   gives prompt feedback;
5   emphasizes time on task;
6   communicates high expectations; and
7   respects diverse talents and ways of learning.

Source: Chickering and Gamson (1987)

I experimented somewhat haphazardly with strategies recommended in McKeachie *et al.* (1986), always trying to incorporate Chickering and Gamson's principles, but I developed a more systematic approach after reading Weimer (1990). Weimer offers a helpful five-step approach to improving instruction (Box 9.2). She begins by pointing out that 'Instructors who equate good teaching with divine gifts need first to be confronted with the research-identified characteristics of effective instruction' (Weimer 1990: 7). This argument that good teachers are made, not born, and that research is available to guide improvement is very reassuring. Weimer's recommendations for assessing the effectiveness of teaching methods were very useful and reinforced the comforting notion that working on teaching could be like working on a research problem – the literature review provides the theoretical background, data is gathered, and results are evaluated.

Although my concern with becoming a better teacher stemmed primarily from a desire to make classes more enjoyable for me and for students and to improve their learning, I was also concerned about having good student evaluations to put in my promotion and tenure file. I teach at a public university that places high value on both teaching and research (as well as service). Since I was in my pre-tenure stage I had to maintain a reasonable but steady level of research, so the increased time I was spending on teaching was a concern.[2] Fortunately, I had continued going to workshops on teaching by colleagues in the Education Department at my university. At one of these, Jeff Trawick-Smith, an expert in early childhood education with several major textbooks, grants and scholarly publications, talked about how he organized his courses so they supported rather than competed with his research. As I revised my courses I kept in mind his argument that good teaching does not have to come at the expense of research.

So what were the changes that I made in light of all of this inspiration and information? First, following Chickering and Gamson's third principle, I relied less on lectures and built more active learning into classes. I think scientists

---

Box 9.2 Weimer's five steps in an instructional improvement process

1 Develop instructional awareness (enlarge, clarify and correct my understanding of how I teach).
2 Gather information (compare my understanding of how I teach with the feedback of others).
3 Make choices (decide what to change and how to change it).
4 Implement alterations (incorporate changes in my teaching).
5 Assess effectiveness (determine the impact of the alterations).

Source: Weimer (1990)

(with labs) and visual artists (studio classes) have a natural advantage when it comes to active learning. With one exception, all of the economics classes I'd taken as a student were straight lecture or discussion (generally dominated by the instructor). I enjoyed these lectures and learned from them, but the evidence is clear that for many students this is not the most effective mode of instruction:

> When measures of knowledge are used, the lecture proves to be as efficient as other methods. However, in those experiments involving measures of retention of information after the end of a course, measures of transfer of knowledge to new situations, or measures of problem solving, thinking, attitude change or motivation for further learning, the results tend to show differences favoring discussion methods over lecture.
>
> (McKeachie *et al.* 1986: 70)

Not being good at leading discussions, and finding them often unproductive given an average class size of about 40, I replaced lecture time with in-class group problem-solving exercises, analysis of cases and simple experiments about economic behaviour. General (for example, Hatfield 1995) and discipline-specific publications such as *The Journal of Economic Education* proved helpful as I searched for techniques that promote active learning and for evidence about their effectiveness.

Some of the best active learning exercises that I use apply two other Chickering and Gamson principles – cooperation among students and time on task. In-class group 'progressive' problem-solving exercises, where each student has to do one piece before the next student can do theirs, are particularly effective. They help students to identify what they know and don't know (prompt feedback – Chickering and Gamson's fourth principle), use peer pressure to nudge them to prepare for class and pay attention, and indicate to me which concepts students are finding difficult.

One challenge is that this type of exercise uses up a lot of class time and, as a result, fewer concepts can be addressed in class. This seems like a sacrifice but it has the very positive side effect of forcing careful thought about the concepts, models and principles that are most important – the course 'take-aways'. Bain (2004: 50) lists specific planning questions that effective teachers address as they prepare to teach (see Box 9.3). The first of his questions gets answered in the process of figuring out how to find time for teaching methods that are less 'efficient' than lectures.

The solution to my second teaching problem (the dread of reading hundreds of similar papers several times a semester) was largely solved with 'authentic assessments'. In the interest of providing frequent and prompt feedback to students and to promote attendance, I continued to give short quizzes,

Box 9.3   Ken Bain's 13 questions that the best college teachers ask as they prepare to teach

1   What big questions will my course help students answer, or what skills, abilities or qualities will it help them develop, and how will I encourage my students' interest in these questions and abilities?

2   What reasoning abilities must students have or develop to answer the questions that the course raises?

3   What mental models are students likely to bring with them that I will want them to challenge? How can I help them construct that intellectual challenge?

4   What information will my students need to understand in order to answer the important questions of the course and challenge their assumptions? How will they best obtain that information?

5   How will I help students who have difficulty understanding the questions and using evidence and reason to answer them?

6   How will I confront my students with conflicting problems (maybe even conflicting claims about the truth) and encourage them to grapple (perhaps collaboratively) with the issues?

7   How will I find out what they know already and what they expect from the course, and how will I reconcile any differences between my expectations and theirs?

8   How will I help students learn to learn, to examine and assess their own learning and thinking, and to read more effectively, analytically and actively?

9   How will I find out how students are learning before assessing them, and how will I provide feedback before – and separate from – any assessment of them?

10   How will I communicate with students in a way that will keep them thinking?

11   How will I spell out the intellectual and professional standards I will be using in assessing students' work, and why do I use those standards? How will I help students learn to assess their own work using those standards?

12   How will the students and I best understand the nature, progress and quality of their learning?

13   How will I create a natural critical learning environment in which I embed the skills and information I wish to teach in assignments (questions and tasks) that students will find fascinating – authentic tasks that will arouse curiosity, challenge students to rethink their assumptions and examine their mental models of reality? How will I create a safe environment in which students can try, fail, receive feedback and try again?

Source: Bain (2004: 50–60)

but I developed new assignments that incorporate the skills and technology students will use after college at the same time that they help students master course content. Montgomery (2002: 35) provides guidelines and examples for developing and evaluating assignments that emphasize 'the application and use of knowledge' and that require 'higher levels of cognitive thinking such as problem solving and critical thinking'.

One of the first assignments I revised was in a course for non-majors that focused on work and workers in the USA. I had always had students do a standard research paper on a common topic and although it required that students do some research and that they write several drafts, the product did not resemble materials they would likely be asked to produce after college. The new assignment required that each student pick a particular textile mill in Connecticut, research its history, put that history into the context of the typical pattern of economic development in Connecticut, create a website depicting their findings, and then make a short presentation explaining their findings as depicted in their website. Students enjoyed this project – many did much more research than I anticipated, they produced websites much better than I expected, and during and after their presentations they made thoughtful observations connecting their findings to the history we'd discussed in class. Years later students still send me updates on their mills. In another class that focused on the history of economic thought, students created social networking sites to detail connections between economists and their ideas. Again, students were enthusiastic about the work and they demonstrated deeper understanding of critical concepts. At the same time, they were mastering new technologies, honing their presentation and verbal communication skills, and writing in a style and format that they were more likely to use after college.

Keeping in mind Jeff Trawick-Smith's argument that teaching can be complementary to research, I redesigned assignments in advanced classes too. Several years ago I started doing research on inter-state variation in the ratio of female to male earnings. There is significant variation, with the ratio being much higher in some US states than in others, even in adjacent states. Standard econometric methods and variables explained a disappointingly small amount of the variation. Clearly there were unique factors in some states that were driving the ratio up or down but, with 50 states, identifying them would be a challenge. This then became the basis for several semesters' worth of work by students in advanced labour classes. Students picked a state and explored why the ratio was above or below the average. Their findings often pointed to variables that needed to be added to the model or to explanations for outliers. From these advanced classes some students would go on to graduate school so a standard academic paper was an authentic assessment. But even more authentic was the experience of being part of a research team. Students knew they were contributing to a larger project and developed the habits and practices of a group working on a common problem. They shared information, were creative in using theory to identify factors that may have been important, and brought insights from courses in other disciplines to the problem.[3] My experience supports the recommendation of Hattie and Marsh (1996: 533) that universities should 'aim to increase the circumstances in which teaching and research have occasion to meet'.[4]

In *Scholarship Reconsidered*, Ernest Boyer (1990) emphasized the importance of assessment of teaching – self-assessment, student assessment and peer assessment. Weimer (1990: 66–7) describes a number of formative feedback instruments that can help an instructor evaluate what works in a class and what doesn't. Using some of Weimer's techniques, I found, for example, that having students stay in an assigned group for the whole semester for in-class active learning exercises had a positive effect on attendance compared to groups that changed every class or when students picked their own groups. I found that group 'progressive' problem exercises resulted in higher quiz grades while providing 'guided notes' and using PowerPoint slides instead of drawing graphs on overheads or on the board did not.

Hutchings and Shulman (1999: 13) argue that:

> *All* faculty have an obligation to teach well, to engage students, and to foster important forms of student learning – not that this is easily done. Such teaching is a good fully sufficient unto itself. When it entails, as well, certain practices of classroom assessment and evidence gathering, when it is informed not by the latest ideas in the field but by current ideas about teaching the field, when it invites peer collaboration and review, then that teaching might rightly be called scholarly, or reflective, or informed.

The ample literature on effective teaching practices makes it relatively easy to develop strategies for improving teaching and learning. Executing those strategies requires a certain amount of risk taking and refining of course content, but viewing the experience as a research problem aimed at identifying techniques that work and those that don't makes it a little less threatening. And sharing the results of these teaching experiments provides both opportunities for further refining techniques and for participating in an important area of scholarship.

New technologies and techniques for evaluating the impact of various teaching methods on learning create ongoing opportunities to review the latest evidence on teaching. While each instructor's discipline, personality, teaching responsibilities and students will influence the teaching methods they find most effective, the abundant research offers vast scope for experimenting with major or minor modifications to current practice. Keeping up with one's discipline and with technology and balancing teaching, research and service make it difficult to take the time to consider how classroom teaching can be improved. As I found, however, it can be time well spent – making class preparation, time in the classroom and time spent assessing student work more rewarding, more supportive of research, and, most important, more effective in promoting student learning.

Notes

1   McKeachie and Svinicki (2007), which is the 12th edition of McKeachie's *Teaching Tips: Strategies, Research and Theory for College and University Teachers*, is a wonderful newer source of inspiration and practical advice.
2   Hattie and Marsh (1996) provide a very complete review of literature and offer some interesting findings. For example: '. . . those who spend time on research do have higher research outcomes, but those who spend time on teaching do not have similar returns from their teaching. There does seem to be a non-reciprocal effect, in that time on research is more critical to outcomes than time on teaching. Following Feldman (1987a), we would agree that time on research probably comes from non-teaching times and that there is, at best not a one-to-one trade-off between time on teaching and time on research' (p. 529).
3   One paper that benefited from student work is Free and Clifford (2003) Analysis of interstate differences in gender earnings ratios, paper presented to the Eastern Economics Association Annual Conference, New York, 20–23 February.
4   Hattie and Marsh (1996: 534) provide a very helpful list of strategies that reduce competition between research and teaching.

References

Bain, K. (2004) *What the Best College Teachers Do*. Cambridge, MA: Harvard University Press.

Boyer, E.L. (1990) *Scholarship Reconsidered: Priorities of the Professoriate*. Menlo Park, CA: Carnegie Foundation for the Advancement of Teaching.

Chickering, A.W. and Gamson, Z.F. (1987) Seven principles for good practice in undergraduate education, *The American Association for Higher Education Bulletin*, March, http://www.aahea.org/bulletins/articles/sevenprinciples1987.htm, accessed 24 May 2009.

Free, R.C. and Clifford, M. (2003) Analysis of interstate differences in gender earnings ratios, paper presented to the Eastern Economics Association Annual Conference, New York, 20–23 February.

Hatfield, S. (ed.) (1995) *The Seven Principles in Action: Improving Undergraduate Education*. Bolton, MA: Anker Publishing Company.

Hattie, J. and Marsh, H. (1996) The relationship between research and teaching: a meta-analysis, *Review of Educational Research*, 66 (4): 507–42.

Hutchings, P. and Shulman, L.S. (1999) The scholarship of teaching: new elaborations, new developments, *Change*, September/October, 31 (5): 10–15.

McKeachie, W.J. and Svinicki, M. (2007) *Teaching Tips: Strategies, Research and Theory for College and University Teachers*, 4th edn. Boston, MA: Houghton-Mifflin.

McKeachie, W.J., Pintrich, P.R., Lin, Y. and Smith, D.A.F. (1986) *Teaching and Learning in the College Classroom: A Review of the Research Literature*, Technical Report No. 86-B-001.1. Ann Arbor, MI: University of Michigan.

Montgomery, K. (2002) Authentic tasks and rubrics: going beyond traditional assessments in college teaching, *College Teaching*, 50 (1): 34–9.

Weimer, M. (1990) *Improving College Teaching*. San Francisco, CA: Jossey-Bass.

Wiggins, G. (1990) *The Case for Authentic Assessment, ERIC Digest*. ERIC Clearinghouse on Tests Measurement and Evaluation, Washington DC. American Institutes for Research Washington DC, ED328611. http://eric.ed.gov:80/ERICDocs/data/ericdocs2sql/content_storage_01/0000019b/80/22/c5/e7.pdf, accessed 5 July 2009.

10 Destinations and pathways: the curriculum challenge

Ian Cameron

Beginnings

It was Argentina, April 1982. With impeccable timing we arrived just one day after the start of the Falklands War or *Guerra de las Malvinas*, if you were Argentine. Having arrived in the country as a UNIDO (United Nations Industrial Development Organization) process engineering consultant, attached to a university-based research and development institute, there were expectations besides the industrial project work. The director of the institute was soon to declare, 'Of course we expect that you will teach a subject or two in the coming academic year around design, modelling and maybe risk; and in Spanish'! This, as you can imagine, requires some serious thought and organization for a novice in both teaching and Spanish. How would I approach this task? What should be covered? How could we move through the concepts in an engaging manner? What should the students learn in such subjects? These were just some of the immediate thoughts that flooded through my mind.

In my reflections I recalled the best and the worst of my previous higher education experiences in learning and also the attitudes and commitment of those teachers. Some memories never leave you, for better or worse, and I was determined not to replicate some of the practices inflicted on me, but instead to mirror those of the best, most dedicated teachers I had experienced in Australia, the USA and the UK.

Having finished doctoral studies at Imperial College London on aspects of process systems engineering, I also pondered how the concepts of this research area might apply in the educational environment. The systems area was a fruitful domain for thinking through the challenges of engineering higher education. Indeed, it has continued to provide a powerful conceptual framework informing my developing practice as an engineering educator.

Needless to say, I did develop, deliver and enjoy the initial educational challenge that the institute director put to me. The students survived my gringo Spanish and were pleased with my first foray into higher education as a teacher. However, experience and gut feeling only gets you so far in engaging students. My Argentine experiences made me acutely aware that the educational enterprise in engineering required strategic planning, careful development, engaged learners and the growing realization of the vital role of relationships, realism and relevance. I'll return to this later.

Depth in understanding student learning styles, appreciating education research, accepting professional peer advice and serious personal contemplation were needed to help me move forward. Other significant aspects around subject design, curriculum architectures and pedagogies were to start upon my return to Australia, some three years later.

It has to be said that I had some distinct educational advantages through doing my undergraduate engineering degree in Australia under a company-sponsored arrangement. I completed my degree over five years and embedded more than two years of full-time industry work within that period. I knew early on what it meant to contextualize learning and relate theory to practice. A further five years in a wide range of roles in engineering research, design, construction, operations and management certainly didn't hurt my understanding of the world of professional engineering. These are experiences that I now treasure and which, regrettably, are increasingly rare in many higher education institutions.

Enlightenment

In the middle of 1985 I was appointed to a teaching and research position within Chemical Engineering at the University of Queensland (UQ). It was a small department, but one characterized by a passion for excellence in research as well as teaching and learning. It had a culture that valued innovation and calculated risk taking. There was also a strong departmental partnership with the UQ Tertiary Education and Development Institute (TEDI). This turned out to be instrumental in moving me from gut feeling to informed educational practice.

Part of my appointment expectations in teaching and learning were centred on the areas of process systems and engineering design. This started me thinking strategically about engineering education pathways. In those days, the chemical engineering department had commenced a resource-based education (RBE) initiative across major areas of the curriculum, which focused on the deployment of the most appropriate pedagogies and resources to support student learning. It had a strong emphasis on moving away from a major reliance on traditional lectures towards more active learning strategies, be they advanced simulation techniques, industry-based experimentation or computer-aided learning environments. The initiative had strong industry support and many of my colleagues had immediate or current industrial experience that fed into considerations around active learning strategies. I too was able to add my experience of a wide range of industry consulting, research and development projects under the auspices of UNIDO. This helped to drive authentic learning experiences for the students – a common call often made in contemporary engineering education.

In this enlightened educational environment I was encouraged to spend a full half year embedded with TEDI staff to develop design-based subjects in Years 2 to 4 of the curriculum. It was a seminal period for understanding some of the basic educational philosophy and practice that undergird curriculum design and the formation of educational pathways. Issues of outcomes-based subject design, matching desired outcomes, processes and assessment in a constructive alignment (Biggs 1999), plus engaging students with authentic engineering experiences throughout their learning journey, were paramount in devising and implementing subjects. My early developments of a pathway of systems-based design subjects continue to form a significant part of the current curriculum: it testifies to the fundamental and abiding nature of the original ideas.

The opportunity to work intensively on a pathway of process systems-based subjects was enhanced by enthusiastic colleagues who continued to probe, question, critique and encourage educational innovation. It was an inherent aspect of the culture in which I worked, and have continued to work, despite massive changes to life in the academy. Creativity accompanied by critical thinking around significant socio-technical challenges brings forth the fruits of the educational process.

In these engineering systems-focused developments, the fundamental issues revolved around: *relationships* among key conceptual components, coupled with systems thinking; *realism* in the design applications; and *relevance* to engineering practice. This tripartite mix of relationships, realism and relevance can be a powerful set of learning motivators and subject design ideas. This R^3 (R cubed) framework has remained for me a basic set of ideas for thinking strategically about the teaching and learning journey. It provides a platform for subject creativity and innovation – reflecting professional engineering as in my words 'the ingenious application of sciences and technologies to meet the needs of society'.

The role of influential and committed people can never be underestimated. I was indeed fortunate to work with talented individuals who had a passion for establishing educational pathways that prepared students for creative exploits. These enlightening experiences were not just local and national but were global in scope (Cameron *et al.* 1990, 1994).

My enlightenment has been a steady progression, punctuated by moments of revelation where profound insights and connections occur, most often through going completely outside the engineering discipline and seeing teaching and learning ideas from radically different perspectives. It has also been driven by insights into how students visualize, theorize, conceptualize and integrate ideas through cognitive and other processes. It has forced me to think more deeply about what I do in subject design and how students can engage in the learning process. This personal journey has continued to take shape through wider reading in educational philosophy, a renewed appreciation of engineering education history and animated discussions with colleagues and friends in corridors of the academy, industry and the wider community. There's a need to be both aspirational and inspirational in order to excel in the education endeavour. Read widely, think deeply, engage globally, act locally. Push the conventional boundaries and, above all, step back from the daily rush of academy life to reflect on the why, what, how and when of the educational enterprise. I encourage myself and others to create the time and space in busy lives for this to occur. It will repay the investment many times over.

Developing and deploying

I learnt a vital lesson early in my fledgling academic career about engineering education as a 'team sport'. What I do as an engineering educator, in concert with my colleagues, should reflect the student learning approaches proposed by the curriculum. Educational practice must for me approach and mirror the way professional engineering is practised. This continued reflection and commitment to this idea is often in stark contrast to many other disciplines where the teaching role is almost a 'private' academic practice, where the individual 'owns' the subject and regards their domain as inviolable. My own engineering field would be all the poorer if it were totally fragmented into personal, private practice.

There are two issues that I would touch on here: development of learning pathways and deployment of those pathways. Just like engineering itself, development and design of the learning pathways for a subject or curriculum is exciting because it affords the exercise of creativity to drive innovation. However, just as in professional engineering practice, a development that is not well deployed ends up being a disaster!

I've always taken the view that since development is a very creative activity I should be particularly critical of the *status quo* and be adventurous in my thinking. In many cases this has involved asking myself deep questions around how engineering theory and practice can be more intimate partners for enhanced student learning. Is it theory first and then practice? Hardly! In many cases, I have used my own consulting and engineering practice to provide initial challenges for student thinking and learning – an explosion of a gasoline tanker or a tsunami incident can drive curiosity and learning in thermodynamics. Heading to an informal laboratory session to set up, run and observe the dynamic behaviour of a complex chemical separation or an on-site visit during a hot summer's day to a major gas terminal where the emergency deluge system is activated, with students getting a nice cool drenching, can be powerful starters to a learning pathway.

It's not sufficient for me to develop learning pathways that deal simply with knowledge and application issues. So much of my professional engineering life has been dominated by careful listening, speaking, communicating and engaging with other engineers, disciplines and the public. Engineering has to be seen as a deeply social and human endeavour and this professional orientation has pervaded my approach to the education enterprise. It needs weaving into the pathway in seamless and convincing ways – not just an afterthought or ignored completely. I keep asking myself: where should this learning take place? How can the students be immersed in the learning? What should be the learning destination? Who should be available to facilitate learning? What physical and technological resources are needed?

In all these development activities I have to mentally step outside my personal world, take on the role of learner and see what this looks like from another perspective. Being willing to run the 'crazy' idea past critical colleagues for an honest opinion and not being concerned about hearing a definite 'no' is a worthy personality trait! Pride so often comes before a fall.

The role of contextualization has always been an indispensable design concept. Heightening curiosity to drive learning through challenging, realistic engineering problems or projects has been a major theme in my academic teaching role. Students rise to the occasion and meet the challenge. They display great creativity in tackling major issues when given the opportunity. Give students the space to be creative and see what happens. It is often amazing to witness the outcomes.

Development has a soulmate in deployment. Deployment needs to be strategic in nature. So often, innovation falls flat or languishes because of a lack of shared vision or when the innovator departs or even dies. How many of you have seen this occur? I've found over many years that where there has been no shared vision around the individual subject or curriculum pathways, things die a painful death. My role in many cases has been that of mentoring other staff by bringing them into the deployment strategy so that a new generation of academics can move the enterprise forward. A shared vision of educational excellence is essential for longevity of innovative practices.

Innovative subject and curriculum deployments should not be locally contained. I've always taken the view we should have a national and international vision for sharing best practice. This had led to global impacts in some of my specific discipline areas: process systems modelling, industrial risk management and the like. Be willing to share what has been done (see Hangos and Cameron 2001; Cameron and Raman 2005). I hold lightly to learning resources, case studies and insights, such that numerous individuals and institutions deploy and use approaches and supporting resources that I have freely given away. Those I have mentored have taken, adapted and creatively deployed some of these educational ideas nationally and internationally. That's been most satisfying.

Finally, what continues to excite me is not just the subject-level engagement but the whole of curriculum challenge in engineering education. It brings me back to my commitment to the idea of the 'teaching team'. A manifestation of this has been the major curriculum changes to a project-centred curriculum architecture that has placed emphasis on vertical and horizontal integration within the programme (see Crosthwaite *et al.* 2006). It is an internationally recognized exemplar. Students are challenged in each semester with at least one team-based project that extends their knowledge, pushes creativity and innovation while developing personal professional skills. Integration occurs vertically as projects become more ambiguous, uncertain and challenging. Where possible, the curriculum integrates horizontally to capture parallel learning in other courses into the project spine. Committed collegiality has been essential to achieving and sustaining this innovation.

Collegiality, joint ownership, development and deployment of curriculum are characteristics of the academic team to which I am fully committed. I readily acknowledge the tremendous debt I owe to so many colleagues, past and present, local and international.

Reflection, 25 years on

Reflection on teaching and learning is not generally a strong point in engineering academe – it certainly gets a rough reception by student engineers! However, reflection on a range of issues over the last 25 years has been vital to appreciating the significant changes that have been made to engineering education. My commitment to systems thinking in engineering has remained an underlying principle within curriculum and subject design. The tripartite aspects of relationships, relevance and realism remain, but have been complemented by more expansive views of curriculum: in particular, the important roles that learning places and spaces play, together with pedagogy and the people that engage in and facilitate learning activities. After all, I should have really grasped earlier in my academic career the underlying etymology of curriculum, namely the Latin word *currere*, to run. The curriculum is the track on which students move to the finish line of their programmes. It features goals, it has coherent pathways, and traverses a learning landscape.

Thinking strategically about that journey, the places and spaces where learning occurs and how professional attributes develop, is vital in facilitating an education for twenty-first-century students who will need to grapple with the 'grand challenges in engineering' (see National Academy of Engineering

2009). Confronting students with authentic challenges that are drawn from fundamental and industry-based research as well as engineering consulting provides opportunities to drive student creativity and learning. Given the important affordances of learning *places*, the *people* we encounter in the education journey, and the *processes* by which we design curriculum and challenge students, I've now added a P^3 (P cubed) to my strategic thinking: people, places and processes. They all figure intimately in a holistic view of curriculum architectures.

It's essential that we engage outside our discipline area to see the learning landscapes and smell the flowers that bloom in different knowledge domains. Myopic attitudes can easily develop, stunt our insights and distort our perceptions. We need to work actively against those attitudes. Our personal worldview, *weltanschaung* or *cosmovisión*, whichever language you prefer, determines how we approach our teaching tasks. As a Christian, I aspire personally to 'be transformed by the renewing of my mind . . .' (Romans 12: 2), so that students may in turn be transformed in how they think about their engineering world and its interconnectedness to the world in which they live and move.

However, it's not simply knowledge that counts, it's the need to combine this with passion and love in seeking to excel and see others do the same through their educational journey. That commitment, as an aspect of our relationship with students, makes all the difference.

I started an academic journey as a teacher and researcher many years ago. I'm still on the journey and continue to find it intellectually stimulating, of decided value to others and accompanied by personal satisfaction. I trust that my students will likewise find their educational and personal journey to be fulfilling, both now and into the future.

References

Biggs, J. (1999) *Teaching for Quality Learning at University*. Buckingham: Open University Press.

Cameron, I.T. and Raman, R. (2005) *Process Systems Risk Management*, 6, Process Systems Engineering Series. Maryland Heights, MO: Elsevier.

Cameron, I.T., Douglas, P.L. and Lee, P.L. (1990) Towards a process systems engineering curriculum, *American Society for Engineering Education Annual Conference Proceedings*, Toronto, 24–28 June: 514–17.

Cameron, I.T., Douglas, P.L. and Lee, P.L. (1994) Process systems engineering – the cornerstone of a modern chemical engineering curriculum, *Chemical Engineering Education*, 28(3): 210–13.

Crosthwaite, C.A., Cameron, I.T., Lant, P.A. and Litster, J.D. (2006) Balancing curriculum processes and content in a project centred curriculum: in pursuit of graduate attributes, *Education for Chemical Engineers, Trans IChemE, Part D*, 1(1): 39–48.

Hangos, K.M. and Cameron, I.T. (2001) *Process Modelling and Model Analysis*, 4, Process Systems Engineering Series Maryland Heights, MO: Elsevier.

National Academy of Engineering (2009) *Grand Challenges for Engineering*, http://www.engineeringchallenges.org/, accessed 8 October 2009.

PART 3
Approaches to Assessment and Feedback that Foster Independent Learning

This part of the book takes as its prompt approaches to assessment and feedback that foster independent learning. Contributors were asked to think about, for example, assessment methods appropriate to different contexts and to diverse student needs; the ways in which they use formative and summative assessment strategies; and how these strategies are aligned with learning aims. As with the other chapters of this volume, contributors were asked to focus on their personal 'how and why' accounts.

In inimitable style, Welby Ings reviews his 32 years of teaching experience to crystallize approaches he has taken to assessment and feedback that support independent learning. Within his discussion he makes the telling observation that assessment is often not as much about how one *thinks* but about how one *performs*. In his own teaching he endeavours to remedy this problem. He eschews cut-and-paste assessment sentences and check-a-box rubrics, focusing instead on letters to each student, reviewing their work in relation to themselves and their peers. He is distrustful of 'constructive criticism', instead preferring to encourage and lead students to analyse and reanalyse their own work. In his chapter Welby presents us with a remarkable and highly readable word-picture of a multifaceted teacher embedded in particular time and space configuration – a real person with a geography and a history.

This holism is something that geographer Sue Wurtele explores in detail in her chapter on assessment for independent learning. Following bell hooks (1994) in conceiving of education as the 'practice of freedom', she focuses on some of the ways she has shaped assessment to take account of and challenge students' own diverse life experiences and learning styles. The chapter sets out and explains a range of the assessment formats Wurtele uses. But she expands the topic and draws further from hooks to argue the need for teachers as well as students to be 'present' in the classroom as whole people, with multifaceted identities, and not just as academics defined by institutional tenure and promotion systems – a view echoed elsewhere in this book by Wesch (Chapter 3) and Loeffler (Chapter 4), for instance. And though she refers in this chapter to the work of hooks and other scholars of higher education (e.g. Weimer 2002), Wurtele makes it clear that her development as a teacher has largely been the result of personal observation, conversation and careful reading of course evaluations, rather than the result of systematic research into what works and what does not work in her classes.

In Chapter 13 clinical ethicist Wendy Rogers recounts her experiences teaching and assessing medical ethics in an Australian university. In that role she found herself in a quite remarkable position, able to take a sole charge, whole-of-degree, whole-of-curriculum perspective for a graduate-entry medical programme. And in this chapter Rogers sets the rationale for the four-year framework she developed in that programme. Among her observations, she reminds us of the critical role assessment can play in motivating learning, especially in highly competitive educational contexts. She also makes some pertinent comments about the day-to-day practice of assessment and the ways it can shape the kinds of learning exercise students are offered and how it can be constrained by (un)available resources (e.g. time and money for marking). Finally, she revisits and comments on some general principles of (ethics) assessment that are extant in the literature.

The final chapter in this part is by Peter Schwartz who, after a long and distinguished career, 'still teaches medical students' – as he puts it! Peter sets out a marvellous account of how and why his approaches to assessment have changed over 40 years of teaching and makes clear the deeply scholarly approach he has taken to that enduring transformation. The secret to Schwartz's sustained contributions and his ceaseless quest to find new and better ways of assessment lies, I think, in the emphasis he so clearly places on caring about students.

References

hooks, b. (1994) *Teaching to Transgress: Education as the Practice of Freedom.* New York: Routledge.

Weimer, M. (2002) *Learner-Centered Teaching: Five Key Changes to Practice.* San Francisco, CA: Jossey-Bass.

11 An assortment of small anomalies

Welby Ings

It is late at night. Outside you can hear the low hum of commuters as they make their exodus from the city. Their tyres swish through a black skin of water still clinging to the street.

In the half-light, the wall of my office is graced with small objects . . . eclectic scavengings, the detritus of many journeys . . . small gifts I have been given because students know my penchant for the unusual and neglected.

They help me to think.

I am going to use some of these things to explain my approaches to assessment and feedback and their relationship to independent learning.

A photograph of me, aged ten, at Pukeatua Primary School

This is a bit tattered. It hangs just above my computer. In this photo I am the kid in the back row, standing up straight and smiling with a fixed grimace into the camera.

At school, while my sisters were Cheetahs and Tigers, I was the sole member of the Rhinoceroses group. Rhinoceroses, we all knew, weren't a bottom group. We were all wonderful and could do anything and to prove it I was relegated to the position of rubbish monitor. Bumbling in my dance with the great gods of literacy and numeracy, I ended up at the close of each term with a report card that listed a line of Ds and a flutter of mildly irritated comments.

Assessment, I learned early, was not about how you thought; it was about how you performed.

Let us think about that for a moment.

The measurement of performance is *not* the measure of learning. Learning goes well beyond performance; it is an integrated and subtle transition. One, I would argue, that is best measured by learners themselves.

In my teaching I try to restore a learner to the position of assessor.

To this end, and with the assistance of my students, I design assessment formats that generally provide three layers of reflection.

The first involves a personal critique by the learner. This is normally written and outlines perceived strengths and limitations in their work. It also discusses how any weaknesses might be addressed in upcoming study.

The second layer involves an in-class, peer group critique of work. This gives an outsider viewpoint and also involves other learners in objective considerations of other solutions to the assignment they have just completed. Small panels of peer reviewers are asked to critique three other submissions (not their own). They write an agreed review. In return each receives a panel assessment of their work.

Finally, students submit their personal critical evaluation and peer review to me for consideration and comment.

At that point I take time to write each student a carefully considered, individualized letter. It has no cut-and-pasted sentences or ticked boxes. It talks about what they did and about where I see them in relation to their self- and peer evaluation. The letter reflects back upon their personal evaluation of their work. These letters take a long time to write and are sometimes seen as a bit excessive by some of my colleagues. But students rarely get this kind of personalized, detailed consideration of their thinking. Writing about their work, their critiques and their learning enables feedback to engage directly with the nature of each submission. This kind of assessment circumvents prescribed frameworks of performance and enables a deeper consideration of what has been submitted.

A broken bicycle light from the Cultural Revolution

I don't know how this object works. I have taken it apart a few times, soaked the wick in paraffin oil and kerosene but it still won't light. It is a living question.

I am a strong believer in the power of a question.

As a result, all learning surfacing out of my teaching is processed through inquisitive group or individual tutorials. These allow students to test ideas on somebody who will ask them questions to help clarify their thinking.

Beneath this lies a principle I try to model in the way I work with individuals and groups.

I try never to criticize.

This may seem a little unusual for someone who values critical thinking but it has been my experience that 'constructive criticism' is a much overrated phenomenon. It is the teacher giving advice rather than drawing out a critical analysis from the learner. Often when we are criticized we magnanimously thank the critic but in our heart we think that they didn't understand.

Questioning rigorously and constantly reflecting back responses stimulates analysis in a learner (rather than gracious reception). Generally when a piece of work is being assessed I ask, 'What is effective and why?' and 'If you had half the time again, what would you change and why?' This kind of questioning helps learners to dig into the nature of their work. You will notice I do not ask, 'What is wrong with your work?' This is because questioning is not concerned with identification as an end point but with deeper analysis and rectification.

In the long run, it is the ability to analyse and critically appraise their work that learners will walk out of the education system with. Without it we can end up 'training' students to seek external evaluation of what they create. They learn not to think, but to acquiesce. They become acolytes instead of generators of knowledge.

A Russian train driver's certificate of proficiency

Above the bicycle light is this mundane document. When I found it I was intrigued by its officialness and the obedient, passive stare of the man whose photograph had been glued and stamped into place. He looked well trained.

I worry a lot about training. I think poor assessment has the propensity to turn education into a ballet of Pavlov's dogs. This is a state where the 'successful' completion of assessment tasks takes prominence over the development of learning. We train people to perform for listed criteria and they jump for the marks.

Training can take subtle forms, and discipleship and imitation are two of its most pernicious seductions. But in the long run, acolytism has little to do with independent learning. In many cases it is simply a symptom of faulty feedback. However, if we place an emphasis on asking questions, then students see themselves as the thinkers and resolvers of problems. If we give advice they simply credit us with the solution.

Assessment can be deeper than advice. It can be something that is lived by a student. If we consider Aristotle's concept of phronesis, we come close to appreciating how this might actually work. Phronesis is the virtue of practical wisdom. It involves learning the principles of action and applying them in new situations.

By reframing assessment so it is something developed by learners as action *upon* thinking, this process becomes active rather than passive. Assessment grows from the learner and is utilized by the learner; in so doing Garrison (1997: 73) suggests we call 'into existence a new and better self'.

The 'new and better self' is a very deep objective of learning, and by nurturing the generation *and* evaluation of thought we may move learners closer to it.

Phronesis involves a process of knowing and doing in problem solving where one is, to use Alan Fletcher's phrase, 'trading beyond experience' (2001: 31).

If people *trade beyond experience* they often utilize intangible ways of thinking. Tacit knowing, heuristic inquiry and what Douglass and Moustakas (1985: 63) call 'the internal pathways of the self' are all processes of thinking that we as educators cannot evaluate on our own. Effective assessment has to occur in discourse with the learner. But assessing everything in tandem with individual learners can take a long time.

As a consequence, in my teaching I keep formal assessment to a minimum.

What this leads to are courses that are designed as opportunities to create cumulative bodies of thinking. This is because the best thinking developed by students occurs when they have opportunities to reflect upon and revisit work.

In my Honours and Masters programmes learners process thinking in a number of different ways (posters, seminars, artefacts, essays). Through the year, these formats do not receive fixed grades. They are a journey through a spiral of experiences involving making work and supporting its development with self-, peer- and tutor-questioning. Each assignment folds into the next one. Constructed thinking can be reused, extended and refined. As a thesis or dissertation builds, the only purpose of assessment is to clarify and support the development of thinking.

Because moving tradition in universities can be like trying to move a cemetery, courses still generally require a final assessment. Therefore I construct courses so there is only one, final submission to be marked. Any assessment requirement that does not involve active discourse with the learner is pared back as far as possible.

At undergraduate level assessment never appears as a list of grades for discrete tasks. There is one grade, given at the end of the course. This is for a portfolio of work that has been developed and revisited many times as the learner progresses through the course. This portfolio normally contains a selection of three or four pieces, and a reflective statement. This statement describes and reviews their learning journey, critiques the outcomes of the study and lays the groundwork later in their academic career for discussions of method and methodology.

An old felt heart, frayed at the edges and stuffed with lavender

On my wall, half hidden by a vase of flowers, hangs this old heart. One of my students gave it to me many years ago. It is suspended next to a feathered fish and a Julia Kristeva voodoo doll. These were all gifts.

At the end of each year I give gifts too. Generally I give a small (often obscure) plant. I try to find something for each person that helps to describe the kind of learner I have experienced in them. With each plant I try to explain why its growth is like them. In some cases I know these plants won't make it through the summer holidays; they will die on the windowsill of an unkempt flat, or will be planted in conditions that would stunt the growth of a radioactive cockroach. But in other cases they grow and years later I hear back from people. You go to their weddings and attend the births of their babies and they remember these small things. This is not feedback as measurement and evaluation. It is feedback as a consequence of learning together. It accepts that we are not learning information and skills but using these things to develop as human beings. In universities we rarely feed back to people about the things that really matter.

Strangely, years later, it is this feedback that people remember.

* * * * * * * *

It is quite dark now. The cocoa I made halfway through writing this has gone cold and outside it has stopped raining. The city is a silence of lights.

I have not tried to offer here 50 great tips for improving your teaching. I'm sorry if this is what you were looking for, but I would not have the audacity.

I can, however, summarize a few techniques I use to lift the evaluation of learning beyond an assessment of performances.

- I design learning systems so learners appraise their own work and the work of others.
- As an extension of this, and in response to these critiques, I provide additional comments. These do not take the form of a tick box report. They are personalized letters. This takes some time, but it allows one to tie feedback into the unique endeavour and content of each person's project.
- I don't criticize and I actively avoid giving advice. Instead I question as a way of drawing solutions to the surface.
- I do everything in my power to structure courses so the allocation of marks is kept to a minimum. In doing this, a final grade is normally assigned to a composite body of work that has gone through an integrated process of review and reworking. This means feedback has been folded back into projects during the process of their refinement.
- I try to make feedback personal and connected not just to the submitted work, but also to the learner and the uniqueness of their journey. At the end of the year this approach becomes a gift, a metaphor that is used to explain the relationship between a teacher, a learner and a point in time on a life's journey.

Now, you might ask, 'Why should I think about these things?'

Well, let me be honest here. Maybe you shouldn't. I am a guy who got expelled from secondary school, suspended from teachers' college, and failed to achieve teacher registration. I spent years in my profession being hauled before boards of governors and education inspectors. I make a lot of mistakes and I know that when one's teaching is based in a paradigm of values that sits outside convention, one is not a lot of help to people looking for a survival package.

A tattered piece of paper

Reform is a lonely path and one I suspect may be best actualized by example. Despite the tone of this chapter, I rarely proselytize. I try to show the power of questioning convention by the quality of learning that surfaces from the people with whom I work.

But it can be hard.

That is why, on my wall . . . just within reach here, is a little quote by Oscar Wilde. It sits between photographs of students spanning 32 years of teaching. It is growing old now and the paper has begun to yellow a little. At times when teaching reform and experiment have met with opposition or misunderstanding, I have sat quietly in front of it. I think it is tied to a kind of vision based on glimpses of the extraordinary limits to which people can take themselves if they learn that someone cares about them and believes in their ability to take control of their own thinking. Wilde's (1976: 1058) quote acts as a kind of arm around my shoulder. He said, 'A dreamer is one who can only find his way by moonlight, and his punishment is that he sees the dawn before the rest of the world.'

What a wonderful thing.

If we approach assessment and feedback so learning really becomes independent, we probably do so without the comfort of recent tradition at our shoulder. In fact we often challenge in universities the very foundations upon which current paradigms of assessment have been built. But in doing so, perhaps we do something much more important.

Perhaps we help to turn a learner's face towards a dawn on their own horizon.

References

Aristotle (1934) *Nicomachean Ethics* (trans. H. Rackham). Cambridge, MA: Harvard University Press.

Douglass, B.G. and Moustakas, C. (1985) Heuristic inquiry, *Journal of Humanistic Psychology*, 25(3): 39–55.

Fletcher, A. (2001) *The Art of Looking Sideways*. London: Phaidon.

Garrison, J. (1997) *Dewey and Eros: Wisdom and Desire in the Art of Teaching*. New York: Teachers College Press.

Wilde, O. (1976) The critic as artist, in J.B. Foreman (ed.) *The Complete Works of Oscar Wilde*. London: Book Club Associates.

12 Beyond the classroom walls: using assessment strategies to foster independent learning

Susan Wurtele

> The academy is not paradise. But learning is a place where paradise can be created. The classroom, with all of its limitations, remains a location of possibility. In that field of possibility we have the opportunity to labor for freedom, to demand of ourselves and our comrades, an openness of mind and heart that allows us to face reality even as we collectively imagine ways to move beyond boundaries, to transgress. This is education as the practice of freedom.
>
> (hooks 1994: 207)

When education is conceptualized as the 'practice of freedom' it cannot be confined to the four walls of the classroom. Not only does education as the 'practice of freedom' require that we leave behind the figurative space of the traditional classroom with its unidirectional communication and learning but hooks's view of teaching requires a 'classroom' which tolerates and indeed embraces transcendence of the limited roles traditionally ascribed to students and teachers. All participants in such a 'classroom' must be present as holistic beings. As hooks says, we must 'teach in a manner that respects and cares for the souls of our students', but doing so requires that we also promote our own well-being (hooks 1994: 13). As a teacher engaged in such an endeavour, I cannot allow myself to be defined only by the ever-tightening boundaries of an academic tenure and promotion system that is focused on research grants and publications. I am required to be present in the classroom as a cyclist, a concertgoer, a mother, a dogwalker – in other words a whole person – a citizen of my many intersecting communities. Likewise the classroom must be a place that welcomes the holistic student. Without this, it is not possible to create the classroom that hooks imagines – a 'classroom' that is the starting point of education, a 'classroom' that encourages the liberation of knowledge, that encourages students to bring *their* personal lives into the classroom, to critically analyse their experiences, but most importantly to take what they learn out of the classrooms into their communities, however defined. This for me is at the core of what I am trying to achieve when fostering independent learning.

My writing here is based on reflections on over 15 years of teaching in a small, primarily undergraduate, Canadian university. I have not engaged in 'systematic' research into what works and what doesn't work in my classrooms. And other than one foray into a formal study, which I will describe later, most of my observations are just that – observations; they are derived from years of conversations with students, from digesting their qualitative course evaluations and from comments they offer years after they have graduated when I meet them on the street.

Creating space for students' diverse life experiences by necessity includes embracing the challenges of creating a classroom that is accessible to students with a range of learning styles. Before I go on, I should note that I use the term learning styles in a looser way than most. I recognize there are many approaches to identifying and understanding learning styles and their impact on learning outcomes, but I use the term to reflect the blatantly obvious fact that not all students learn in the same way and not all students share the same cultural background and life experiences.

Finally, I should add that intertwined with an emphasis on creating a classroom that respects students as individuals and one that encourages independent learning is my deep belief that education must be about improving our world and that we do this by insisting that students see themselves as citizens who have the power to effect change in their communities. This should not be confused with citizenship education that promotes a specific political agenda. Rather it is a view that education must be focused on critical thinking, that students should be encouraged to embrace advocacy within their communities, and that when they graduate they should be capable of taking informed and responsible action within their worlds.

The assignments I discuss in this chapter are all presented in courses I teach to upper year Human Geography students (all of these courses are also open to Canadian Studies and Environmental Sciences or Women's Studies students). The courses are 12 weeks long and run in one semester; they have typical enrolments of between 60 and 80 students. The university at which I teach has a student body comprised of roughly 58 per cent women (a figure that is comparable to the Canadian average) (Canadian Association of University Teachers 2010). We draw students mostly from non-metropolitan areas in eastern Ontario and have a racially homogeneous student body (albeit reflecting a significant range of life experiences including a range of ages, work experience, family experience with post-secondary education and cultural differences).

There are indeed many schools of thought with regard to learning styles. Some believe that students learn best when they can target their learning to their particular strengths, while others believe that students learn best when they employ a variety of approaches (for examples of each see Weimer 2002 and Carson 2009). In my classrooms, I employ a combination. I typically use small assignments such as those I describe in this chapter to expose students to a range of assessment types as well as more substantial, flexible assignments as a means for students to select assignments that 'play to their strengths.'[1]

One of my goals in designing my courses is to offer a wide range of choice for students both in terms of how they can gain access to the course material and how they can demonstrate that they have mastered it. I will discuss the latter in the next section, but in terms of access to course material, I approach this in a number of ways: extensive use of a course management system (e.g. Blackboard, WebCT) to post all course materials including readings (where copyright permits), lecture slides, assignments and support materials. In addition, I encourage students to make use of 'accessibility' software that is available on our university computing system (at times this has included programs such as Inspiration, Kurzweil or Dragon Naturally Speaking). One year, I received a small grant that allowed me to scan all course readings and make them available to all students in an audio format.

Students are challenged to rise to their potential and to share responsibility for their own learning. They also learn that I am as excited as they are about this and that I will do all I can to ensure their success. I describe for students the course material, but also describe what past students have studied and where they have taken their learning. For example, in my Urban Environments class, students have worked with local school boards and the public health unit to increase active transportation among elementary students and others have contributed materials that were ultimately incorporated into the municipal transportation master plan (Wurtele and Ritchie 2005). In every course I teach, I encounter students who push me to grow, not just as a teacher but as a person. For bell hooks this is part of the beauty of the exercise: 'Engaged pedagogy does not seek simply to empower students . . . [Such a] classroom . . . will also be a place where teachers grow, and are empowered by the process' (1994: 21). What more could we ask of education than a system that builds community and citizens, and nurtures and empowers learners and teachers alike?

Assessment strategies

My goal is to offer a wide range of choice for students both in terms of how they can gain access to the course materials (as described above) and also how they can demonstrate that they have mastered it. I have chosen to highlight three different types of assessments to illustrate strategies for encouraging independent yet holistic learning and at the same time to illustrate strategies for ensuring integration between material presented in the lectures, seminar discussions, field trips and assignments.

Reading assignments

To understand my approach to reading assignments, it is first necessary to note that most of the courses I teach involve some kind of readings-based seminar discussions. To encourage advanced preparation, I employ a method based on informal weekly reading summaries prepared by the students and submitted at the beginning of their seminars. These summaries are not assessed, but rather serve as a 'ticket' to the seminar. Students who don't submit them at the beginning of class may attend the seminar but they are not eligible for grades. My primary goal is a simple one: to get the students to do the reading. At the risk of stating the obvious, let me say that, as virtually anyone who has led seminars can attest, the quality of seminar discussions is greatly enhanced when the students have done the readings. The reading summaries encourage such preparation. In addition, however, I add a further dimension by using integrated readings-based assignments to introduce my students to different ways of processing the material they are being asked to read for the seminars. Students are required to choose three weeks in which to submit short reading assignments, each comprising one of the following forms:

Concept map:[2] In this exercise, students choose an assigned reading and create a visual representation of the ideas, issues and important facts discussed therein. Although many students are visual learners and struggle with rendering their ideas in the linear form required by a traditional essay, few have been introduced to the idea of visually representing the core ideas or argument presented in a reading. In addition to summarizing the author's argument, the students are encouraged to use colours and shapes to structure their concept map and to incorporate their own opinions and reflections on the reading. Students are invited to experiment with software programs such as Inspiration that allow them to 'play around' with the visual representation of ideas. This exercise helps them to see how to identify and conceptualize a core idea and it assists them as they explore how authors support their ideas with their writing. In addition to honing their critical reading skills, this exercise introduces students to an accessible mechanism for structuring their own ideas. Many students go on to use concept maps to help them organize their thoughts prior to embarking on their own writing projects. For those wishing to learn more about concept maps, Nesbit and Adesope (2006) offer a good meta-analysis of their use.

Letter: In this reading assignment, students are asked to take on the role of a concerned citizen and write a formal letter to a Municipal Councillor/Employee, a Member of Parliament or a person involved with a non-governmental organization. Students choose a reading that introduces an idea they believe the recipient of the letter needs to understand better. They then use the reading as their primary source of information to write a letter convincing the recipient of the importance of these ideas. The letter is short (maximum two pages) but students are encouraged to add a page documenting additional resources. While much of the material covered in my courses lends itself to such practical applications, I have also used this assignment in courses where this is not the case. In such situations, I ask the students to think about their personal reactions as they read the article and then consider who else might be interested in the ideas introduced by the author. The goal in this assignment, as with the others, is to encourage students to make links between what we are studying in the classroom and the lives they lead. While the students are not required to send their letters, some do. In some cases, I hear from former students that the exercise introduced them to the idea that representative government requires engaged citizens who are willing to communicate with employees and elected officials and that they can be such citizens. Although many university and college teachers use letter-writing assignments that go beyond those incorporated into writing composition courses, there is little research available assessing their effectiveness. My own experience has found them to be very effective pedagogical tools. Doyle's Government Writing course website offers particularly useful resources for students tackling letter-writing of this sort (Doyle 2010).

Personal reflections: The final readings-based assignment is the freest of all. Students are asked to choose a reading they found particularly provocative (in either a positive or negative way) and then write a personal reflection on it. I intentionally leave the parameters of this assignment vague, asking students only that they explain how and why the reading was relevant to them. They can explore how the reading fits into the larger scheme of their world view, or they can present their opinion on the subject and what the article made them think about or question. I encourage them to explore links between the ideas presented in the reading and ideas they are encountering in other courses, thus reinforcing the notion that their learning doesn't just occur in isolation.

Student conferences

As part of my interest in ensuring that students see their university experiences in the context of the world outside the academy, I make regular use of student conferences in my courses. These conferences allow students to present the results of their research in an accessible manner and in a format that allows us to invite other students, academic staff and community members to hear about their work. The conference structure is flexible enough to allow for different presentation styles, including poster presentations, video clips, photo essays, brochures, formal papers and workshops. One issue that presents itself with such a flexible format is how to provide comparable or 'fair' assessments for different assessment exercises. In some years, I have allowed students to slide the weighting of the research and presentation component of the course (so, for example, the entire assignment may be worth 30 per cent of their final course grade, but the student could choose to have the presentation component worth anything from 5 to 15 per cent). A presentation worth 15 per cent would allow a student to dedicate considerable time and effort to it. In other years, I have left the presentation component worth the same for all students (usually 5 or 10 per cent of the grade) and I explain that the presentation is assessed on a combination of effort and its effectiveness in terms of communicating the ideas beyond the classroom.

The breadth of student backgrounds and interests contributes to a fascinating range of research topics (for example, recent topics in my Gender, Society and Space course include: 'Breaking gender boundaries: analysis of gender roles in summer camp'; 'Visibility and invisibility: the creation of gay and lesbian spaces'; 'Wailing at the Western Wall? The gendered experiences of visitors to Jerusalem's Kotel'; and 'Gender and the gym: an analysis of Trent University's Athletic Facility'). Providing an opportunity for the students to hear about each other's research also helps to ensure that the wealth of material is not lost once the course is over. Self-reflection that supports independent learning is enhanced by encouraging students to research and then report on topics that take them beyond traditional library-based essays. Allowing them to share this research with their peers is a further reinforcement. This format allows students to gain experience presenting a 'conference paper' in a supportive environment. Students are not required to make an oral presentation but I do urge them to see this as a safe environment in which to hone their skills. The fact that the students know they will be sharing their work with their peers also encourages them to work to a high standard, and in this way their research is no longer an anonymous endeavour seen only by their professor. Some students have gone on to present their research to interested community groups, while others later attend undergraduate student conferences.

Final examinations

I end this exploration of assessments with a discussion of final exams. I am of two minds as to whether a cumulative assessment of learning in the form of a final exam is a useful instrument (Ory 2003 offers a good summary of the issues at stake in this decision). When I do include a final exam, I use a model that continues my emphasis on catering to different student learning styles.

My exams provide students with the opportunity to answer questions from three of six equally weighted sections each containing a different type of question: multiple choice and true/false questions; definitions; short answers; a concept map; discussion of a quote of their choosing; and a traditional essay question. Students are provided with the exam structure at the beginning of the course and then again during the exam review. They are invited to reflect on how they learn and, therefore, which types of question are best suited to them.

Without doubt, the most challenging element of this approach to exams is writing a set of multiple choice and true/false questions that provides a comparable assessment with an essay question or a series of definitions. Care in composing questions is required and I devote considerable time to crafting questions. I try to balance scope and detail in the questions. My confidence that this format is fair to students regardless of which sections they choose is enhanced by my consistent observation that the type of questions answered does not affect the grades the students achieve. The one exception to this is the multiple choice and true/false section. Although this section is selected by the largest number of students, it also consistently gives the students the most trouble, as evidenced in their test results. To counter the impact of this, I always warn students and encourage them to give careful consideration to their choice.

To assist with their consolidation of course material, the exam structure I employ includes at least one section that allows students to prepare in advance for their specific response. So, for example, I often let students choose a quote from the course readings that they believe captures the central dimensions of the course themes. They bring this quote to the exam and use it either as the base for preparing a concept map, or as the base for an essay question. This encourages an integrative approach to learning and also accommodates students who find the time pressure of exams stressful. Students who tend to focus on and absorb details can weigh their exam towards short, factual-based questions, while those who think conceptually typically choose essay questions. In this way students can proactively structure their own exam in such a way that they 'play to their strengths', but at the same time the requirement that they answer three of six sections ensures that they can't avoid the essential material as I define it.

For many of us teaching is a passion. We are motivated by concern for our students and we are driven by a desire to ensure the best possible environment for learning. But for all of our idealistic motivations, at the end of the day most of us operate within relatively rigid structures that require us to assess student progress by assigning grades to work. In this chapter I have charted my approach to ensuring a balance between the pragmatic and the idealistic. And I have laid out some of the strategies I employ to support my determination to foster holistic, independent learning that is accessible to all students.

Notes

1   I haven't described these larger assignments in this chapter, but in addition to traditional research essays, I encourage students to consider preparing: a teaching unit for students in the teacher education programme; a website; an anthology/annotated bibliography; community-based research; legislation trail; photo or acoustic essay; or a video or radio documentary.
2   Also known as node-link maps, knowledge maps and mind maps.

References

Canadian Association of University Teachers (2010) *2009–2010 CAUT Almanac of Post-Secondary Education in Canada*. http://www.caut.ca/pages.asp?page=442, accessed 8 January 2010.

Carson, D. (2009) Is style everything? Teaching that achieves its objectives, *Cinema Journal*, 48(3): 95–101.

Doyle, S. (2010) *Writing for Government Course*. http://web.uvic.ca/~sdoyle/E302/Notes/Letter%20Writing%20tips.html, accessed 8 January 2010.

hooks, b. (1994) *Teaching to Transgress: Education as the Practice of Freedom*. New York: Routledge.

Nesbit, J.C. and Adesope, O.O. (2006) Learning with concept and knowledge maps: a meta-analysis, *Review of Educational Research*, 76(3): 413–48.

Ory, J.C. (2003) The final exam, *Association for Psychological Science Observer*, 16(10). http://www.psychologicalscience.org/observer/getArticle.cfm?id=1414, accessed 20 January 2010.

Weimer, M. (2002) *Learner-Centered Teaching: Five Key Changes to Practice*. San Francisco, CA: Jossey-Bass.

Wurtele, S. and Ritchie, J. (2005) Healthy travel, healthy environments: integrating youth and child perspectives into local municipal transportation planning, *Children, Youth and Environments* 15(2): 356–70.

13 In the lion's den: teaching and assessing medical ethics

Wendy Rogers

Introduction

Teaching ethics in a medical school can be a challenging process. Commonly, ethics courses are compulsory; almost as commonly, students see ethical issues as common sense, too difficult to resolve, or a matter of opinion, and may resist the teaching. The perceived lack of relevance is compounded by a mismatch between allocation of curriculum space and students' readiness to engage with ethical issues. In early years, when teaching time is freely available, students are keen to master 'hard science' and are relatively unaware of the ethical issues they will face in practice. This realization comes in later years when there is less curriculum time and students are often widely dispersed on placements, limiting face-to-face teaching. When I started teaching medical ethics at Flinders University in South Australia, I was blithely ignorant of these and other challenges. After a couple of years and some disastrous student feedback, the onus was on me to develop imaginative teaching methods that would be educationally sound, informed by best practice in ethics teaching and, most importantly, engage the students. Assessment had to play a key role in all of my courses, from first year through to final year, for without assessment, ethics courses risk marginalization. It is of course a truism in education that assessment drives learning. This is especially true in the extremely competitive atmosphere of a medical school (Mitchell *et al.* 1993; Goldie 2000; Boon and Turner 2004).

Background

My approach to assessment was tempered by a number of factors. First, there is no agreed approach to assessing medical ethics in the literature (Boon and Turner 2004). Indeed, the very aims of medical ethics teaching are contested: is the aim to mould the character of students into 'good' doctors, or to provide students with the relevant knowledge and skills to respond adequately to the issues they encounter (Eckles *et al.* 2005)? I took the latter path, and linked the assessment methods to my goals of teaching, which were to produce graduates who:

- understood basic ethical concepts;
- were competent in ethical debate;
- were competent in ethical analysis; and
- applied relevant ethical concepts in practice.

In designing the assessment, I drew upon Miller's hierarchy of learning, by progressively requiring students to demonstrate that they know, know how, can show how and finally perform the skills in question (Miller 1990). Initially this was an intuitive process, driven by my beliefs about the need for logical progression in the ethics teaching process. At the start of my tenure, existing ethics teaching was linked to the clinical problems studied by the students each week. The medical course at Flinders University was modelled upon problem-based learning (PBL). This was a process that left almost no control over the content or order of the ethics material presented to students, as the weekly problems were set by other disciplines. As I designed my ideal curriculum and developed arguments for teaching ethics outside the PBL framework, I started to develop some theoretical insights, and was able to use Miller to argue my case. The medical course as a whole embraced the hierarchy of learning, which made it easier for colleagues to appreciate my teaching and assessment requirements.

As I was the sole academic responsible for ethics teaching in the Flinders University Graduate Entry Medical Program (GEMP), I was able to take a whole-of-degree, whole-of-curriculum perspective to develop an assessment pyramid that integrated and built upon preceding knowledge and skills from Year 1 to Year 4. Being the sole academic, I also had an interest in developing assessments that did not result in endless piles of marking, or in gratuitously easy opportunities for plagiarism. That ruled out essays, and too many exams. My other goal was to develop assessments that not only tested ethical learning but also fostered and tested generic skills. There were two reasons for this. The first was that some of these generic skills, such as accurate referencing or review of website materials, were not formally taught or assessed elsewhere in the course. Adding them to my assessments remedied this. Second, I was battling the perception that ethics was unimportant or irrelevant, therefore I hoped that linking ethics assessment with assessment of generic skills would increase the value of the learning in the eyes of the students.

Year 1

In Year 1, I replaced a series of lectures and a short-answer written exam with research-based group work. Although there does not seem to be definitive proof that small-group activities enhance learning in ethics, there is some consensus in the literature about the value of this teaching mode (Goldie 2000; Dingle and Stuber 2008). In addition, feedback from evaluation had shown that students wanted small-group activities as an alternative to lectures, a finding that is consistent with the literature (Eckles *et al.* 2005). Lacking a budget for tutors, I developed a topic that required students working in small groups to:

- engage in research, gaining familiarity with major resources and the methods of ethics research;
- gain skills in use of ethics terminology and analysis of issues;
- debate within their group to develop their presentations;
- listen to opposing viewpoints; and
- practise two kinds of presentation skills (oral and written).

Students were allocated to paired groups, each of which researched a set topic. Topics were carefully selected to promote controversy, passion, discussion and learning. These included using organs from anencephalic babies, removing feeding tubes from patients with post-coma unresponsiveness, creating saviour siblings and prescribing performance-enhancing drugs for athletes. The students researched and debated topics within their groups, in preparation for public presentations, with one group in each pair preparing the 'for' side and the other the 'against' side.

Students created superb presentations, going far beyond my expectations with their depth of learning, originality and enthusiasm. The assessment for this was based upon each group's oral presentation to the whole class, and the preparation and presentation of a conference-style poster. A panel including senior clinical staff and bioethicists evaluated the posters. Grades were awarded by group, to a 'non-graded pass' or 'fail' standard, in keeping with the assessment philosophy of Years 1–2 of the medical course. Assessments were completed on the day of the presentations, with no additional marking required. The students' evaluations were extremely positive:

- The independent learning aspect and the air of competition stimulated us to know the topic as best we could. This was great for our own knowledge.
- The group discussion was particularly stimulating and beneficial.
- Issues were interesting, use of active participation was a great method of learning.

> (Students' comments, from evaluation of the
> Year 1 topic in 2006)

Year 2

Prior to my revisions, the Year 2 course also consisted of lectures, with assessment by essays on pre-set topics. The standard of the essays was variable, with considerable opportunities for plagiarism. I abolished the essays and replaced them with reviews of websites, a method adapted from a colleague in Speech Pathology at Flinders University. The task involved students identifying two ethics websites (that is, with content related to medical ethics), and writing a short review of each. In their reviews, students were asked to address credibility, quality of content and ease of navigation, and to describe briefly what they learned from the sites.

This assessment method engaged the students and was relevant to ethics and medicine in a realistic way. The task fostered independent learning by teaching students to critically evaluate websites using a number of criteria. This is a skill that is useful in practice when patients bring in materials from websites to discuss with their doctor. Students engaged enthusiastically with the task:

> This website review task has been a really good one. As a former secondary teacher I find it beneficial (and more enjoyable!) from a pedagogical perspective to have a range of assessment styles . . . making assessments for ethics varying and creative in nature.
>
> (Unsolicited feedback, Year 2 student 2007)

Following completion of Years 1 and 2, the students had been assessed on their understanding of basic ethical concepts, and their nascent skills in ethical analysis and debate, in preparation for the practical analytic work awaiting them in Year 3.

Year 3

At Flinders University in Year 3 of the GEMP, the students' learning was based around clinical attachments that varied according to site, and were either a series of rotations through hospital specialities, or a longitudinal community attachment. Irrespective of site, Year 3 offered students their first intensive immersion in clinical practice and, as such, could be quite confronting. Because of this, Year 3 offered unparalleled opportunities for teaching and learning based upon the students' own experiences of ethical issues as they arise in practice. To this end, I designed an assessment that required students to identify and analyse ethical issues arising in the care of their patients, thereby

Table 13.1 Clinical ethics analysis framework

Case summary	Brief description of the patient's history with relevant clinical information
Problem list	Identification of the ethical, legal and social issues arising from the case
Case analysis	i Patient's perspective
	ii Practitioner's duties and obligations
	iii Consequences for
	• patient
	• practitioners
	• health care team
	• hospital
	• community
Alternatives	Discussion of alternatives, and their respective advantages and disadvantages
Conclusion	Statement of preferred course of action, with reasons
References	Four up-to-date and relevant references

Source: Adapted from Rogers and Braunack-Mayer (2009: 16)

demonstrating 'shows how' in Miller's hierarchy of learning (1990). Every student identified both an adult and a paediatric case, each of which was anonymized and written up using an ethical analysis framework (Rogers and Braunack-Mayer 2009), summarized in Table 13.1.

This task relied upon integration of clinical and ethico-legal knowledge. The cases were discussed at tutorials that were co-taught with senior clinicians, thereby emphasizing the importance of ethics for clinical practice. The assessment criteria related to specific skills, as in Table 13.2. Each numbered criterion, including the six parts of criterion 3, was graded from 1 (falls far short of requirements) to 7 (of excellent standard). This method of grading was developed on the advice of the medical school assessment expert, and used for other upper-level assignments.

After an introductory trial, the grades from this task were allocated to form a substantial part of the overall Year 3 assessments, which focused the students' attention considerably. Students could not proceed to the next year of the course unless they achieved a satisfactory grade in this task. In addition to the ethics case analyses, there were also ethics questions in the Year 3 end-of-year objective structured clinical exam (OSCE) or in the multiple choice papers. The marks from these questions were linked to the associated specialities rather than attributed to the ethics component of the course (for example a consent question based on a clinical example in general practice would be graded as part of general practice).

Table 13.2 Assessment criteria for ethical case analysis

Criterion	Descriptor
Case summary	Brief, well-organized, allows reader to understand issues
Identification and definition of issues	Demonstrates capacity to identify and list relevant issues
Case analysis	i Demonstrates ability to use ethics terminology appropriately ii Demonstrates understanding of ethical concepts iii Demonstrates sensitivity to differing perspectives (patient, professional) iv Demonstrates knowledge of relevant legal and professional guidelines v Considers impact upon health care team, institution and wider community vi Reaches a conclusion stating preferred resolution and reasons for this
References	Demonstrates capacity to find up-to-date, relevant references and use the Harvard system
Global competence score	Overall impression of student's competence at task

Year 4

Assessment in Year 4 mainly focused on the students in practice, and was addressed through reflective portfolios, in-training assessments and an interactive web-based module on whistle-blowing (Palmer and Rogers 2005). The latter was assessed by taking a short multiple-choice test on the material, which was marked automatically. Again, a pass in this assessment was required to graduate.

All of these changes to assessment were implemented simultaneously. This was hard work, but one of the benefits was the opportunity to observe the changes in engagement, attitude, knowledge and skills as the cohorts progressed through each year. Not unexpectedly there were noticeable improvements in the analytic skills of students who had completed all four years of the ethics curriculum, compared with those who were already in Year 2 or 3 at the time of implementation.

Discussion

This brief description of teaching and assessment methods in medical ethics raises a number of issues that are recurrent in the medical ethics literature. At this point, it is worth noting that teaching and assessing medical ethics in medical courses is a relatively recent phenomenon. Goldie (2000) traces the recent history of the introduction of ethics teaching in English-speaking countries, noting the emergence of ideal curricula, for example, the Consensus Statement (1998) in the UK, later joined by that of the Association of Teachers of Ethics and Law (2001); and the evolution of teaching strategies. In particular, Goldie (2000: 116; see also Mitchell *et al.* 1993; Boon and Turner 2004) notes the 'widespread consensus on the importance of assessment for medical ethics education'.

While, however, there is agreement about the importance of assessment, there is to date little consensus about the best methods of assessment (Boon and Turner 2004). This may relate, in part at least, to the lack of consensus about the aims of medical ethics teaching. As I mentioned in the introduction to this chapter, curricular aims vary from seeking to engender good character in medical students, through to the acquisition of specific cognitive skills in ethical problem solving; this is known as the virtue/skill dichotomy (Eckles *et al.* 2005). Boon and Turner (2004) describe concerns in ethics assessment including lack of objectivity, problems with validity of methods, and the difficulty of assessing beliefs and intentions. A final challenge is that of evaluating the overall effectiveness of medical ethics education, studies of which present 'varying and conflicting results' (Eckles *et al.* 2005: 1146).

From the literature, it is clear that it is important to assess medical ethics teaching, and that, despite the difficulties, there are general principles to follow. First, my aim was to design assessment methods that would engage the students, and be linked to the teaching methods in creative ways. Student surveys, as well as pedagogical principles, indicate the value of variety in teaching methods (Harden *et al.* 1984; Mattick and Bligh 2006; Johnston and Haughton 2007). I followed this principle in the development of the Flinders course and extended it to provide variety in the assessments. Variety in assessment methods in ethics has not to date been discussed in the literature; in my courses it seemed to work well, as demonstrated by student engagement and positive feedback.

Second, learning outcomes should be matched to methods of assessment. As students progress through the hierarchy of learning (Miller 1990), the emphasis in assessment should change from demonstrating knowledge and understanding through to competency in clinical ethics (Campbell *et al.* 2007). This requires devising assessment tasks that are appropriate for the learning outcomes at each level of the pyramid. The assessment tasks in Years 1 and 2 of the Flinders course were designed to test students' developing knowledge and skills, with their clinical ethical competency assessed through activities in the final years. In the curriculum design, I attempted to match learning opportunities with educational needs. At each stage of their course, students had the chance to master the necessary skills, at a time when the students themselves could see the relevance of this.

Third, there is a need for the development of reliable and valid tools for ethics assessment. The clinical ethics analysis framework used in Year 3 assessment was refined over a number of years, both for inter-marker reliability and for validity, thereby meeting some of the requirements of an ideal tool (Savulescu *et al.* 1999). This does not of course address the broader challenge of ascertaining the long-term impact of medical ethics education, for which dedicated longitudinal studies are necessary.

Fourth, ethics teaching and assessment should be integrated both horizontally and vertically across the medical course (Eckles *et al.* 2005). I designed my course around student-centred learning, occurring when and where the students needed it in the course, and anticipated the learning needs of students to deliver resources and learning opportunities at times when they could take advantage of them. This required a growing level of integration with the clinical teaching, such that by Year 3, the ethics teaching was part of the speciality clinical teaching, with the cases for assessment identified through clinical attachments. This level of integration was supported by creative use of flexible delivery methods and, at times, travel to remote sites to deliver and support teaching.

Finally, and most importantly, the teaching and assessment of medical ethics must engage students, fire their imaginations and generate enthusiasm. This is not always an easy task, for the student body can be critical to the point of hostility, especially if they feel 'preached at' in any way. But once students make the connection between ethics and medicine, the rewards are immense. Medical students are capable of operating at very high levels, bringing fresh perspectives and providing new insights into challenging problems. In addition, the field of medical ethics evolves constantly, creating a never-ending supply of new and interesting problems for analysis and discussion. Creative and meaningful assessments add to the strength of the teaching and learning, and support student engagement.

References

Association of Teachers of Ethics and Law in Australian and New Zealand Medical Schools (2001) An ethics core curriculum for Australasian medical schools, *Medical Journal of Australia*, 175: 205–10.

Boon, K. and Turner, J. (2004) Ethical and professional conduct of medical students: review of current assessment measures and controversies, *Journal of Medical Ethics*, 30(2): 221–6.

Campbell, A., Chin, J. and Voo, T. (2007) How can we know that ethics education produces ethical doctors? *Medical Teacher*, 29(5): 431–6.

Consensus Statement by Teachers of Medical Ethics and Law in UK Medical Schools (1998) Teaching medical ethics and law within medical education: a model for the UK core curriculum, *Journal of Medical Ethics*, 24: 188–92.

Dingle, A. and Stuber, M. (2008) Ethics education, *Child and Adolescent Psychiatric Clinics of North America*, 17(1): 187–207.

Eckles, R., Meslin, E., Gaffney, M. and Helft, P. (2005) Medical ethics education: where are we? Where should we be going? A review, *Academic Medicine*, 80(12): 1143–52.

Goldie, J. (2000) Review of ethics curricula in undergraduate medical education, *Medical Education*, 34(2): 108–19.

Harden, R.M., Sowden, S. and Dunn, W.R. (1984) Educational strategies in curriculum development: the SPICES model, *Medical Education*, 18: 284.

Johnston, C. and Haughton, P. (2007) Medical students' perceptions of their ethics teaching, *Journal of Medical Ethics*, 33(7): 418–22.

Mattick, K. and Bligh, J. (2006) Teaching and assessing medical ethics: where are we now? *Journal of Medical Ethics*, 32(3): 181–5.

Miller, G.E. (1990) The assessment of clinical skills/competence/performance, *Academic Medicine*, 65 (Suppl.): S63–S67.

Mitchell, K., Myser, C. and Kerridge, I. (1993) Assessing the clinical ethical competence of undergraduate medical students, *Journal of Medical Ethics*, 19(4): 230–6.

Palmer, N. and Rogers, W. (2005) Whistle blowing in the medical curriculum: a response to Faunce, *Monash Bioethics Review*, 24: 50–8.

Rogers, W. and Braunack-Mayer, A. (2009) *Practical Ethics for General Practice*, 2nd edn. Oxford: Oxford University Press.

Savulescu, J., Crisp, R., Fulford, K. and Hope, T. (1999) Evaluating ethics competence in medical education, *Journal of Medical Ethics*, 25(5): 367–74.

14 Upgrading teaching and assessment in a traditional medical course

Peter Schwartz

My early days in teaching and assessment

I sometimes wonder whether my students are as grateful as I am that my teaching practice has evolved the way it has – particularly when it comes to assessment. In hindsight, it surprises me somewhat that I have changed so much, since the traditional assessments I experienced at university and medical school suited me so well. I could even say that almost everything I needed for doing well in these assessments I learned in – English classes! I learned spelling, grammar, composition, how to write decent essays, and how to express myself clearly. So when it came to typical essay questions that essentially asked us to 'write everything you know about X' or 'write everything your teacher has told you in lectures about X' (in 10? 15? 30? minutes), I had little trouble obliging.

When I first started teaching at the University of Otago Medical School in 1971, I had no training in and little insight into the principles or practice of education. I was relying on my own experiences at university and medical school. However, I was keen to learn from educational workshops and books. In those early days I was particularly influenced by books by Michael Simpson (1972), George Miller *et al.* (1961) and Donald Bligh (1972). What I saw in those volumes stimulated me to try novel approaches and led to one of the major recommendations I have routinely made during educational workshops for new teachers: *dare to be different*, even from the start of your teaching career.

Building on ideas gleaned from workshops and readings, I introduced changes to the teaching in my course: improvements to lectures (Schwartz 1980), to laboratory classes (Schwartz 1975), and even to the methods for delivering the course material (self-instructional units, study guides, tape-slide programmes; Schwartz 1980).

Everything I saw or read emphasized the key roles of feedback (for example, Simpson 1972: 94–5) and of rehearsal/reinforcement (for example, Bligh 1972: 62–3) in promoting successful learning, and the importance of valid, reliable assessment of student performance (for example, Miller *et al.* 1961: 205–6;

Simpson 1972: 133–7). Accordingly, I implemented several changes to the traditional practice in my course:

- brief formative quizzes at the ends of lectures so that students could see whether they had picked up the main points (and incorporating simple, homemade audience response cards so that I could see whether any points had been missed by more than a few students; Schwartz 1980);
- self-assessment quizzes to accompany sets of notes and self-instructional units; and
- replacement of the 'all or nothing' final examination, comprising ill-defined long essays, with multiple assessments throughout the teaching term consisting of a variety of types of question (short essay, short answer, multiple choice), although most of the questions were still traditional in content.

On teaching evaluation questionnaires, students found my methods highly acceptable, and examination performance was at least as good as it had been before my initiatives, so I was feeling pretty good about my teaching after five to ten years at Otago. Fortunately (or too bad, depending on your point of view), things were about to change dramatically.

As I reflected on what I read (with especial influence now coming from an insightful article by Dennis Fox, 1983, and Stephen Abrahamson's articles later collected in his book, 1996) and what I observed in my own teaching, I recognized that what I had felt was wrong with my own medical education was being replicated in many courses (including my own) at the Otago Medical School. I concluded that medical students:

- were spending too much time sitting and listening in lecture theatres rather than thinking, engaging, applying or solving problems;
- were being done a great disservice by being taught by teachers who seemed to think that medical education consists solely of the transmission of large numbers of isolated facts;
- routinely lacked adequate feedback on their progress; and
- were sitting examinations that mainly required recognition, recall or repetition of the same masses of isolated facts presented to them by their teachers.

As was neatly summarized by Abrahamson (1996: 104), 'There seems to be too much attention to what is perceived as "teaching" and not nearly enough to "learning".'

When I carefully considered the objectives of my teaching, I realized that what I wanted was for my students to be able to *do* things, not just *know* things. For my course, this meant that they should be able to interpret information

and apply knowledge. It has long been acknowledged even by their propo-
nents that lectures are very poor for developing these abilities in students
(Bligh 1972). To learn these skills, students need opportunities to apply and
practise them, not just hear them described by a lecturer. It appeared only
logical to move to a teaching method that would encourage this application
and practice, supported by opportunities for feedback, answers to questions,
and close contact between teachers and students.

So despite my own success as a student with traditional teaching and
assessment, and despite the apparent success of my early efforts to improve
teaching and assessment in my course, I was forced to conclude that major
change was needed.

My responses to this conclusion can be encapsulated in three of the dozen
or so principles of good teaching that I believe in most firmly and that I endorse
for all teachers:

- recognize that what students put into, do during and get out of classes
  are more important for learning than what the teacher does. I believe
  that the teacher's role should be to organize activities and experiences
  that are important, interesting, motivating, enjoyable and challenging for the students;
- arrange for the students to obtain feedback on their performance and
  progress as frequently as possible; and
- assess not just what the students know but what they can do with
  what they know.

A more enlightened teaching philosophy

Based on insights gained from workshops, reading and reflection on my own
experiences, my model of the role of the teacher had become one of the 'developed' models proposed by Fox rather than one of his 'simple' models (Fox
1983). In the developed models ('travelling companion or guide' and 'grower'),
the teacher recognizes the important role played by students in the learning
transaction. In contrast, in the simple models ('transfer of information' and
'shaper' of students' minds), the focus is almost solely on what the teacher
does. If our teaching sessions were to be truly a shared, interactive experience,
it would be essential that students prepare for class sessions and participate
actively during those sessions. When an opportunity arose for curricular revision in 1988, I worked with my departmental colleagues to replace all of our
lectures and laboratory classes with a series of small-group, problem- and case-
based sessions that built on the principles of problem-based learning (Barrows
1985; Kaufman 1985) and emphasized application of knowledge rather than
information transfer (Schwartz 1989, 1997).

This new programme proved highly popular with the students and with my colleagues from its first trial. Observations included:

- much more enthusiasm, dedication, curiosity and cooperation among the students during class than were present in the old course;
- strong positive reactions by the students on course evaluation questionnaires;
- positive responses by the teachers, who all actively sought to take as large a part as possible in the teaching programme each year;
- an incredible improvement in the educational atmosphere, with much better interaction and communication between teachers and students than in the old course; and
- 15–20 per cent better performance by the students in problem-solving examinations that were at least as difficult as those in the old course.

Responses and results have remained comparable since then, even with the application of an identical style of teaching to new courses that we have prepared and taught. Content and activities are deleted, modified or added to conform with changes in knowledge or in medical technology, but the process of the class is retained.

Assessment in the new programme

With such a dramatic change in the style of teaching and learning, it would have been unfair (if not downright criminal) to retain the assessment practices we had employed in the old course. So, since 1988, I have applied an array of assessment and feedback processes that are much more in accord with my more 'enlightened' approach to teaching.

Style of question

Even in our old course, assessment questions had always been closely aligned with our objectives for content, but they required little more than memory and reproduction of that content. With the new teaching approach, it seemed sensible that they should demand something more: interpretation, application and problem solving. I was quite comfortable with this, as it was consistent with one of the principles already enunciated: the importance of assessing not just what students know, but what they can do with what they know. (This principle has been adopted by no less a body than the National Board of Medical Examiners for the medical certification examinations in the United States; NBME 2002.) In all examinations that 'counted', therefore, I totally replaced traditional questions with problem-solving questions that demanded the same sorts of skills as those required of the students during class sessions. In practice, this meant for example that students had to interpret data to arrive at a diagnosis, choose among sets of laboratory data to match lab findings with descriptions of patients, or identify an inconsistent result among a series given for a hypothetical patient. In most instances, students had to give brief explanations for their conclusions, allowing examiners to see whether their reasons for a correct answer were right and to allow some credit to be given to students who applied relevant information but for some reason drew the wrong conclusion. (In one large experiment, however, we found that it was unnecessary for students to explain their answers: if they got the correct answer, it was usually for the correct reason. Without requiring explanations, therefore, we could ask more questions during the same examination time, allowing wider sampling (and hence improving test reliability) and more opportunity for students who had drawn an incorrect conclusion in one question to 'redeem' themselves in other questions; Schwartz and Loten 1999.)

An example of the sort of question I routinely use in final examinations is shown in Box 14.1. Although the content may mean little to those outside medicine, I hope that you can see how little it resembles a traditional open-ended, rote-memory essay.

The response of students to this type of question has been remarkably positive. While they frequently report finding the questions challenging, anecdotally they find them both fair tests of the skills that we expect of them and a refreshing contrast to the traditional essay questions asked in other disciplines.

Practice/preparation

During small-group sessions, students get the opportunity to apply information and develop the sorts of skills we want to encourage. One of the responsibilities of the course tutors is to ensure that all students in the group grasp relevant concepts and develop the appropriate skills in applying them. This can be difficult when students, for reasons of cultural background, shyness or fear of exposing lack of understanding, don't ask questions, contribute to the group's deliberations, or venture answers to the problems posed. Yet on the final examinations, *each* student will have to demonstrate his or her abilities. Therefore, I try to ensure that all students have opportunities to practise the skills that are at the heart of our course's objectives and obtain feedback on their skill development. In the first instance, this practice and feedback comes from a self-assessment quiz that students complete before each session (during which model answers are provided) and from the class exercises and oral feedback on the group's responses during class sessions. For those students who require something more, there are additional cases, puzzles and games that, while tackled in class by the whole group, are accompanied by written feedback that clarifies issues and explains the answers. One session even specifically includes

---

Box 14.1 Example of a final examination question (medicine)

Mr Y, a 48-year-old department store manager comes for consultation with his GP because of nausea and vomiting, abdominal distension and loss of appetite. The symptoms began approximately six weeks ago. He denies having lost weight or having noticed any change in his intestinal habits. The patient reports enjoying 'a glass of wine or two' with his meals, and some whisky in the evenings. On examination, his temperature is 38.2° C, pulse is 96/min, respirations are 10/min and blood pressure is 120/70. There is a yellow tinge on his skin and sclerae, and spider angiomata on his chest. Palmar erythema is present. The liver is enlarged and palpable at 6 cm below the right costal border; the spleen is palpable at 2 cm below the left costal border. Ascites is present and he has bilateral pitting oedema to his knees.

Mr Y was given a battery of biochemical tests. Among them were the ones listed below.

In this list of tests and results, **ONE OF THE RESULTS DOES NOT FIT** with what would be expected for Mr Y's condition. Which is the result that does not fit?

EXPLAIN YOUR CHOICE AND BRIEFLY EXPLAIN THE UNDERLYING MECHANISM OF EACH OF THE OTHER RESULTS. (10 minutes)

	result	reference range
plasma calcium (total)	1.90 mmol/L	(2.05–2.55)
plasma cholesterol	2.9 mmol/L	(3.0–5.5)
plasma alanine aminotransferase (ALT)	975 U/L	(8–40)
plasma gammaglutamyl transferase (GGT)	220 U/L	(1–50)
prothrombin time	12.3 seconds	(7.6–10.6)
urine bilirubin	positive at 1+	(nil)

---

time for students to attempt several questions that have appeared in recent final examinations, followed by a run through of the correct answers and explanations, and an indication of what examiners would have been looking for in various grades of answer.

More opportunity for practice and feedback

To accompany a new pre-clinical medical curriculum that began at Otago in 1997, a programme of regular, frequent computerized testing of all course modules was introduced. This was mainly to be formative, with feedback on correctness or incorrectness of answers and indications of areas of weakness to be given to each student on completion of each test. Students were required to reach a level of around 70 per cent correct to pass, but they had up to three opportunities to pass equivalent versions of each test.

I saw these tests as an opportunity to give students more practice and feedback in the skills that we expected them to develop in our course. Notwithstanding assertions by some of my colleagues that questions testing recognition of isolated facts were the only sort that could be asked in menu-driven computerized tests, I was determined to demonstrate otherwise. For each of the two computer tests for the third year module that was my responsibility, I designed a preliminary 'basics' component that included terminology, definitions, basic facts, and so on, that students *had to* grasp before they could do any 'applying'. Students had to answer 90 per cent of these questions correctly to complete the test. They had an unlimited number of opportunities to reach this level on the sole version of the basics component of each test. Once passed, they didn't have to repeat the basics component, regardless of their performance in the subsequent 'applied' section, which had the usual three versions and maximum of three attempts to reach the passing level of about 70 per cent. The applied section consisted solely of questions that demanded the same sorts of application of concepts as was required in class sessions and in final examinations, but no explanations for the answers were required. An example question is shown in Box 14.2.

Box 14.2   Example of a computerized, in-course test question (applied knowledge in medicine)

END 1.36	Below are listed 6 conditions related to thyroid function. You will be given a series of laboratory results

Marks: 7

END 1.36 Below are listed 6 conditions related to thyroid function. You will be given a series of laboratory results for a patient who had signs of disordered thyroid function. **Assume that the patient had only one of the listed conditions**. After each result you are to indicate which of the diagnoses **are eliminated** by the result by dragging the corresponding letter or letters (A to F) into the empty box beside the result. You can return diagnoses to the list by clicking on the box where you have put them, or you can start again by clicking on the button at the lower left. At each step any number of diagnoses (including 0) may be eliminated. **There may be more than one diagnosis still possible after the last result. NB: Consider the laboratory results in the order shown.**

A   excess administration of exogenous thyroid hormones
B   toxic multinodular goitre
C   Graves' Disease
D   an inherited defect in one of the enzymes for synthesis of thyroid hormones
E   iodine deficiency
F   pituitary failure

This laboratory result..........

......**eliminates these diagnoses (0 or more)**

The plasma TSH level was low.

The plasma total T_4 and free T_4 were high.

An injected dose of TRH led to no rise in plasma TSH levels.

The patient was given a small oral dose of radioactive iodine (^{125} I). The subsequent scan gave the results shown below on the right. A normal scan is shown on the left for comparison.

Start Again

Mark Now   Next Question

Again unlike many of my colleagues in other modules, I felt that these computerized tests offered the chance for students to obtain 'warrants of fitness' in my module, analogous to the certificates given to cars that have passed their inspections for roadworthiness. In the computer tests I was able to sample the students' abilities much more widely than was possible in final examinations. Thus if students could pass the applied sections of my tests at a 70 per cent level, they should be able to feel confident that they were 'fit' to pass in my module, and only if something went drastically wrong might they fail my component of the final examination.

From the students' perspective, these tests were very successful. In one of the three years that students were asked by a faculty administrator to identify the two 'most helpful' computer tests for the year, the two tests for my module received about 80 per cent of the votes, with none of the other 19 tests for the year attracting more than 3 per cent. Results from the other two years were comparable. From my perspective, the tests achieved their purpose, as very few students failed in my component of the final examination.

Finale

In this chapter I am not suggesting that my methods are unique or revolutionary. Most of them have built upon insights obtained from the variety of sources I have named. The fervour and passion for improving medical education that were so obvious in those sources closely matched and further stimulated my own commitment. Although most of my favourite sources are now quite old, their basic messages are being reiterated even today in books and other resources such as the 29 separate booklets in the Understanding Medical Education series from the Association for the Study of Medical Education (ASME 2006–08) and the ABC of Learning and Teaching in Medicine from the *British Medical Journal* (Cantillon *et al.* 2003). What I will state quite categorically, however, is that my methods have resulted at least in part from another of my basic principles of good teaching: I care about students and about teaching and I try to do the best job of it that I can.

References

Abrahamson, S. (1996) *Essays on Medical Education*. Lanham, MD: University Press of America.

ASME (2006–08) *Understanding Medical Education* (29 booklets). Edinburgh: Association for the Study of Medical Education.

Barrows, H.S. (1985) *How to Design a Problem-Based Curriculum for the Preclinical Years*. New York: Springer.

Bligh, D.A. (1972) *What's the Use of Lectures?* Harmondsworth: Penguin.

Cantillon, P., Hutchinson, L. and Wood, D. (eds) (2003) *ABC of Learning and Teaching in Medicine*. London: BMJ Publishing.

Fox, D. (1983) Personal theories of teaching, *Studies in Higher Education*, 8: 151–63.

Kaufman, A. (ed.) (1985) *Implementing Problem-Based Medical Education. Lessons from Successful Innovations*. New York: Springer.

Miller, G.E., Abrahamson, S., Cohen, I.S. *et al.* (1961) *Teaching and Learning in Medical School*. Cambridge, MA: Harvard University Press.

NBME (2002) *Constructing Written Test Questions for the Basic and Clinical Sciences*, 3rd revised edn. Philadelphia, PA: National Board of Medical Examiners.

Schwartz, P.L. (1975) A laboratory course in clinical biochemistry emphasizing interest and relevance, *Journal of Medical Education*, 50: 903–5.

Schwartz, P.L. (1980) Teaching methods down under, *Biochemical Education*, 8: 16–20.

Schwartz, P.L. (1989) The right place at the right time. An example of innovation in medical education, *Teaching and Learning in Medicine*, 1: 171–5.

Schwartz, P. (1997) Persevering with problem-based learning, in D. Boud and G. Feletti (eds) *The Challenge of Problem-Based Learning*, 2nd edn. London: Kogan Page.

Schwartz, P.L. and Loten, E.G. (1999) Brief problem-solving questions in medical school examinations: is it necessary for students to explain their answers? *Medical Education*, 33: 823–7.

Simpson, M.A. (1972) *Medical Education. A Critical Approach*. London: Butterworths.

PART 4
Respecting and Supporting the Development of Students as Individuals

For the book's fourth part, I asked authors to set out their thoughts and experiences on respecting and supporting the development of students as individuals. How and why, for instance, do they help students from minority and disadvantaged groups participate successfully in their courses? How do they build students' confidence? And how do they guide and advise students? Although the authors have taken quite different paths, several of the chapters in this part reveal teachers grappling with the relationships or tensions between the needs of individual students, classrooms as communities of learners, and institutional systems and procedures.

To begin, in a thoroughly engaging and uplifting chapter, New Zealand author Lisa Emerson reflects on her teaching, beginning with the experiences teaching writing to resistant horticulture students that truly started her career as a teacher. With strong links to the work of Parker Palmer (2007) and bell hooks (1994, 2003) she takes up three issues vital to the theme of this part: acknowledging and attending to the uniqueness of students; dealing with the fears and anxieties all students bring to the class; and finally, developing the classroom as a safe, supportive community. Lisa is keen to make the point that it is these, and not the specific teaching tools we use, that support the development of students as individuals.

Kathleen Regan's chapter offers a fascinating insight to the ways in which she has drawn together two major inspirations to review and shape her Spanish teaching. The first inspiration was a professor who had influenced Kathleen when she was a graduate student by likening the role of a teacher to that of a gardener who must cultivate an environment in which students can flourish and bloom. The second inspiration comprises principles of good teaching practice set out in the work of Ken Bain (2004). In her chapter, Kathleen gives particular attention to the role of the teacher in creating communities of learners. She acknowledges issues taken up in the previous chapter by Lisa Emerson and sets out in detail ways she has strived to address those. But whatever specific teaching tools she uses, Kathleen makes it evident that in her work she remains guided by the powerful metaphor of the gardener who not only tends individual beings but who also seeks to create an environment that fosters the full variety of things in that environment.

Beginning with a quite different metaphor – that of the biblical Good Samaritan – psychologists Jerusha Detweiler-Bedell and Brian Detweiler-Bedell emphasize processes that encourage students to become skilled collaborators with professors and other students in the creation of new knowledge. For these authors, what matters in great teaching is being attentive educators and mentoring students effectively and efficiently. Drawing evidence from social psychology, they argue that this requires professors to slow down – avoiding being consumed by all of the day-to-day tasks that typically confront us – and they illustrate approaches that guide and support students to take responsibility for, and possession of, the learning endeavour.

In his chapter, Canadian psychologist Dennis Krebs recalls an eminent colleague's observation made to him early in his career about the relative power of individual and institutional ways of improving the lot of those who need help. From that point, Dennis resolved to work at both scales, supporting students individually and directly and also improving institutional arrangements to achieve those ends. The case being made here is important: supporting the development of students as individuals is not achieved solely by engaging with students on a one-to-one basis or even in the context of a university classroom. Instead, support can be realized through, for instance, structural changes in curricula, institutional reform, and efforts to heighten the perceived value of teaching.

Finally, the chapter by New Zealand educationalist Roger Moltzen takes up in more detail some of the matters set out in the previous chapter by Dennis Krebs. Roger notes that supporting and acknowledging students as individuals has significant implications for institutional systems and procedures and observes that this has led to significant systemic change in many universities. However, he cautions that without parallel shifts in teaching practice, institutional reform will be only partially successful. He then goes on to take up ideas set out by Leadbeater (2004) distinguishing between 'individualizing' learning and 'personalizing' learning. He emphasizes approaches built on personalization, and drawing from his own experiences shows how students can be engaged in devising their own learning plans and targets and determining how they will demonstrate their learning. And he hopes personalization will move us from the prospect of universities producing graduates who can run the world, to producing graduates who can change the world.

References

Bain, K. (2004) *What the Best College Teachers Do*. Cambridge, MA: Harvard University Press.

hooks, b. (1994) *Teaching to Transgress: Education as the Practice of Freedom.* New York and London: Routledge.

hooks, b. (2003) *Teaching Community: A Pedagogy of Hope.* New York and London: Routledge.

Leadbeater, C. (2004) *Personalisation through Participation: A New Script for Public Services.* http://www.demos.co.uk/publications/personalisation, accessed 2 April 2010.

Palmer, P. (2007) *The Courage to Teach,* 2nd edn. San Francisco, CA: John Wiley and Sons.

15 'I am a writer': unlocking fear and releasing possibility in the classroom

Lisa Emerson

> The academy is not paradise. But learning is a place where paradise can be created. The classroom, with all its limitation, remains a location of possibility.
>
> (hooks 1994: 207)

Three angry, disruptive students were the spark that set alight my passion for teaching writing.

In the early 1990s I was a new teacher in my first 'real' job, running a university writing centre, armed only with the dubiously relevant qualification of an MA in Victorian poetry. In New Zealand universities at this time, writing was just emerging as a new, contested aspect of the curriculum, and I was one of the first 'homegrown' university teachers to start my career in this field.

To acquire some skills in teaching writing, I volunteered to teach into a first-year writing course where it was soon clear I was in trouble. Three students seemed determined to dismantle what little confidence I had and carve it into small decorative pieces of their own design. They came to class unprepared. They sighed heavily whenever I spoke for more than two minutes. They wouldn't participate in any classroom activities.

Attempts to engage them were all rejected. So I spoke to the person running the course, who sighed wearily and said, 'Don't worry, they're *horticulture students*'. She went on to explain that all horticulture students had to take this course even though they uniformly hated it. 'What's baffling', she said, 'is that in class evaluations they rate the course highly on *This course helps me to write better*, but they mark it low on *This course meets my needs*. They don't know what they want.'

Next day, I ended the class early and asked my horticulture students to stay behind. With the air of innocents preparing for interrogation by police in a totalitarian state, they stayed. Yes, they were horticulture students, and yes, they hated this course. Because, they explained, 'if we wrote like you're teaching us in our horticulture papers we'd be mincemeat'.

They talked and then we talked. We wrote complex sentences on the whiteboard and reshaped them into bullet points. We worked through their assignments, removing qualifiers, reshaping sentences, cutting transitions. Within 15 minutes we were all laughing from the sheer exhilaration of discovery.

Later, when I spoke to the horticulture faculty, they agreed with the students. 'I don't want any of that flowery English department crap', said one person, 'I just want them to get their ideas down'. So, I visited the office of the person who made this course compulsory for horticulture students. 'It's a great course', he said. 'I'm so glad our students are being taught to write by the experts'.

On my way back to my office, I stopped at the library and discovered the literature on writing across the curriculum that was to become the basis of my teaching and research career.

I could have just failed those students. Just 12 weeks of gritting my teeth and it would have been over for them – and for me. That thought still makes me shiver. Because this was the day my career as a teacher began – and I could so easily have missed it. In that half hour I spent with those students, I began to learn so many things: that writing classes never come in a 'one size fits all' model, that there is no such thing as a generic writing course any more than there is a generic student writer with generic learning needs. That miracles, when they happen in a classroom, are not caused by the teacher but are part of an exquisite interchange, sometimes between teacher and students, sometimes (as I later learned) just between students. And that persevering in listening and paying attention to students can be a life-changing activity – can lead to learning that 'gets [so gloriously] out of hand' (Torrence 1975, cited in Gibbs 2006) that I can still feel the shock waves almost 20 years later.

I tell this story because it illustrates the theme of this chapter, showing what can happen when we honour our students as individuals. The question that then emerges for me is this: as a writing teacher, how can I sustainably support my students' development as individuals and as writers?

It is beyond the scope of this chapter to discuss why we should see our professional role as supporting students' development as individuals rather than just teaching to a series of learning outcomes. It is also beyond the scope of this chapter to discuss the multiple pedagogical practices and learning strategies that can be used for this purpose. Instead, I have chosen to discuss just three issues that are vital for me in answering this question.

Acknowledging and attending to uniqueness

In New Zealand, because of the contestable and emergent nature of writing as a discipline, the writing teacher must be a jack-of-all-trades. Over my 20 years of teaching, I have taught writing in a range of contexts: from running one-on-one programmes for pre-degree students (Emerson and Clerehan 2009), developing a WAC (writing across the curriculum) programme in a university's College of Sciences (Emerson *et al.* 2002, 2006) and teaching large lecture-based writing courses, to running workshops for PhD students.

Through this work I have recognized that embracing diversity is at the heart of teaching writing. Student writers I have worked with have had ambitions (among other things) to be poets, agricultural consultants, sports therapists, research physicists, amateur family historians, teachers and financial advisers. They have wanted to write farm reports, lyrics, medical reports, academic papers, business plans, PhD theses, and life stories for their grandchildren. Some have had a burning ambition to be a writer since childhood; some simply see that they need a professional skill; others are sure writing is a skill they cannot learn.

In the face of such diversity, I see clearly that, if I am to support each student's development, I must first see each student as an individual (Moss and Walters 1993). This may seem so obvious as to be a truism, but it is a truth we easily forget. Some years ago, I visited the principal of our local high school to ask for a special dispensation in the school programme for my eldest daughter. The principal didn't think this was possible, and by way of explanation added, 'She's not unique, you know.' My face must have been a picture, because she quickly laughed away her choice of words.

We all know that each person in our class is unique, but the weight of that understanding is something we may set aside in the practical world of delivering outcomes and working with multiple pressures. But we cannot afford to do this if we want to support and respect our students' development.

I find that when I focus on the uniqueness of each student, the way I relate to them changes. First, I find myself paying attention in new ways: why does this student perform poorly in assessment, but ask great questions in class? Is there something in the assessment that confuses her – and why? How can we climb over this? Why is this student so tired and restless in class, and his work so fragmented, yet showing dazzling moments of insight? How can I help him develop those insights in new ways? Thus, as with the story that opened this chapter, I find myself engaging in dialogue and problem solving with my students.

And something happens to students when someone pays attention to them (Palmer 2007). I have had as my mantra for many years that we can all fly higher than we think we can, and that sometimes it takes just one person to pay enough attention to see that, and to support us through the process. Our universities are big places where students, especially in their first year, can feel faceless (Hall 2005). As Palmer (2007) says, students, whether they are young or mature, are marginalized people in both our society and in our classrooms. By paying attention to each student's uniqueness, we communicate to our students, 'In this big university, *you matter.*' It's a great place for learning to start (hooks 2003).

Acknowledging and addressing the pervasiveness of fear

The second critical issue I have found important if I am to support my students is to understand the fear and anxiety each student brings into a class. As Palmer puts it, 'Students . . . are afraid: afraid of failing, of not understanding, of being drawn into issues they would rather avoid, . . . of looking foolish in front of their peers' (2007: 37). But it has taken me many years to recognize the pervasiveness of fear, and why it takes particular root in a writing classroom – or, indeed, in relation to any academic writing in the disciplines.

On some levels the fear is simple: some students give up careers to follow a vocation which involves acquiring and using specialist writing skills. Often these dreams are laid down in childhood and recovered after many years of pragmatism, and pursuing them may put these students and their families under considerable strain. The fear of failure is therefore a powerful issue.

Students who have English as a second language or specific learning disabilities may fear shame in relation to writing. For these students, who may have advanced cognitive skills or knowledge in their field, writing can feel like an insurmountable barrier. These students have often experienced shame because of their writing skills at school, where writing expertise may have been judged through the lens of error frequency (Rose 1985). Shame inhibits learning primarily because its impact on students is such that they withdraw from the connectedness that makes learning possible.

But there is also a more intrinsic and pervasive form of fear in relation to writing. The ability to use the language (written or oral) of a specific group defines the extent to which we belong to that group (Porter 1986). Any written assessment confronts students with the knowledge that they do not yet belong to the group to which they aspire. The ability to succeed in written assessments then becomes a high-stakes exercise since their ability to acquire specific and appropriate discourse skills will, to a large extent, determine their academic and future careers (Bourdieu *et al.* 1994).

Our students must therefore acquire the rhetorical skills of their discipline, a task fraught with difficulty.

> Students have to appropriate . . . a specialized discourse, and they
> have to do this as though they were easily and comfortably . . .
> members of the academy . . . They have to invent the university by
> assembling and mimicking its language . . . They must learn to speak
> our language. Or they must dare to speak it, or to carry off the bluff,

since speaking and writing will most certainly be required long before the skill is 'learned'. And this, understandably, causes problems.

(Bartholomae 1985: 382)

The most obvious problem, or danger, of this necessary bluffing is plagiarism (Howard 1999), which is presented to students as the ultimate academic sin. Is it any wonder that students in a writing classroom, or writing assignments in their disciplinary courses, are filled with anxiety?[1]

The outcome of this fear can be cynicism ('When I have a job I'll have a secretary, so my writing skills don't matter'), resistance ('Scientists don't need to write'), silence and excessive caution (e.g. putting a reference in every sentence or quoting large segments of secondary tests) (hooks 2003), all of which inhibit learning.

Recognizing that these behaviours are rooted in justifiable fear allows a teacher to come alongside the student in a particular way: 'If I want to teach well in the face of my students' fears, I need to see clearly and steadily the fear that is in their hearts' (Palmer 2007: 46). As teachers, we need to be strongly motivated as enablers rather than gatekeepers into academic, professional or scientific discourse communities. For example, we must resist being cast – or casting ourselves – into the role of the Grammar Police (Rose 1985), or the Plagiarism Police (Howard 1999; Hall 2005) and become interpreters of specific discourses – or, better, facilitators who enable our students to become interpreters of discourse. We must never forget, as Bourdieu *et al.* (1994) remind us, that academic writing is nobody's first language. Not even our own (Hull and Rose 1989).

The classroom as a community of writers

So far I have discussed teacher attitudes as central to supporting students as individuals. The final issue I wish to highlight is what I consider to be the central pedagogical tool needed: developing the classroom as a community.

For students to feel confident enough to share their writing, they have to feel they are in a safe, supportive community. For on-campus students, this involves developing a classroom where the teacher models attentiveness, empathy and an openness to sharing critique. For distance students, online environments can encourage community in exciting ways. In my online writing courses, we have developed websites that nurture a community of writers not only through 'work' activities (peer review and the like), but also through social interaction features. These include a 'writer's café', where students publish their work or discuss anything from the joys and trials of distance study to the best use of punctuation in a particular sentence; a private messaging system, so students can develop friendships; and a comical 'writing prompt' page, which generates challenging or humorous writing exercises.

Developing a community of writers is vital to my approach to teaching writing: not only does it help students gain skills (e.g. learning to critique and support other writers), but it also helps them to grow in a social context, to gain confidence in their own voice, and to feel free to experiment with genre and voice in a safe, supportive environment with other developing writers. Such a community is characterized only partly by what happens in the community (e.g. reviewing each other's work, sharing of ideas) but primarily by how the members of that community relate to, support and challenge one another.

Supporting the development of students as writers

When I first faced the question of how a teacher can support the development of each student as an individual, my first thought was to write about the plethora of teaching techniques and pedagogical tools that would make this possible. Yet as I thought more deeply, it seemed that none of those tools could have impact unless the fundamentals were in place: that unless we honour the uniqueness of our students as individuals, understand and empathize with their fear, develop for ourselves an 'interpretive' role, and create our classrooms as communities, nothing else could empower our students to realize their dreams.

bell hooks (2003: xi) says we should acknowledge our weaknesses and celebrate our joys as teachers. So let me end in this way. I don't always manage to practise my ideals. Sometimes in large lecture classes, or when time pressures seem overwhelming, I am unable to meet my own expectations of what it means to be a teacher who values and supports each of her students as individuals and as writers.

But there are moments when the ideals I've written about here all slot into place. In 2007 I was invited to teach an advanced undergraduate science writing course at the University of Michigan. These students were the brightest I'd ever met – and all openly terrified of writing science. The rapport we developed was based on an acknowledgement of that fear, and soon the class was so dynamic and fluid I could arrive at class with three lesson plans in my hand, only to throw them all aside so we could pursue a question asked by a class member. It was an exhilarating experience. The day before I returned to New Zealand, I found my office full of Christmas cards, cookies and mementoes of Michigan. One Christmas card said, 'You have made us into a family.' But best of all was the note from a young man whose struggles with a learning impairment meant he believed he would never meet the writing requirements of his major and realize his dream of going to medical school. He wrote simply this: 'I am a writer.'

Note

1 And is it surprising that the students in the opening story were behaving badly? They were being taught the rhetorical conventions of the humanities while aspiring to enter the discourse community of the applied sciences. Thus they were having to learn and unlearn one set of rhetorical conventions, while acquiring a different set (which were not being actively taught)!

References

Bartholomae, D. (1985) Inventing the university, in M. Rose (ed.) *When a Writer Can't Write: Studies in Writer's Block and Other Composing Process Problems*. New York: Guilford.

Bourdieu, P., Passeron, J-C. and de Saint Martin, M. (1994) *Academic Discourse: Linguistic Misunderstanding and Professorial Power*. Cambridge: Polity Press.

Emerson, L. and Clerehen, R. (2009) Writing program administration outside the North American context, in D. Strickland and J. Gunner (eds) *Interrupting the Program: Essays on WPA Theoretical Dissensus*. Portsmouth, NH: Boynton/Cook Heinemann.

Emerson, L.E., MacKay, B.R., MacKay, M.B. and Funnell, K.A. (2002) Writing in a New Zealand tertiary context: WAC and action research, in S. McLeod (2002) *Language and Languages Special Edition: WAC in an International Context*, 5(3): 110–33.

Emerson, L.E., MacKay, B.R., MacKay, M.B. and Funnell, K.A. (2006) A team of equals: teaching writing in the sciences, *Educational Action Research*, 14(1): 65–81.

Gibbs, C. (2006) *To Be a Teacher: Journeys towards Authenticity*. Auckland: Pearson Prentice Hall.

Hall, J. (2005) Plagiarism across the curriculum: how academic communities can meet the challenge of the undocumented writer. *Across the Disciplines: Academic Perspective on Language, Learning, and Academic Writing*. http://wac.colostate.edu/atd/articles/hall2005.cfm, accessed 3 August 2010.

hooks, B. (1994) *Teaching to Transgress: Education as the Practice of Freedom*. New York and London: Routledge.

hooks, B. (2003) *Teaching Community: A Pedagogy of Hope*. New York and London: Routledge.

Howard, R.M. (1999) *Standing in the Shadow of Giants: Plagiarists, Authors, Collaborators*. Norwood: Ablex.

Hull, G. and Rose, M. (1989) Rethinking remediation: toward a social-cognitive understanding of problematic reading and writing, *Written Communication*, 6: 139–54.

Moss, B.J. and Walters, K. (1993) Rethinking diversity: axes of difference in the writing classroom, in L. Odell (ed.) *Theory and Practice in the Teaching of Writing: Rethinking the Discipline.* Carbondale, IL: Southern Illinois University Press.

Palmer, P. (2007) *The Courage to Teach*, 2nd edn. San Francisco, CA: John Wiley and Sons.

Porter, J.E. (1986) Intertextuality and the discourse community, *Rhetoric Review*, 5: 34–47.

Rose, M. (1985) The language of exclusion: writing instruction at the university, *College English*, 47(4): 341–59.

16 Seeing the tree in the midst of the forest: respecting and supporting the development of students as individuals

Kathleen Regan

> . . . It is all around
> Fertile ground
> For planting.
>
> The lush green
> That grows inside
> Us.

(Johnston 2009)

When I was a graduate student in Spanish literature, I took a course in foreign language pedagogy. One of my teachers enjoyed gardening and hence, when she spoke of the role of teachers, she likened it to that of a gardener who cultivates an environment that will be rich and fertile ground for students to thrive. As a novice language instructor the garden analogy made sense and I embraced it. The comparison helped me understand the covenant an instructor makes with each of the students who enrol in a class: the commitment to cultivate the rich potential that exists deep within each student. An educator, much like a gardener, cultivates an environment that supports student learning, finds strategies that support development, assesses the effectiveness of the strategies and revises the approach in order to have that *fertile ground* for the plant/ individual to thrive.

I am fortunate to teach classes with enrolments between 20 and 25 students. Small class sizes allow for a learning environment that is intimate and connected. We get to know each other. Based on my experiences in the classroom and research I have read on effective teaching, I have established three basic principles that inform the way I start every new semester and teach. To begin, I believe in each student's potential to succeed. Everything is possible and my task is to create a learning environment that invites risk taking and exploration. Next, each new class is an ongoing experiment. I have my game plan in the form of a syllabus, reading materials, websites and lesson plans but I do not know how each new group of students will respond to the information, where they will struggle and what they will master easily. Therefore, I am flexible and experiment with new ways to present materials and find the path to create dynamic exchanges that ignite the students' interest in the subject at hand. Finally, it is important to recognize and capitalize on the knowledge students have acquired and provide final projects that reveal the ways they have learned and mastered the material. The ideal goal is for them to see their growth and be able to apply their education in service projects and study abroad programmes in Spanish-speaking countries. Using these principles to support student learning nurtures the unique connections and relationships between the teacher and student as we embark together on the adventure of discovery and growth.

In his book, *What the Best College Teachers Do*, Ken Bain (2004) presents extensive research and examples regarding teachers who effectively inspire students to learn. One characteristic that all the teachers shared was their ongoing *learning* about how to teach better for the benefit of their students:

> (They) struggled to *learn* how to create the best learning environments. When they failed to reach students, they used those failures to gain additional insights. Most important, because they subscribed to the *learning* rather than *transmission* model of teaching, they realized that they had to think about ways to understand students' learning.
>
> (Bain 2004: 173, emphasis added)

Successful teachers do not simply *transmit information*; rather, they invest in creating a *community of learners*, a community based on mutual respect and dignity and dynamic exchange between students and teacher (Engle and Conant 2002: 400). In this exchange, students are active learners who explore a disciplinary question, receive support as they examine and analyse their question, are accountable to use resources well and share their findings with their peers. Professors ask the 'whats' and 'hows' to teach the material, track students' grasp of information, and create activities that challenge students to *use* their new knowledge. Students delve more deeply into topics in ways that prove more accessible, interesting and ultimately more lasting in their everyday lives.

Creating a community of learners cannot happen by chance. Like a gardener who proceeds with a plan to create a lush environment to support plant growth, so too a teacher must map out a strategy that will effectively support student learning. Bain's (2004: 99–116) principles for generating a community of learners can be grouped under three different headings:

1   Creating *fertile ground* for lush growth. This involves:
    • seeking commitments;
    • getting (students') attention and keeping it; and
    • starting with the students rather than the discipline.

2 Cultivating the environment to support student learning. This involves:
- generating a natural critical learning environment;
- engaging the students in disciplinary thinking; and
- creating diverse learning experiences.
3 Evaluating and assessing student learning. This involves:
- creating final projects that have students present their findings within the context of disciplinary issues; and
- helping students think beyond the classroom and having them apply their knowledge.

After reflecting on Bain's principles of best teaching practice I assessed my own teaching and challenged myself to incorporate them. I started the experiment using my Spanish for Business Purposes class (henceforth Spanish 305) in spring 2007. The course gives me and the students – who come from multiple disciplines – a unique opportunity to explore and examine linguistic and cultural practices in business settings with Spanish speakers in Spain, Latin America and the United States. Bain's principles stimulated creative ideas and made the class more engaging for the students and me. Here's how it unfolded.

Creating fertile ground for lush growth

Spanish 305 lacks the array of diverse topics students might encounter in an advanced conversation course, where topics can vary from tango singers of the past to the culinary delights of Spanish paella. In Spanish 305 the topics are rather standard and conventional: terminology and discussions relate to offices, banking, accounting, marketing and international trade. Vocabulary and expressions are coupled with business practices and ideas. Cultural sections relate to conducting business in Spain, Latin America or the Hispanic communities in the United States. Given the focus on business, I make sure from the very beginning to learn of the students' commitment to this material. At the beginning of the semester, I conduct informal interviews and have students complete a short questionnaire about their interest in the material and their learning objectives. This brief assessment proves successful in that students have a concrete opportunity to state their learning objectives in the beginning and evaluate their accomplishments at the end of the course. In the final student evaluations at the end of term, one student noted: 'My initial interview with Dr Regan made me decide whether this was the class for me. I felt less anxious about the course and ready to learn.' Another student commented: 'I work part-time in a bank and I took this class to learn more business vocabulary. I've done this and so much more!' The students who decide to enrol in Spanish 305 have goals in mind and feel committed to the class; they are eager to have a positive educational experience and invest in being involved in building a community of learners.

To be as relevant as possible to my students and society as a whole, I must provide the tools that help students navigate the Spanish language and the range of issues of our cross-cultural world. The class has to make a difference in some way to the student who is enrolled. Many of the students in the class use business Spanish in their work places. Some are bank tellers with Spanish-speaking clients. Others volunteer in service programmes in Latin America. Despite the diverse backgrounds of the students, their desire to use Spanish beyond the classroom environment provides a built-in motivator I can leverage. All of these students come to the class with a desire to develop inter-personal communication skills that will provide them with cultural under-standing. The class helps in developing sensitivity and understanding in order to better navigate the rich diversity within Spanish-speaking communities. The course can then give students the terminology and expressions to read online newspapers from Spanish-speaking countries and understand the impact economic, political and social factors have in the various professional environments in the regions.

Cultivating the environment to support student learning

Spanish 305 is enhanced and enriched when I can create a learning environ-ment that involves students in the learning process. Rather than seeing my role as transmitter of information, I see myself as a facilitator of information and encourage students to use the material they are learning (King 1993). One effective way to get students involved is to create intellectual bridges from the classroom to industries and professionals involved with cross-cultural issues and global markets. Careful planning of the readings and class discussions, invited speakers and excursions to businesses can effectively immerse students in real-life issues in the business world and foster a critical learning environ-ment where students acquire information based on in-class readings and discussions, use this information to put questions to professional business leaders, and reach informed insights about the business world. They see and experience first-hand the application of theory in professional contexts.

The Spanish 305 section on marketing brings together a number of elements that enhance the foreign language and cultural understandings students acquire in the class. Students learn important vocabulary, expressions and concepts that they practise in small-group activities. Once students have learned vocabulary and terminology, I invite a guest speaker from a major corporation who specializes in international marketing and promotion. A day before the presenter comes to share her experience with the class, the students in SPN 305 prepare questions that are emailed to the visitor and help serve to organize the class. After the in-class presentation, students have an on-site visit to the guest speaker's corporation where they meet with the Director of Marketing and Research and learn about launching a product and maintaining market share. After the on-site visit, students are placed into groups of four, and assigned the task of preparing a product launch into a Spanish-speaking market. They must work together to create an ad, write a business plan, and present the details of how the product will be launched into a Spanish-speaking community. The students work together and at the same time each one in the group takes responsibility for overseeing and completion of one aspect of the presentation.

One of the student groups did an excellent job promoting a Spanish version of a small Weber barbecue grill. Their presentation included a catchy tune with a rhythmic jingle; an explanation of Spaniards' love for grilling outdoors; an illustration of the scarcity of affordable and efficient small grills that are portable; and a competitive price point. The students successfully used the terminology and readings we had covered in the unit on marketing together with information obtained from the business presentation and excursion. They combined this learning experience with their passion for barbecuing and Spanish customs. The student audience marvelled at how well their peers had integrated the material into such an engaging presentation and gave them the ultimate compliment: they dared them to execute their idea. Although the students in the group did not take up the challenge to launch the Weber grill in Spain, their project did provide them with insight into their own ability to gather data, examine the facts, create a game plan and launch a product. They saw the power of applying their learning experience to make a difference in the world outside the classroom.

Evaluating and assessing student learning

In all of my classes, especially Spanish 305, I stress the need for students to be active learners and think of innovative ways to apply classroom readings and discussions to situations in the professional world. One activity that helps students build a bridge into the professional world is to have them go out and interview business leaders to learn how they provide services to Spanish-speaking communities. I created this kind of activity as a way to encourage students to network with professionals in their prospective fields. Whenever possible, I assist students in making contacts with professionals in their field. The benefit of this activity is that it allows students to gain useful perspectives on how to apply their linguistic skills and cultural understanding to professional situations. In one instance, I advised and assisted a student (double major in Spanish and Political Science) to meet with and interview the director of a housing centre that assisted many Spanish-speaking first-time home buyers. The centre provided classes on buying a house, understanding mortgages, and legal issues involved in purchasing a home. The centre was a wonderful place for the student to see the interconnections between business, teaching and social service outreach. He loved this experience because of the self-awareness he gained and insights he gained about Spanish in a professional setting. This student had thought that teaching would be the only way to use his Spanish, but visiting the centre and talking with the director gave him insights into different ways in which he could use his linguistic and cultural skills.

Student presentations during the semester are another way I bring together students' interests with business and/or economic practices or issues in Spanish-speaking countries. These presentations are a perfect way to have students apply their learning to real business and/or economic issues and practices in Spain or Latin America. Topics include examining the social and economic costs of immigration; the economic struggles of communities dependent on tourism; cost analysis of study abroad programmes on small communities; and entrepreneurship initiatives in developing nations of Latin America. One student group who needed to organize their presentation came to me in a quandary. They wanted to combine their study abroad experience in Michoacan, Mexico, with the issues we had covered in class but they did not know how to focus their topic and make it relevant. They came to my office to discuss their problem and find a relevant and meaningful topic. Knowing they wanted to include their study abroad experience, I asked them what was one of the most memorable moments during their studies in Michoacan. As both were guitar aficionados, they agreed that it had been a visit to a town noted for making guitars. The luthiers live at home and spend their days in their workshops building guitars. We discussed some of the business challenges these craftsmen faced in maintaining their cottage industry. A plethora of ideas surfaced: ecological issues that affect availability of materials such as wood; marketing and promotion of the guitars; balancing cost and profit margins; the challenges of creating an efficient export market. The students created an informative, engaging presentation that provided a comprehensive look at this regional guitar industry. Furthermore, they were clearly engaged with this topic and provided fascinating and unique insights to the multiple challenges this community faced in being viable economically in the midst of being solely dependent on one mode of production. Everyone in class enjoyed this presentation and benefited from it: the student presenters used their love for guitars to explore a regional industry that faced serious challenges; the student audience learned about a tradition they did not know existed; I enjoyed seeing how the student presenters used terminology and expressions they had learned in class, applied cultural concepts they had read in cultural readings in the book and, most importantly, connected their personal interests with real social and economic issues in Michoacan.

Conclusion

The learning environments we create in our classes mirror the gardens that flourish around us. Whether in the classroom or the garden, we not only have to tend to the individual being but also nurture an environment that will foster the good health of the full variety of living beings in that environment. In teaching, I work to connect with all the students who enrol in my classes. I do this by meeting with them, finding out the personal interests and motivations that have led them to enrol, seeing their learning objectives and goals, and creating an understanding that invites them to be active participants. As an educator, excitement comes from finding different ways to cultivate the lush green within each student and inviting them to contribute to the learning community of which they are members. This community encourages personal growth, understanding and a desire to generate innovative ideas that create positive changes beyond the classroom. What better way to accomplish this than through the interpersonal connections we can create in our classes?

References

Bain, K. (2004) *What the Best College Teachers Do*. Cambridge, MA: Harvard University Press.

Engle, R. and Conant, F. (2002) Guiding principles for fostering productive disciplinary engagements: explaining an emergent argument in a community of learners classroom, *Cognition and Instruction*, 20(4): 399–448.

Johnston, M. (2009) Unpublished poem.

King, A. (1993) From Sage on the Stage to Guide on the Side, *College Teaching*, 41(1): 30–5.

17 A classroom of colleagues

Jerusha Detweiler-Bedell and
Brian Detweiler-Bedell

All too often, teachers and students speed through the academic year hoping to connect with one another, but a productive collision of minds seldom occurs. Those seemingly ideal and striking Socratic moments are few and far between. For insight into why this is so, we turn to the parable of the Good Samaritan, a biblical story in which robbers accost and beat a man, leaving him for dead at the side of the road:

> Now by chance a certain priest came down that road. And when he saw him, he passed by on the other side. Likewise a Levite, when he arrived at the place, came and looked, and passed by on the other side. But a certain Samaritan, as he journeyed, came where he was. And when he saw him, he had compassion. So he went to him and bandaged his wounds, pouring on oil and wine; and he set him on his own animal, brought him to an inn, and took care of him.
>
> (Luke 10: 31–4, New King James Version)

The parable of the Good Samaritan offers two lessons to those of us who teach. The first lesson envisions the student as a bystander, that is, the priest or the Levite. As we all know, it is quite possible for students to be passive bystanders to their own education, yet research on learning indicates that students who are active, not passive, learn more (Bransford, Brown and Cocking, 1999). Although teachers can energize a student by modelling their own passion for a topic and by being enthusiastic and interactive in the classroom, this is not enough. Great teaching systematically guides students to take *responsibility* and *ownership* of the endeavour of learning itself. As a result of this kind of engagement, students will learn to join professors in the creation of new knowledge by becoming our collaborators.

But how can this be accomplished? How can professors rally students to be valuable, skilled and effective collaborators rather than bystanders in the process of learning? This brings us to the second lesson of the parable of the

Good Samaritan. The second lesson envisions the *professor* as the ineffective bystander. Indeed, it's far too easy for a professor to be either the priest or the Levite. Professors are busy, and the demands of our jobs have us rushing from task to task. One of those tasks, of course, is lecturing, which is wonderful but arguably self-indulgent. It is quite possible to ignore our students' unique needs on the road to delivering our lectures or rushing between service and other obligations. How can we support the development of students as individuals (and not just as individuals, but as skilled collaborators) when there are so many of them and so little time?

In this chapter we take you along on our journey to find a solution to this dilemma. Although we have not found a way to add more hours to the day, we have focused very deliberately on ways that professors can attend to what matters most in the pursuit of great teaching: being attentive educators and mentoring students more effectively and efficiently. We hope to persuade you that creating a classroom of colleagues is much more than an ideal. It can become a tangible and deeply rewarding reality for every teacher.

We set off on this journey by underscoring the parable of the Good Samaritan's caveat to those of us with good intentions – whether priest or professor, we often fail to translate our ideals into effective action. Still, there's a ray of hope within the parable. Someone comes to the rescue. The Samaritan, a lowly outcast, surprises us and leaps into action. Inspired by this parable, John Darley and Daniel Batson (1973) conducted a famous social psychological study that helps us glean the simple yet powerful reason for the Samaritan's actions, and this meaning goes well beyond the nature of altruism. It speaks to how each of us can become better mentors, the type who treat students with empathy and help them to develop a deep sense of confidence and competence.

In Darley and Batson's study, Princeton University seminary students were asked to come individually to the research laboratory to participate in a study on 'vocational careers'. Half of the students were asked to prepare a speech on jobs that seminary graduates would be particularly skilled at, while the other half were asked to prepare a speech on the parable of the Good Samaritan. All of the students were told they would be giving their speech in a neighbouring building, and as they walked from one building to the next, they passed a moaning 'victim' slumped in a doorway. Would the seminary students be more likely to intervene if they had just prepared a speech on helping? And by translation, can we become more effective mentors by routinely reminding ourselves of the importance of attending to our students' individual needs and development?

To answer these questions, we must highlight another detail of the study. As the seminary students were leaving to give their speech either on job skills or on the parable, some were told, 'Oh, you're late. They were expecting you a few minutes ago . . . so you'd better hurry.' Others were told, 'It will be a few

minutes before they're ready for you, but you might as well head on over . . .'
(Darley and Batson 1973: 104). Those who were told 'You're late' were pushed
to accomplish a very *concrete* goal (getting to the next location). In contrast,
those who were told they had a few minutes to spare were able to keep their
minds on more *global* goals (ranging from being a good study participant and
effective speaker to being an upstanding seminary student and person). The
distinction between having a concrete, hurry-induced goal versus a more
relaxed, global goal might seem trivial compared to the urgency of helping
someone slumped in a doorway. Most of us would like to believe that seminary
students, especially those primed to think of the helping parable, would stop to
aid a person in desperate need. Hurry and irrelevant 'goal focus' should matter
little, if at all. But this wasn't the case. There was no difference in the likelihood
of the seminary students stopping to help the victim depending on whether
they had just prepared a speech on jobs or on the parable of the Good Samaritan.
The only thing that mattered was *time*. Those in a hurry failed to stop. Those
who believed they had a few extra minutes extended a helping hand.

The social psychology of the Good Samaritan leads us to a simple conclusion, one that directly informs our vision of how to mentor students. Even if
we have the best intentions in mind, we cannot mentor students if we are in a
hurry, perpetually focused on the concrete goal of getting from one place to
the next. We must slow down to mentor effectively. When we feel the pressure
of time it is all too easy to be consumed by *how* we meet the demands of each
pressing task. Our most important global goal – attending to students – gets
lost in this context. Being an effective mentor requires that we focus on the
bigger picture of *why* we are educators: to create a new generation of lifelong
learners and scholars.

The process through which a student becomes a scholar is a gradual one,
and it develops as a result of the student working effectively with other people,
setting challenging yet achievable goals, and developing a sense of ownership
over compelling intellectual questions. In our experience, we have found that
one of the most efficient ways of mentoring the individual student along this
path to becoming a scholar is to capitalize on one of the greatest resources we
have – other students. Carefully crafted, well-supervised, team-based learning
experiences are among the most important tools we use in the systematic
development of our students' confidence and abilities as scholars. Indeed, we
have come to recognize the serendipitous compatibility between the student's
ability to learn from peers and the mentor's need to slow down. When students
work together, they find independent solutions to many of the small problems
that would otherwise occupy the professor's time. And extensive research on
cooperative learning suggests that team-based work enhances college students'
relationships with other students, builds self-esteem and confidence, and leads
to greater academic success (Johnson *et al.* 1998a). By harnessing the exciting
synergy of collaborative work, professors can focus their efforts on the bigger

issues associated with mentoring, including team-building, goal-setting, and promoting each student's higher-level reasoning skills.

In order to put this overarching approach in action, we design our classes and our research lab based on three key principles – teamwork, laddering of experiences and ownership. In each of our courses, students design and conduct projects in teams, rising to the next level of challenge as their expertise grows. Ultimately, this allows students to own and then share their new ideas with individuals outside the classroom community. For example, in Clinical Psychology (taught by JDB), students are immersed in a semester-long collaborative project that gives them the opportunity to engage in clinical practice in a controlled setting. Before the semester begins, each student studies the autobiography of a person who has a psychological disorder and then creates a persona (e.g. symptoms, life history) similar to the character he or she read about. Each individual is teamed up with another student, and each pair schedules a weekly 'therapy session' outside class hours, trading off in the role of therapist and client and putting into practice the therapeutic techniques they are learning. Academic guidance is provided throughout the semester, and students learn how to conduct a comprehensive diagnostic interview, plan for treatment, apply empirically supported therapeutic techniques, write weekly session notes, and participate in case presentations. The students' experiences are meant to mirror, as closely as possible, the actual work of clinicians because, as the Aristotelean saying goes, 'What one has to learn to do, we learn by doing' (*Nicomachean Ethics* 2006: 1103a). Feedback from graduates who have pursued careers in social services suggests that this semester-long project gave them confidence in their own individual skills while at the same time enhancing their ability to collaborate closely with another person over time. This gave them a significant head start when they began their own professional work.

In Advanced Statistics (taught by BDB), workgroups of three to four students are assigned challenging problem sets that even the best students are unable to complete on their own. It takes a collaborative blend of student strengths (e.g. perseverance, insight, organization, creativity, experimentation, and even humility) to tackle these projects. The expectation is that each student will at some point in the semester experience a 'crumbling of their house of cards', that is, a moment when their understanding of statistics seems to evaporate in the face of one challenge or another. Together, the students help each other rebuild a renewed and deeper understanding of statistical concepts. All the while, the class as a whole and each workgroup is supervised closely. Significant course time is dedicated to group work, enabling the instructor to 'infiltrate' groups, pepper them with questions and seed an idea here and there. The result is a course experience that is frustrating by design, yet tolerates frustration only so long. At critical moments, the students themselves make breakthroughs or the instructor steps in to ensure that the students recognize which tools will enable them to surmount a particular challenge and therefore ladder their learning toward greater expertise. Many students have translated this expertise into paid positions at a nearby research university, where they take charge of analysing national datasets, and a few students have gone on to graduate programmes and industry jobs specializing in quantitative data analysis.

Community Psychology (taught by JDB) is dedicated to the idea of ecological validity, that is, getting out into the community and seeing how things 'really' are. In this class, students are assigned to a community lab group at the start of the semester, and this class-based lab group becomes a forum for students to apply the concepts they learn to real-life settings. Each lab group consists of four to five students who together investigate a relevant problem for peers on their own college campus. Throughout the term various assignments help the students focus their projects; these include literature reviews, interviews with stakeholders and professionals, data collection, and the design of an intervention to help solve the problem. The project culminates with a formal, campus-wide presentation of findings to administrators, professors and other staff, and students. In past years, these projects have contributed directly to changes such as the restructuring of the Career Centre and the redesign of the Student Centre. As a graduate noted in an email: 'I heard that there is now a 10-year plan to completely re-do the Student Centre. It's pretty much our Community Psych project coming to life, which makes me very excited.'

The same principles – teamwork, laddering of experiences and ownership – serve as the foundation of our research laboratory, the Behavioural Health and Social (BHS) psychology lab. Rather than having undergraduate students take on the role of either solo 'honours' students or, alternatively, low-level worker bees, we treat them as individuals worthy of serious, deliberate involvement in professor-driven research. Their involvement is team-based, with responsibilities that systematically increase over time as their expertise and ownership of the research grows. Each student on one of our three-person laddered research teams fills a specific role: team assistant (typically a first- or second-year student who is new to psychology), team associate (a mid-level student who has taken many of the core classes of the major), or team leader (an advanced student who has a history of working in the research lab).

Students typically join the lab as assistants, but they advance over time to more rigorous levels of inquiry and challenge by becoming associates and then leaders. The more senior students in our lab model the skills and knowledge necessary for the advancement of the more junior students. But just as often, the more junior students find they have particular areas of interest or strengths that complement those of the more senior students. We recently surveyed 35 alumni from the BHS Lab, and one former student observed, 'A strength of the lab model is that any old clueless freshman can be dropped into the equation and oriented as he or she participates. I certainly never expected that my involvement in lab would become such a significant part of my educational experience and even a defining part of my life.' Another former student remarked, 'I had wonderful experiences collaborating with my research team. We became colleagues and friends, and we learned that we each had different styles of time management, interpersonal communication, and work ethic. We utilized our differences to make an excellent team.' Over time, students engage in every aspect of the research process and evolve from novices into accomplished graduate-level researchers. What has been most rewarding to us is seeing our students gain confidence in their skills and begin to treat these real-world, scholarly pursuits as their own.

This kind of excitement within and beyond the classroom is, quite simply, contagious. The use of carefully structured, team-based work allows each student to do a great deal more than they could ever do alone. There are, of course, realistic risks associated with creating teams of students. Professors must be deliberate in their formation and support of teams. Simply assigning students to groups and expecting them to 'work together' will not lead to the efficiencies and accomplishments we have discussed. As Smith and colleagues describe, 'Cooperation is more than being physically near other students, discussing material with other students, helping other students, or sharing material among students, although each of these is important in cooperative learning' (Smith *et al.* 2005: 9). In order to maximize the conditions for successful teams, professors must create a culture of positive interdependence, intervene when needed to assist teams with specific tasks or teamwork skills, and actively evaluate students' learning while simultaneously helping them to assess the strengths and weaknesses of their group's functioning (Johnson *et al.* 1998b). A professor also must plan for potential setbacks within well-constructed groups. As one of our students described in her reflection on our joint mentoring of a research project:

> What I really appreciate is that they never held so tightly to the reins that they prevented us from falling on our faces. I remember one time when lack of attention to detail resulted in almost a semester's worth of work being virtually unusable. Jerusha and Brian did not coddle us about this issue. They discussed with us the time and resources lost, they pointed out how conscientiousness could have prevented the error, and they helped each team member see how important individual and collective responsibility is to successful research. I identify that one failing as the single best learning experience in all of my years of lab. And to be sure, we never made a mistake like that again.

Challenging the abilities of students effectively requires the teacher to know when and how to let go, accepting risks such as the one described above. It also requires the teacher to know when and how to subsequently intervene. In laddering students' experiences, we ensure that each project (in the classroom and research lab) includes barriers to surmount, complexities to disentangle and, perhaps most importantly, the tools and guidance that ideally lead to success or, at other times, to a deeper understanding as a result of failure. As mentors, we would echo the words of Harvard professor Richard Hackman (2002: 38), 'Our job is to figure out what makes the difference between teams that inspire and those that embarrass – and to do so in a way that invites constructive action.'

The pinnacle of helping individual students become scholars is to allow them to cultivate a sense of ownership over the work they produce. To encourage students' sense of ownership, we treat them not as passive recipients of knowledge, but as scholars, practitioners and researchers in their own right. We challenge them to investigate multifaceted, real-world puzzles, and in taking up these challenges they become extraordinarily skilled, earning their place as our collaborators. In embracing this approach to teaching, we find that the role of the hurried bystander, who is focused solely on how to get from one place to the next, is no longer viable for student or teacher. How can students be bystanders when their teams depend on them and they routinely receive the constructive attentions and respect of their peers and their professors? Engaging in team-based work excites students and enables them to see that they are capable of teaching one another many of the skills necessary to become lifelong learners. Likewise, how can teachers be bystanders when their system of mentoring makes them accountable to teams of students, allows them to spend less time on mundane tasks, and emphasizes the global aim of developing students into accomplished scholars? By carefully structuring team-based efforts, laddering each student's experiences over time, and giving students a true sense of ownership over something that matters, we foster capabilities in our students that free up just enough of our own resources to attend to the bigger picture. This efficiency helps allay some of the hurried pressures that can be so distracting and counterproductive and, by focusing more on what matters, we continually reignite our own passion for teaching.

The reward of mentoring effectively and efficiently is deep and long lasting, and it is with great pleasure that we follow the lives of our students long after graduation. Fittingly, the very last response we read in our stack of alumni questionnaires was, 'I wish I could come back!' But come back as an undergraduate? We don't believe so. That would suggest a return to a precarious state in which both student and professor are potential bystanders. This student wanted to return to our community of colleagues, an environment that enables each individual to embrace the immersive, gratifying challenges associated with a scholarly life. These are the challenges, once surmounted, that cause you to step back and admire the person you have become: a better individual, a skilled team member, and a true colleague on the road to learning.

References

Aristotle (2006) *Nicomachean ethics* (trans. C.C.W. Taylor). Oxford: Oxford University Press.

Bransford, J.D., Brown, A.L. and Cocking, R.R. (eds) (1999) *How People Learn: Brain, Mind, Experience, and School*. Washington, DC: National Academy Press.

Darley, J. and Batson, D. (1973) From Jerusalem to Jericho: a study of situational and dispositional variables in helping behaviour, *Journal of Personality and Social Psychology*, 27(1): 100–8.

Hackman, R.J. (2002) *Leading Teams: Setting the Stage for Great Performances*. Boston, MA: Harvard Business School Press.

Johnson, D.W., Johnson, R.T. and Smith, K.A. (1998a) Cooperative learning returns to college: what evidence is there that it works? *Change*, 30 (4): 26–35.

Johnson, D.W., Johnson, D.T. and Smith, K.A. (1998b) *Active Learning: Cooperation in the College Classroom*, 2nd edn. Edina, MN: Interaction Book Company.

Smith, K.A., Sheppard, S.D., Johnson, D.W. and Johnson, R.T. (2005) Pedagogies of engagement: classroom-based practices, *Journal of Engineering Education*, 94 (1): 1–15.

This material is based on work supported by the National Science Foundation under Grant No. 0737399. Any opinions, findings, and conclusions or recommendations expressed in this material are those of the authors and do not necessarily reflect the views of the National Science Foundation.

18 Extending the reach of higher education inside and outside the classroom

Dennis L. Krebs

Early in life, I intended to pursue a career in psychology that would enable me to work one-on-one with troubled people. While in graduate school, an eminent psychologist interrupted my aspirations by asking how many people I thought I could help in my lifetime as a psychotherapist. He pointed out that although individual forms of psychotherapy may (or may not) be beneficial to troubled people, there are other, farther reaching ways of improving the lot of those who need help – by changing social institutions and cultural norms. The overriding wisdom in this point lingered in my mind through the years. When I became a university professor, I resolved to try to reap the best from both worlds by supporting the intellectual development of students directly, in the classes I taught, and by supporting it indirectly, by helping my colleagues improve their teaching, by making structural changes in curricula, by improving institutional support for teaching and learning, and by increasing the value of teaching in the academic community. In this chapter, I will recount some of the things I have learned about how best to foster the education of college and university students inside and outside the classroom.

Inside the classroom

When people think about the ways in which university and college teachers support the educational development of students, they tend naturally to think of what happens inside classrooms. The image of a learned professor standing in front of a large class purveying his knowledge is familiar to us all. As an undergraduate student, I sat in many such classes. Maybe I'm a poor listener, but the truth is I learned relatively little in them.

When it was time for me to stand in front of my own class, I adopted a traditional lecture style. The course was an utter failure. It was featured in the students' handbook of teaching evaluations under the heading, 'For Masochists Only.' What went wrong? I valued teaching highly; I was a good public speaker;

I cared about students; I was highly motivated to teach well. I spent many sleepless nights trying to figure out how to make myself a better teacher. I tried many strategies, including reading my lectures to the class (this one died a quick death!). Slowly but surely, I found ways to capture my students' attention and inspire them to learn.

I would like to say that I found a golden key to becoming an effective teacher that I could pass on to others, but that was not the case. Developing an effective teaching style is an individual matter that, in large part, entails finding one's own groove. There is no one secret to becoming a good lecturer. For me, it involved attending to the feedback of students, responding to their suggestions, and making a large number of small changes.

I think that my early failures as a teacher stemmed in large part from an incompatibility between the format of traditional lectures, on the one hand, and my teaching philosophy and teaching style on the other. My goal as a teacher is to inspire students to think about challenging problems and to help them develop their general cognitive skills. Although I encourage students to respect the ideas of experts, I also encourage them to beware of their limitations, and to evaluate accepted ideas and theories in constructively critical ways. I feel uncomfortable professing the knowledge I have acquired as though it were the truth, because I do not believe that anyone knows the truth about important things, and to truly understand ideas, students must engulf themselves in them, grapple with them and put them together in their own ways.

Among the ways I have found to foster the intellectual development of students inside the classroom, several stand out. Perhaps most importantly, I make it clear to students that I take their education very seriously, and am highly motivated to invest in it. I explain in the first meeting of my courses that students and professors sometimes engage in an implicit and insidious conspiracy. Professors profess the content of their courses in superficial ways, investing little effort in teaching the material. In turn, students meet the requirements of the course (often a single multiple choice test or term paper at the end) in ways that enable them to get good grades with minimal demands on their professors. I make it clear that I will not join this conspiracy, and that my goal is to help every single one of my students improve their knowledge and thinking abilities in deep and enduring ways. I tell them that I am willing to make the commitment necessary to achieve this goal, and that I expect a commensurate commitment from them in return. I explain that the high standards I set for them reflect my confidence in their ability to learn.

When professors profess their ideas to large classes, it is difficult to treat their students as individuals, and this fosters what social psychologists call a 'diffusion of responsibility' (Darley and Latane 1968). To focus responsibility on individuals, I attempt to learn students' names, and call them by name as often as possible. I also attempt to learn what issues are important to them, so I can customize the content of my courses to accommodate to their interests. I encourage students to share their knowledge with me and other members of the class, blurring the distinction between teacher and learner. Finally, I encourage students to debate issues with one another in a respectful manner. Obviously, it is easier to achieve these goals in small classes than in large classes.

The individual attention I give students is not welcomed by all of them. Although most students appreciate the commitment I make to teaching them and the value I put on their education, those who are accustomed to getting by with as little effort as possible soon learn that they will not be able to sit back invisibly and let their classmates carry the load.

Outside the classroom: extending the reach of educational influence

However beneficial to students and rewarding to professors it may be to inspire students to learn inside the classroom, this is not the only, nor necessarily the most effective, way of fostering their intellectual development. Teachers (and administrators) also can foster students' intellectual development in a variety of indirect ways, such as revising the courses in their departments, creating teaching resources for other instructors, mentoring new faculty, organizing groups to exchange ideas about teaching, ensuring that those who invest in good teaching are rewarded appropriately, making university-wide changes in curriculum and teaching support structures, and increasing the value afforded to teaching in their institutions.

Consider, for example, changes that my colleagues and I made in one of the most popular courses in our university – Psychology 100, or Introduction to Psychology. In the old days, several academic staff from the Psychology Department taught Psych 100. Each of them used a different textbook and left it up to the graduate student teaching assistants, who met with students enrolled in the course once a week in small tutorials, to review the assigned readings and to answer students' questions. Some years ago, I joined forces with two colleagues to standardize the textbook for this course, produce a set of resources for the teaching assistants, and create projects for the tutorials designed not only to help students understand the content of psychology, but also to improve their writing, quantitative and critical thinking skills. We obtained a grant to set up a lab for the tutorials that contained computers loaded with state-of-the-art software. We shared these resources with other Intro Psych instructors from our department and with colleagues from other universities and colleges as well.

Without question, the many undergraduate students who took this revised course enjoyed a better learning experience than those students who took the old course. In addition, the revisions made the course easier to teach. The graduate student teaching assistants were armed with interesting exercises and tips for promoting active learning. New instructors were able to avail themselves of the lecture notes, structured tutorials, labs and other resources that my colleagues and I had assembled. Thus, we were able to contribute to the educational experience of large numbers of undergraduate students whom we never met, and indeed would ever meet, as well as providing graduate student teaching assistants with a structured introduction to the art and craft of teaching.

In addition to revising courses, university and college professors can extend the reach of the educational influence indirectly by revitalizing curricula, helping ensure that students acquire a broad general education, good writing abilities, and the quantitative skills necessary to participate effectively in an ever more technological society, and developing resources that help their colleagues improve their teaching effectiveness.

Left unattended, there is a natural tendency for curricula to lose coherence. Individual academic staff members attend to the courses they have created or have been assigned to teach, without attending to the ways in which they fit with the courses taught by other faculty or with the overriding learning objectives of their departments and universities. Members of universities and colleges can make significant contributions to the intellectual development of students in their institutions by asking themselves what forms of knowledge and cognitive abilities they expect students to acquire before they graduate (and what forms their institutions are certifying that they have acquired when they receive their degrees), and taking measures to set requirements, to sequence courses and to create opportunities that enable students to meet appropriate objectives (Doherty *et al.* 1997; Ratcliff 1997).

Consider an example. There is considerable consensus that two essential aspects of education, both of which relate to the ability to reason, are writing and quantitative skills. When a committee that I chaired examined the extent to which students in our university were acquiring these abilities, we were shocked by the dismal results. To correct this deficiency, we recommended the creation of a set of general education requirements to ensure that all students who received degrees would take at least two writing-intensive and two quantitative-intensive courses. To implement this recommendation, it was necessary to develop a large number of appropriately designed courses that would appeal to students, and recruit good teachers to teach them. It took more than two years of hard work to accomplish this (see Strachan 2008 for an account of the many trials and tribulations we suffered in implementing writing-intensive courses in our university). Although members of this committee will not teach most of the students who will leave their university with better writing and quantitative abilities, they will, nonetheless, have contributed to the education of those students in very significant ways.

It is important to acknowledge that creating new courses and implementing new requirements will contribute little or nothing to students' education if the courses are not taught effectively. In the end, structural changes that originate outside classes must produce beneficial educational experiences inside classes. It is disconcerting to admit that at my university virtually nothing is done to ensure that new academic staff are given any training in the art and craft of teaching, and that instructors in our institution are not encouraged to avail themselves of the teaching support services that are available. In response to this deficiency, a committee that I sat on for more than two years has recommended the creation of a university-wide teaching mentor system and the coordination of teaching support services. If all goes according to plan, there will be a designated person in all departments available to help their colleagues improve their courses and become better teachers, and all departments will have teaching advocates and information providers who will aim, on an ongoing basis, to improve the quality of teaching and learning in their domains (Ramsden 2003). If this initiative is successful, members of this committee will have made a major contribution to the education of students at their university – not only during their lifetimes, but potentially for many decades after.

Recommending broadly based changes designed to enhance the educational experiences of students and professors is one thing; persuading the university community to adopt and to support the changes necessary to bring them about is another (Gaff 1997). University cultures that undervalue teaching are notoriously prevalent. The philosophy of educational leadership that has guided my efforts in this respect may best be described as consultation, consultation, consultation and more consultation. For changes to be effective and enduring, they must be supported by those affected by them.

To conclude, my philosophy of institutional change is, in many respects, similar to my philosophy of teaching. It involves a dynamic interaction between 'top-down' and 'bottom-up' strategies. Just as dictating ideas to students does not help them learn, 'top-down' attempts to implement institutional changes are doomed to failure (Lindquist 1997). Just as presenting oneself as an authority discourages creative thought, an authoritarian leadership style discourages creative suggestions for change. Just as students invest in ideas they have played a role in developing, members of the university community invest in changes they have participated in making. And just as it takes a tremendous amount of time, commitment and consultation to improve the quality of education of individual students, it takes a tremendous amount of time, commitment and consultation to gain the support necessary to make effective institutional changes. However, just as students depend on their teachers for guidance, members of university communities depend on those with the most expertise about undergraduate education to outline the most promising options and guide the process of change. After listening to everyone who has an opinion, someone – ideally members of a committee with a representative sample of views – must hammer out decisions, be prepared to defend them, and persuade members of the community to support them.

References

Darley, J.M. and Latane, B. (1968) Bystander intervention in emergencies: diffusion of responsibility, *Journal of Personality and Social Psychology*, 8: 377–83.

Doherty, A., Chenevert, J.C., Miller, R.R., Roth, J.L. and Truchan, L. (1997) Developing intellectual skills, in J.G. Gaff and J.L. Ratcliff (eds) *Handbook of the Undergraduate Curriculum*. San Francisco, CA: Jossey-Bass.

Gaff, J.G. (1997) Tensions between tradition and innovation, in J.G. Gaff and J.L. Ratcliff (eds) *Handbook of the Undergraduate Curriculum*. San Francisco, CA: Jossey-Bass.

Lindquist, J. (1997) Strategies for change, in J.G. Gaff and J.L. Ratcliff (eds) *Handbook of the Undergraduate Curriculum*. San Francisco, CA: Jossey-Bass.

Ramsden, P. (2003) *Learning to Teach in Higher Education*, 2nd edn. New York: Routledge Falmer.

Ratcliff, J.L. (1997) Quality and coherence in general education, in J.G. Gaff and J.L. Ratcliff (eds) *Handbook of the Undergraduate Curriculum*. San Francisco, CA: Jossey-Bass.

Strachan, W. (2008) *Writing-intensive: Becoming W-faculty in a New Writing Curriculum*. Logan, UT: Utah State University Press.

19 Personalizing the student experience

Roger Moltzen

Over the past 20 years, in most western countries at least, the learner as an individual has received considerable interest and attention in the school sector. The message has been similar across these countries, namely that each individual brings to classrooms a unique array of background experiences, culture, interests, abilities, needs and learning styles and will respond to teaching in a similarly unique way. This notion is hardly radical but what has had a significant impact on classroom practice is the principle that learning is greatly enhanced when teachers use the knowledge of individual differences to personalize learning. In fact, some countries, such as New Zealand and the United Kingdom, have introduced national initiatives with this aim.[1]

Traditionally, universities have seen themselves offering and requiring something quite different from schools and a core distinction between the two levels has been the notion that adult learners should be much more independent, autonomous and in need of much less academic and personal support. There is also a strong history in universities of viewing students at the same level and within the same discipline as an homogeneous group. This leads to a belief that failure to keep up and the withdrawal from courses is part of a natural 'culling' process of students who did not 'belong' in the first place. This model sees an acceptance of learning environments that feature large numbers of students and are impersonal in approach. There is almost an implication that if you can survive being treated as one of the masses for long enough, the institution will eventually respond to you more as an individual.

This approach has arguably never been defensible but there are some very compelling reasons as to why this depersonalized approach to teaching and learning is particularly inappropriate in the twenty-first century. First, the intakes to most universities are much more diverse than was the case even a decade ago. The reasons for this are not appropriate to explore in the context of this chapter but this diversity is across a wide range of dimensions, including culture, nationality, language, age, ability and disability, relevant existing knowledge, socio-economic background and expectations. Failure to recognize and accommodate some of these categories of difference will inevitably re-inforce existing social inequities. In institutions that pride themselves on a commitment to social justice such inattention to diversity would seem very hypocritical. Second, the diversity that comprises our university classrooms now, if it is tapped into, has the potential to greatly enrich the learning environment. It is critical that this diversity is not seen as some form of 'deficit' but a 'difference' with the potential to add to the knowledge and experience of students and teachers alike. Third, many of the students who come to our universities from school have been exposed to instruction that has taken cognizance of their individuality. These students have an expectation that the next stage of their education will continue to build on this approach to enhancing their learning. Fourth, the lack of retention of able students represents a large loss of human potential, personally for the individual and economically for a society.

Of course respecting and supporting the development of students as individuals has implications for institutional systems and procedures. In this regard it is gratifying to observe the elevation of the student experience in many universities around the world. This has seen the implementation of initiatives that attend to the whole system with which a student interacts while undertaking study at a university, including academic, financial, physical, emotional, social, spiritual and cultural influences. At many universities this has led to a significant realignment of priorities and to systemic change. Change of this nature is critical but the intended outcomes will remain only partially fulfilled without a parallel shift in teaching practice.

As a teacher, my commitment to 'personalizing' learning is quite different from a commitment to 'individualizing' learning. Personalization is a concept with its origins in the public sector in the UK and was introduced by Charles Leadbeater (2004) in the paper *Personalisation Through Participation*. Leadbeater (2004: 59) defines his personalization as the connection between the individual and the collective by 'allowing users a more direct, informed and creative say in rewriting the script by which the service they use is designed, planned, delivered and evaluated'. Leadbeater maintains that many of the 'scripts' in education have not changed for decades, and, indeed, are written largely by professionals, producers and regulators, not by users: 'The users are expected to fit into the roles given to them by the script handed down from on high' (Leadbeater 2004: 7). Leadbeater believes the education script has to become far more user responsive. Personalizing learning allows learners to be continually engaged in setting their own targets, devising their own learning plans and goals, and being offered some choice in how they learn and how they demonstrate that learning.

One of my priorities with any class is to get to know the participants and what they bring to the learning environment and expect from it. The way I approach this is determined by the level and size of the class. It is also salient to note that I work in the social science area and the manner in which I approach this will not be appropriate across all disciplines. Arnove (2008: 14) cites the distinguished music professor Giorgio Tozzi who said:

> For me a teacher is like a tailor who has just moved to another loca-tion. So he sends out notices to his customers. One customer lives on the northeast side of town; another on the southwest side. Obviously, if he gives both customers [the same] directions on how to get to his shop, one is probably going to make it. The other is going to get hopelessly lost. I feel the teacher has to know where the student is coming from.

In smaller classes this can be achieved easily by allowing students opportuni-ties to share information directly. In my experience, this is best achieved by providing ongoing opportunities to engage at a personal level with topics related to the subject, rather than simply asking students on the first day to introduce themselves. For example, one can compare students' lived experi-ences with the theoretical approaches being studied. Another approach I find effective is asking students to provide an initial personal response to a question (prior to undertaking any reading), a second response that draws from the research, and a final response that is a synthesis of the two. The critical aspect to this process is the creation of a learning environment where students feel that it is safe, appropriate and acceptable to share the more personal. A real challenge for many teachers, and I certainly include myself here, is learning to curb our tendency to dominate interactions. Even where we resist the tempta-tion to interject or redirect, we often assume a physical disposition that gives the same message.

In larger classes the commitment to get to know the students may be less direct. It may be part of assessable tasks where students can engage with a topic in a personal rather than in a detached manner. One often hears students, especially undergraduate students, complain that including personal experi-ences or perspectives in assignments is a recipe for failure, or at least a lower grade. When I have attempted to refute this with my students and reassure them that this does not apply in my classes, I always detect a degree of cyni-cism and certainly a cautious approach to including their own voice in their assignments. Some academics will argue that the personal experiences and perspectives of students have no place in the production of an academic assign-ment. I would argue that this dimension can enhance the learner's engage-ment with the content and that to integrate personal experience and opinion appropriately with theory and research requires advanced academic skill development.

Of primary importance in supporting an individual student is having an understanding of the culture or nationality that he or she identifies with. In my country of New Zealand, the indigenous people are the Maori and as tangata whenua (people of the land) they are entitled to expect that their cultural perspectives will be recognized and valued. This right is enshrined in the Treaty of Waitangi, an agreement signed in 1840 between the Maori and the British but which remains legally binding. In no context is this more important than in education, where Maori continue to be overrepresented among those who fail to achieve. Maori students are at much greater risk of dropping out of university than non-Maori students. A significant contributing factor here is the failure of institutions to understand, value and respond to culturally specific perspectives and practices. My responsibility as a teacher is to become culturally aware and culturally responsive. This means an ongoing commitment to being conversant with Maori culture and language and seeking the input from Maori colleagues to develop culturally responsive pedagogies (Bishop and Glynn 1999; Macfarlane 2004). In the past decade and a half, New Zealand has become much more multicultural and while Maori have a priority right to special consideration, I must extend my cultural knowledge to include all cultural groups represented in my classes. This demonstrates a respect for the individual's culture. I do not expect my students to leave their culture at the door of the classroom. As a teacher, this has not resulted in a radical revision of the curriculum I teach or of my teaching practices but rather an integration of more culturally inclusive ways of selecting, delivering and assessing knowledge.

Personalizing learning is about offering choice and providing opportunities for personal innovation and creativity. This principle has to be applied selectively and in every area I teach there are tasks that are non-negotiable – or at least components of tasks. However, most university courses lend themselves to flexibility in how material is presented, learned and assessed. In both an undergraduate and a graduate paper I teach, for three minor tasks the students are asked to present their understanding of what they have learnt in any manner they choose. I once received an assignment as a knitted cardigan. The student, an older Maori woman, had symbolically represented in design the key features of her culture's approach to human development. In her accompanying oral presentation she contrasted this to the major Western European explanations of development. Other students have submitted board games, interactive games, models, diagrams, recorded mock interviews, computer games and blogs, and presented dramas, roles plays, quizzes and more.

At the core of my teaching is the asking of questions. I give primacy to finding problems and asking questions, rather than offering solutions and providing answers. The challenge is much more about, 'Have you asked a good question today?' than, 'What did you learn today?' There are many reasons for this approach, some of which are obvious, but it is at the heart of personalizing learning. In a third-year undergraduate class I teach, the major assignment requires the students to formulate the question as well as the answer. Obviously the question has to relate to the curriculum of the paper. Students are given in-class guidance on question selection and can seek individual feedback on their choice from their tutors. Each assignment is assessed on the quality of the question and the quality of the related answer. Overall, this has resulted in a higher standard of assignments than those previously submitted in response to questions I had posed, from which the students were required to make a selection.

Students enrolling in university today are much more diverse than their predecessors in the relevant background knowledge they bring to their area of study and in the rate at which they acquire new knowledge and skills. Unfortunately our teaching is often based on a perceived uniformity of prior knowledge and rate of learning. Yet this is contrary to a large body of evidence that clearly demonstrates that learning is more effective when account is taken of the learner's prior knowledge, and the rate of exposure to new ideas matches the learner's capacity to understand and apply. The challenge within the university system is less about how to gauge prior knowledge and skill and more about how to differentiate our content and approaches to match this. As the diversity of our classrooms has increased, the traditional one-size-fits-all approach has become less acceptable. In many ways, our undergraduate class-rooms, at least, are becoming much more like heterogeneous school classrooms and the attention to differentiating the curriculum that many school teachers are skilled at doing must be added to the repertoire of university teachers.

The awareness in universities of the need to respond to the diversity of its learners is often prompted by a concern with the numbers of students whom the institutions fail to retain. The focus is largely on students who have failed because they are considered to have 'lower' levels of prior knowledge and are 'slower' to master new material. While there are needs in this direction that must be addressed, there is also a need to attend to the particular needs of our best and brightest. My areas of research and teaching are intelligence, crea-tivity, eminence and the development of talent. I am equally concerned about the needs of our most gifted students who often report being unstimulated and unchallenged by a university curriculum that is sometimes perceived as designed to accommodate students of more modest ability. My studies into the lives of eminent adults has found evidence that significant numbers of gifted individuals felt let down by university because the content and delivery fell short of their expectations. Some attested to dropping out in frustration. Among our most gifted students it is the most highly creative who often struggle the most. Our emphasis on conformity and the limited opportunities for creative input and response poses a particular problem for this group. Some researchers (e.g. Simonton 1999) contend that creative individuals who continue formal education beyond school place their creative productivity at risk if they remain in tertiary institutions for too long. According to Simonton (1999: 121), 'Such restriction will tend to confine the number and diversity of ideational variations that the individual can conceive.' The challenge to university teachers is to offer opportunities for such diversity of ideas and at early stages in higher education.

As universities are placed under more external scrutiny and face increased levels of 'accountability' and compliance, the response is usually greater standardization of practices. While not wishing to bemoan the passing of an era where academics enjoyed seemingly unbridled freedom, this shift in institutional culture does bring with it a diminished tolerance of difference and a potential diminution of creativity, innovation and spontaneity. The trend towards commodification of education has undoubtedly increased the influence of the extrinsic at the expense of the intrinsic. The place of both those teachers and learners on the margins of the system is probably more tenuous than it has ever been. University teachers must continue to respect and support the students on the fringes and make it safe for them to occupy that space. Part of this support is taking a stand against practices that restrict the opportunities for creativity and innovation. History provides us with innumerable examples of great creators who lived their lives outside the mainstream of society. The relationship between marginalization and creativity is well documented (Moltzen 2009). While most universities would argue that they are safe havens for those with more radical views, the wave of systemic change that has occurred more recently sends quite different messages.

Universities are at risk of becoming institutions focused on producing graduates skilled at running the world, rather than producing graduates who can change the world. While the exception to this may be some who persist through to postgraduate education, the masses will graduate much earlier and it is this group we must empower to be innovators and not simply imitators. Part of the process is valuing and supporting each student's individuality. There was an assumption in the past that if as a university teacher you were an expert in what you taught, how you taught was of minimal concern. The onus was often placed on the student to bridge the gap between teacher knowledge and teacher delivery. Understandably, this variability of pedagogical effectiveness has attracted increased attention recently on teaching quality. To improve our performance here requires a radical change in attitude and approach and the challenging of some long-held assumptions about how tertiary students learn. I believe that such a shift should begin by positioning the student at the centre of the university's vision and mission.

Note

1   In New Zealand in 2006, the then Minister of Education launched *Let's Talk About: Personalising Learning* (Ministry of Education 2006). This book closely mirrors the 2004 UK booklet, *A National Conversation about Personalised Learning*

(DfES 2004). In October 2008, the Department for Children, Schools and Families (DCSF) in the UK launched *Personalised Learning: A Practical Guide*, to support schools in implementing personalized learning. The government made available £1.6 billion for schools to spend on the personalization of learning (and special educational needs) between 2008 and 2011.

References

Arnove, R. (2008) *Talent Abounds: Profiles of Master Teachers and Peak Performers.* Herndon, VA: Paradigm Publishers.

Bishop, R. and Glynn, T. (1999) *Culture Counts: Changing Power Relations in Education.* Palmerston North, New Zealand: Dunmore Press.

Department for Children, Schools and Families (DCSF) (2008) *Personalised Learning: A Practical Guide*. London: teachernet. http://publications.teachernet.gov.uk/, accessed 10 January 2010.

Department for Education and Skills (DfES) (2004) *A National Conversation about Personalised Learning*. London: teachernet. http://publications.teachernet.gov. uk/, accessed 10 January 2010.

Leadbeater, C. (2004) *Personalisation Through Participation: A New Script for Public Services.* London: Demos. http://www.demos.co.uk/publications/personalisation, accessed 25 September 2009.

Macfarlane, A. (2004) *Kia hiwa ra! Listen to Culture: Māori Students' Plea to Educators.* Wellington, New Zealand: New Zealand Council for Educational Research.

Ministry of Education, New Zealand (2006) *Let's Talk About: Personalising Learning*. Wellington, New Zealand: Ministry of Education.

Moltzen, R. (2009) Talent development across the lifespan, in L.V. Shavinina (ed.) *International Handbook on Giftedness*. New York: Springer.

Simonton, D.K. (1999) *The Origins of Genius: Darwinian Perspectives on Creativity*. New York: Oxford University Press.

PART 5
Scholarly Activities that Influence and Enhance Learning and Teaching

In the book's final part four well-regarded contributors from disciplines ranging from computing to law set out their views on scholarly activities that shape and support learning and teaching. They were each asked to present informed autobiographical accounts on matters such as how and why teaching and learning methods can usefully be shared with colleagues, how to link scholarship, research and professional activities with teaching, and how networks of colleagues might be usefully developed and influenced.

To begin, Ursula Lucas provides a remarkable and engaging account of her scholarly journey as a teacher, drawing from personal inner worlds – including the serious illness of her mother – and more public and institutional outer worlds to inform and develop her own career in accounting education. She notes a series of serendipitous circumstances that led her to engage with three attitudes argued by Rogers (1980) to be characteristic of a successful learning facilitator and which resonate with ideas raised by several contributors to this book: (i) genuineness; (ii) prizing, acceptance and trust; and (iii) empathetic understanding. And in the final remarks of her chapter Lucas offers each of us the comforting reminder that through a scholarly approach to teaching and learning, our journeys as reflective teachers are not made alone.

Then, in a chapter that is a bit longer than others in this collection, Australian lawyer Sally Kift moves us to an inspiring explication of ways in which core aspects of a sustainable and successful academic career can be constructed around the scholarship of teaching and learning (SoTL). She does this in a thoroughly scholarly fashion, yet focusing on approaches and strategies she has adopted in her own, highly successful career path. She makes a persuasive case for ending the hoary debate about the relationship between SoTL and what is more commonly understood to be 'real' research. Sally's chapter is a very strong and vital contribution to this book. Yet, as editor of this volume and as someone who regards learning and teaching as critical university activities, at least on par with research and service, I feel obliged to note the irony in a situation where those of us who share at least some of Sally's seemingly boundless passion have to repeatedly justify and point to the importance of learning and teaching in developing academic career pathways.

We then move from Sally Kift to Sally Fincher. Sally Fincher's simply fascinating and thought-provoking chapter covers some of the revelations she made following her work leading the UK's Computer Science Discipline Network, set up to promote and spread good practice in computer science learning and teaching. Among these is the observation that a cosmopolitan, disciplinary research model of dissemination may be less appropriate for transferring practice than a local, institutional teaching model. So, rather than imagining scholarly activities that shape learning and teaching as following a research model, she points to the highly situated nature of teaching practice and reminds us of the successful ways in which other professions transfer practice (e.g. shared studios, master classes, Balint groups) and to work she has undertaken with Josh Tenenberg to develop *disciplinary commons* as a mechanism for useful sharing.

The next chapter – and the final one in this collection – is by a globally central figure in work on SoTL, geographer Mick Healey. He reminds us of the distinction between a scholarly approach to teaching and the scholarship of teaching and then, in reflections on three phases of his career, the most recent of which has seen him seeking ways to embed SoTL in disciplines and institutions, emphasizes five matters as core in supporting high-quality learning and teaching. He describes and exemplifies the importance of providing and developing: motivation and active engagement; authentic case studies and discipline-based examples; a variety of learning, teaching and assessment experiences; an inclusive curriculum; and communities of practice. Mick's perspective on his career offers a fine and fitting chapter with which to conclude the main parts of this volume.

Reference

Rogers, C. (1980) *A Way of Being*. Boston, MA: Houghton Mifflin.

20 Exploring the 'inner' and 'outer' worlds: steps along a scholarly journey

Ursula Lucas

What do we mean when we call something 'scholarship'? Certainly, all acts of intelligence are not scholarship. An act of intelligence or of artistic creation becomes scholarship when it possesses at least three attributes: it becomes public; it becomes an object of critical review and evaluation by members of one's community; and members of one's community begin to use, build upon, and develop those acts of mind and creation.

(Shulman 1999: 15)

Teachers possess the power to create conditions that can help students learn a great deal – or keep them from learning at all. Teaching is the intentional act of creating those conditions, and good teaching requires that we understand the inner sources of both the intent and the act.

(Palmer 1998: 6)

The outer world

It's late 1984. I look earnestly at the four members of the interview panel sitting across the table. With some conviction, I am stating that I can't understand why an 18-year-old would want to enrol on an accounting and finance degree – indeed, should there be such a degree? I am a qualified accountant and have ten years' experience of auditing and accounting in a large professional firm. My own degree was International History and Politics. I have little teaching experience. How did these questions come up? I don't know. I get the job – teaching on the accounting and finance degree.

These questions remain with me now. They are not questions that can ever be answered – even if every student or lecturer had an 'answer', the responses would be many and varied. That interview was the start of a long and fascinating journey of exploration. One step on this road was to register for a PhD in which I found myself conducting phenomenological research into students' and lecturers' lifeworlds: looking at the values and beliefs that underpin their learning and teaching. I started to realize just what different worlds we all inhabit. And I made the joyful discovery of accounts of others who have been there before me (see, for example, Perry's 1988 chapter, 'Different worlds in the same classroom'). And so I set about mapping the worlds within my own subject area of introductory accounting (Lucas 2000, 2001; Lucas and Meyer 2005). As I learnt more about how students experience their learning, so this knowledge provided the foundations on which to base the development of my teaching.

However, at the same time I started to extend my reading about the wider social and political context of education. I immersed myself in more 'critical' accounts of education (Freire 1970; Illich 1973; Mezirow 1991). Consequently, I realized that I was seeking directions for a journey which would have been better started elsewhere. So I found that I had moved on from questioning why a student might want to study on an accounting degree to also questioning why I continued to teach on one.

The inner world

My first experience of teaching – an auditing class in February 1985. My day-release students look at me expectantly. They work in accounting and attend university for one day a week to study for their professional examinations. I am fortunate – the syllabus and examination expectations are clear. As an accountant who endured these examinations myself, I know the syllabus content and the examination pressures. As an auditor of some ten years' experience I also know about the 'reality' of auditing. What do I do? I stand and deliver for 90 minutes, using my carefully prepared lecture notes, sporadically lightened with a few of my auditing tales. The students' heads lower as they work through past examination questions. I am very nervous, I am wholeheartedly glad when the 90 minutes is over. I have 'filled' the slot, I have not been asked any awkward questions. I have survived!

Whether the students did so, is another matter. I knew that this was just, and most immediately, about survival, my survival. Fortunately, I also knew that this must change. I sought help and enrolled on a Postgraduate Diploma in Educational Development. The tutors introduced me to the educational literature and supported me as I attempted to apply that literature's ideas within my teaching. A series of carefully designed interventions followed and I learnt much about the law of unintended consequences (see Merton 1936). I started to realize that teaching is a lifelong process of experimentation, whether formal or informal, and that most often it is the unexpected, and the aspects that one cannot fully make sense of, that provide the most productive episodes.

But looking inwards, I recognized that the notion of 'survival' did not vanish. As I read about the impact of the all-important 'fear of failure' (Fransson 1977) on student learning, I reflected on my own fear of failure and its effect on my teaching. Palmer (1998: 17) vividly describes teaching as a 'daily exercise in vulnerability'. This sums up my feeling exactly. There is much to fear: for example, silence, perceived antagonism, boredom, superiority on the part of students and fear itself. But as Palmer also points out, fear is natural and, once recognized and acknowledged, can be worked with.

This was a considerable inner learning journey for me. I began to understand how my underlying beliefs about myself, knowledge and professionalism frame my teaching. At the same time serendipitous connections led me to the work of Carl Rogers (1980). He identifies three attitudes that characterize a facilitator of learning. The first attitude is *genuineness* in the sense that 'the feelings that the facilitator is experiencing are available to his or her awareness' (Rogers 1980: 271). There is a choice: between mindless reaction to those feelings or acknowledgement and a mindful working with those feelings. Second, there is *prizing, acceptance and trust*. This involves an acceptance of the worth of the learner as a person in his or her own right. It implies an openness to the potential of students and a willingness to set aside presuppositions about their motives, feelings and states of knowledge. This leads on to the third attitude, that of *empathic understanding*, which allows the teacher 'to understand each student's reaction from the inside, with a sensitivity to how the process of education seems *to the student*' (Rogers 1980: 272). I had realized the need for empathy in my own research (Ashworth and Lucas 2000) but I had not, so far, extended this to my teaching.

Strangely, I was thrust into a close encounter with these three attitudes. My mother was seriously ill in hospital for several months – badly affected by a stroke. I would dash from the hospital on a Thursday morning ready for my auditing class. As I stood on the threshold, ready to open the door, I would take a deep breath. The only way through was to 'be there' – be entirely with, and open to, my students and the subject. I would open the door, smile and greet my students and get on with it. That year, feedback from my students was the best ever. One comment struck home 'Ursula is always so pleased to be with us!' I suddenly realized that I had never entered a classroom alone before. I had always been accompanied by the 'students who won't turn up', 'the students who won't have done the prep' and by my own anticipated inadequacies. Now I try to leave them all at the door.

Combining the inner and the outer worlds . . . 'playing' with the subject

Another February class – some 15 years later. It is St Valentine's Day. I look through the window at the grey and misty horizon. I feel detached from my lecture, even as I carry on speaking. I feel my annoyance – at the room layout which does not support student activity. I feel gloomy; the students look rather gloomy. I reflect that they are probably more interested in Valentine's Day cards than audit reports. So, to break into this grey day, I ask them to move the chairs, to form themselves into small groups and to answer this question: 'What is the difference between a Valentine's Day card and an audit report?' Chatter brightens the room. An amazing range of responses emerge – most with a black humour that is killingly to the point.

Months later I saw these responses reflected within some perceptive examination answers – recalling both the gloomy February day and the burst of creativity that lay within it. Contrary to my original question (and expectation), typical responses included more commonalities than differences. For example, 'Neither are worth the paper they are written on', 'It's better to have one than not', 'Don't enquire into their meaning too closely, you might not hear what you want to', and so on.

On a good day, I now respond to a 'dead' situation in a classroom by taking risks. I try out completely new activities, radically revise tried and trusted activities or, even better, ask my students how 'they are' and how we might best move on. Even better still, I find that, over the years, I have developed a repertoire of learning activities that really seem to 'work'.

What do I mean by 'work'? How did these learning activities develop? Despite an anticipated difficulty in achieving publication, I found myself writing a paper that reflected upon the nature of these activities (Lucas 2008). Teaching is, for me, a form of praxis (Freire 1970) – reflection and action upon the world in order to transform it. What is the focus of this transformation? While I want students to become technically skilful, I also want them to engage in, or to come to understand the possibilities provided by, critical reflection. But, as all teachers know, this is not a straightforward matter. So I drew on the educational and broader literature searching for potential frameworks, or a 'lens' through which I could interpret these successful learning activities.

Two such frameworks emerged. The first related to the role of beliefs about knowledge and the way in which they may affect the receptivity of students to the expectation of critical reflection (Baxter Magolda 1992). Students who see accounting knowledge as factual and objective will experience difficulties in coming to view accounting as a process of social construction! I speculated about what made these learning activities 'work'. They comprised moments when students were 'pulled up short' – when the activity exposed their implicit beliefs as insufficient or challenged in that particular situation. But these were playful, non-threatening moments; leaving denial to hit in much later, if at all. So far, so good. A framework identified within the literature came to my aid.

I then went on to ask myself 'how did these moments arise?' Here I had to draw on my inner experience and develop my own framework. I named them 'moments of surprise and possibility' (Lucas 2008). These moments were, and continue to be, characterized in many and several ways, but central to all is that I am relaxed: open to the possibilities of the moment, open to the feelings, mood and relevancies of the students, engaged in what has been described as an 'eros' of learning and teaching (Beckett 2000). As Beckett vividly describes:

> Humour, anecdote, negotiation and spontaneity are the hallmarks of this type of learning, and this sort of teaching. Putting out spotfires, seizing the moment, catching the nuance and making something unique out of human sensibilities as they are inevitably revealed is all part of this too. You have to *be* there.
>
> (Beckett 2000: 73, my emphasis)

These moments also involve a confident and enquiring stance in respect to the subject and a willingness, above all, to 'play' with ideas. The subject of auditing, derided by many within accounting as being 'boring' – comes alive. It is commonplace to read about the contrast between 'teacher-centred' and 'student-centred' learning. Yet the subject must also be at the heart of the 'intentional act' of teaching.

This is not the subject as understood by a technical expert, nor the subject as understood by the professional practitioner. It is the subject as understood by the teacher. The teacher draws on 'pedagogical content knowledge'. This is Shulman's (1987: 8) term for that 'special amalgam of content and pedagogy' that represents 'an understanding of how particular topics, problems, issues are organized, represented, and adapted to the diverse interests and abilities of learners'. It also involves an understanding of what might comprise those 'threshold concepts' that, once grasped or understood, represent a transformed way of understanding or practising (Meyer and Land 2006; Lucas and Mladenovic 2007).

The scholarly journey

A process of critical reflection reveals a scholarly journey. Mine draws on outer and inner worlds to inform and develop my teaching. I have discovered that I can create possibilities that allow me to work within, but extend beyond, an institutionalized higher education and professional curriculum. Each teacher has an individual journey. Sometimes we are great teachers and sometimes we are not, but as scholars we do not have to travel alone.

> Checking our readings of problems, responses, assumptions and justifications against the readings offered by colleagues is crucial if we are to claw a path to critical clarity. Doing this also provides us with a great deal of emotional sustenance. We start to see that what we thought were unique problems and idiosyncratic failings are shared

by many others who work in situations like ours. Just knowing that we're not alone in our struggles is profoundly reassuring. Although critical reflection often begins alone, it is ultimately a collective endeavour.

(Brookfield 1995: 36)

Thank you notes

A list of references is a set of thank-you notes. It is our way of acknowledging that, without the people whom we reference, we could not have done the work we did. We are members of a community of scholars.

(Shulman 1999: 15)

References

Ashworth, P. and Lucas, U. (2000) Achieving empathy and engagement: a practical approach to the design, conduct and reporting of phenomenographic research, *Studies in Higher Education*, 25(3): 295–308.

Baxter Magolda, M. (1992) *Knowing and Reasoning in College: Gender-related Patterns in Students' Intellectual Development*. San Francisco, CA: Jossey-Bass.

Beckett, D. (2000) Eros and the virtual, in C. Symes and J. McIntyre (eds) *Working Knowledge: The New Vocationalism and Higher Education*. Buckingham: SRHE/ Open University Press.

Brookfield, S.D. (1995) *Becoming a Critically Reflective Teacher*. San Francisco, CA: Jossey-Bass.

Fransson, A. (1977) On qualitative differences in learning IV. Effects of motivation and test anxiety on process and outcome, *British Journal of Educational Psychology*, 47: 244–57.

Freire, P. (1970) *Pedagogy of the Oppressed*. London: Penguin.

Illich, I. (1973) *Deschooling Society*. London: Penguin.

Lucas, U. (2000) Worlds apart: students' experiences of learning introductory accounting, *Critical Perspectives on Accounting*, 11(4): 479–504.

Lucas, U. (2001) Deep and surface approaches to learning within introductory accounting: a phenomenographic study, *Accounting Education*, 10(2): 161–84.

Lucas, U. (2008) 'Being pulled up short': creating moments of surprise and possibility in accounting education, *Critical Perspectives on Accounting*, 19(3): 383–403.

Lucas, U. and Meyer, J.H.F. (2005) 'Towards a mapping of the student world': the identification of variation in students' conceptions of, and motivations to learn, accounting, *The British Accounting Review*, 37(2): 177–204.

Lucas, U. and Mladenovic, R. (2007) The potential of threshold concepts: an emerging framework for educational theory and practice, *London Review of Education*, 5(3): 237–48.

Merton, R.K. (1936) The unanticipated consequences of purposive social action, *American Sociological Review*, 1(6): 894–904.

Meyer, J.H.F. and Land, R. (eds) (2006) *Overcoming Barriers to Student Understanding: Threshold Concepts and Troublesome Knowledge*. Abingdon: Routledge.

Mezirow, J. (1991) *Transformative Dimensions of Adult Learning*. San Francisco, CA: Jossey-Bass.

Palmer, P.J. (1998) *The Courage to Teach: Exploring the Inner Landscape of a Teacher's Life*. San Francisco, CA: Jossey-Bass.

Perry, W.G. (1988) Different worlds in the same classroom, in P. Ramsden (ed.) *Improving Learning: New Perspectives*. London: Kogan Page.

Rogers, C. (1980) *A Way of Being*. Boston, MA: Houghton Mifflin.

Shulman, L.S. (1987) Knowledge and teaching: foundations of the new reform, *Harvard Educational Review*, 57(1): 1–22.

Shulman, L.S. (1999) Taking teaching seriously, *Change*, 31(4): 10–17.

21 Integrating a sustainable academic career around scholarly learning and teaching activities

Sally Kift

> A scholarship of teaching is *not* synonymous with excellent teaching. It requires a kind of 'going meta', in which [teachers] frame and systematically investigate questions related to student learning – the conditions under which it occurs, what it looks like, how to deepen it, and so forth – and do so with an eye not only to improving their own classroom but to advancing practice beyond it. This conception of the scholarship of teaching is not something we presume all [teachers] (even the most excellent and scholarly teachers among them) will or should do – though it would be good to see that more of them have the opportunity to do so if they wish. But the scholarship of teaching is a condition – as yet a mostly absent condition for excellent teaching. It is the mechanism through which the profession of teaching itself advances, through which teaching can be something other than a seat-of-the-pants operation, with each of us out there making it up as we go. As such, the scholarship of teaching has the potential to serve all teachers – and students.
>
> (Hutchings and Shulman 1999: 13–14)

In Australia, nominees for the annual national teaching excellence awards administered by the Australian Learning and Teaching Council (ALTC) are assessed on evidence provided against five selection criteria, the fifth of which alludes to Hutchings and Shulman's 'mostly absent condition for excellent teaching'. This criterion, titled 'scholarly activities that have influenced and enhanced learning and teaching', is the one to which particular attention is paid when selecting the recipient of the premier teaching award – the Prime Minister's Award (ALTC 2009: 31). The relevant ALTC's Guidelines (2009: 24) state that such 'scholarly activities' may include:

> advanced skills in evaluation and reflective practice; participating in and contributing to professional activities related to learning and

teaching; coordination, management and leadership of courses and student learning; conducting and publishing research related to teaching; demonstrating leadership through activities that have broad influence on the profession.

These indicia of scholarly practice invoke recourse to the theoretical base that informs effective pedagogical practice. To be scholarly in learning and teaching is rigorous academic work. It demands: currency and command of both discipline subject matter and educational theory; inquiring, methodical and reflective approaches; the collection, evaluation and documentation of evidence of learning and teaching efficacy; and it optimally entails participation in and communication among a community of teaching professionals.

In this chapter, I examine my own practice under this head to explicate the 'how' and 'why' of my scholarly and scholarship approaches, as much as the 'what' and 'where' of that endeavour. In doing so, I make this meta-analysis 'community property', in the same way that Shulman (1993: 6) exhorted we 'change the status of teaching from private to community property' so that teaching might be more greatly valued in the academy.

I begin with an account of my history and context, following which I suggest a framework for approaching these 'scholarly activities'. I then turn to discuss how the staples of academic work might be integrated around scholarly learning and teaching in ways that offer time-poor academics operating in dynamic environments manageable and sustainable career and workload pathways. Throughout the discussion, I offer examples of my own approaches and strategies, drawing on a range of career experiences.

My story and context

I came to a learning and teaching focus early in my career upon being thrust, as many are, into teaching core undergraduate classes with large enrolments, an unstable full-time teaching team, and a large sessional staff contingent. As a junior law academic, I was responsible for designing and managing complex, multifaceted environments to support student learning, engagement and success. The broader professional context was one of constant dynamic change in both higher education and the legal services industry.

From earliest days, I adopted a scholarly and inclusive approach to teaching, research and academic service, and sought to publish from these activities; primarily because I was personally and professionally motivated to do so, but also because it seemed an effective and efficient workload strategy. As I evolved, my scholarship developed in complexity also, often building cumulatively to advance practice within and beyond my home discipline. For example, early work in graduate attributes, student engagement, the training of sessional staff and exploration of online delivery all coalesced to present new ways of enhancing the first-year experience (FYE) for diverse cohorts.

I have negotiated my way through promotion hurdles by prosecuting a case built on a synergistic interpretation of the academic dimensions. My progress has been far from smooth or linear and I cannot pretend that it has been unproblematic, particularly as I was in the vanguard of those making such arguments in the sector. In early attempts to mitigate the risks of this approach, I also published 'safe research' in my discipline area, though the quantum of that activity has recently been diminishing.

Without a primary grounding in pedagogical theory, as Tomazos (1997) has documented, I struggled initially with obfuscatory 'eduspeak'. However, as a critically reflective teacher (Brookfield 1995) who was interested in student learning, I found that my intuitive understandings and instincts – my 'strongly held, pedagogically relevant, personal theories of learning' (Tomazos 1997) – essentially aligned with underpinning 'eduspeak' constructs. I was comforted also that I was contributing to my own discipline's 'pedagogical content knowledge', the pedagogy of legal education (Shulman 1993: 7; Trigwell *et al.* 2000: 163). As Huber and Morreale (2002: 2) reassuringly observe:

> Each discipline has its own intellectual history, agreements, and disputes about subject matter and methods that influence what is taught, to whom, when, where, how, and why. Each has a set of traditional pedagogies . . . and its own discourse of reflection and reform. Each has its own community of scholars interested in teaching and learning in that field, with one or more journals, associations, and face-to-face forums for pedagogical exchange. For good or for ill, scholars of teaching and learning must address field-specific issues if they are going to be heard in their own disciplines, and they must speak in a language that their colleagues understand.

As I moved into more formal learning and teaching leadership roles, I worked hard to be a 'visible advocate' of and 'role model' for learning and teaching excellence; locally, institutionally and nationally. I worked to make a difference to the quality of the 'educational conditions in which we place students' (Tinto 2009: 2) across the spectrum of scholarly activity: through innovative curriculum design, whole-of-programme student engagement, policy formulation, committee work, mentoring and staff development, sessional staff training, grants and scholarship. For example, my first-year teaching led to involvement as a project team member in first-year curriculum renewal to embed graduate attributes and online delivery. I then won a large internal grant to assure the quality and efficacy of assessment practices to support these new skill-based learning objectives. This was followed by another large grant, with a colleague from the Faculty of Information Technology, to investigate enhanced undergraduate transition practice across our two disciplines. As both a project team member and project leader, I sought to ensure that this work benefited both students (through enhanced research- and evidence-based practice and an enabling policy environment) and staff (through scholarship outputs). By the time the assessment grant reported, the project team had generated 55 national and international publications. In 2007, the assessment project received a national ALTC teaching award for its enhancement of student learning. These projects have had demonstrable impact across contexts. McKenzie *et al.* (2005: 64) commented, for example,

> Members of the project team have given numerous presentations on the project. For example, the team member who received an Australian Award for University Teaching has given numerous keynotes and presentations on graduate capabilities development and assessment at conferences. She has also been invited to present the work at a number of other universities, both to Law Faculties and the university more widely. Law curricula in other universities have been influenced by the QUT [Queensland University of Technology] developments.

These are the sorts of metrics that institutions and colleagues understand when making judgements about the worth of scholarly activities – peer-reviewed publications, esteem factors, grant income, speaking invitations leading to national and international visibility, and scholarly work being adopted, adapted and transferred to other contexts. The subsequent award of external grant income adds to the metric mix.

In essence, then, my pedagogical career strategy has been to align my individual interests with intra-institutional priorities and higher education's broader agenda and leadership possibilities. Wherever possible I have sought to engage and influence others collaboratively (Kotter 1990) to enhance student experiences and learning outcomes, within and across disciplines and institutions. Decades of pedagogical research and theory have told us much about what counts for student success and retention and what engages learners in productive learning (most recently, for example, Scott 2006; ACER 2009). The challenge is to take this core university business seriously enough to pursue the often difficult and unglamorous work of translating that knowledge into effective action that is implemented fully, effectively and sustainably, in ways that are measurable, upscaleable, and have continual relevance. This is the challenge I have sought to meet over my career, with varying degrees of success.

A possible framework for scholarly and scholarship activities

This chapter is not the place to debate the dividing line between scholarly teaching and the scholarship of learning and teaching (SoLT), about which much has been written (for example, Glassick *et al.* 1997; Healey 2000; Trigwell *et al.* 2000; Kreber 2001; Kift 2003a). My preference, as a working academic who has had to jump through the promotion hoops, is for Shulman's (1998: 6) definition of the latter, which, by subscribing to standard scholarship values, does much to negate the traditional privileging of 'real', discovery-type, research:

> A scholarship of teaching will entail a public account of some or all of the full act of teaching – vision, design, enactment, outcomes, and analysis – in a manner susceptible to critical review by the teacher's professional peers and amenable to productive employment in future work by members of that same community.[1]

Particularly, I have found Shulman's deconstruction of the 'full act of teaching' helpful because it provides a structure around which to conceptualize this type of scholarship (Kift 2003a).

The formulation of the scholarship question is not necessarily an easy matter. 'No one gets an idea and immediately begins to "do research"' (Shulman 2000: 98), and so too for this type of scholarship. Bass (1999: 1) argues that we should 'make the problematization of teaching a matter of regular communal discourse [and] . . . think of teaching practice, and the evidence of student learning, as problems to be investigated, analyzed, represented, and debated', as occurs routinely for research 'problems'. Some authors frame the classroom (perhaps now more aptly, the entire student experience) as a 'laboratory' and teaching as an 'experiment', where ongoing investigation and inquiry may be conducted into student learning (Cross 1990; Cerbin 1996).

SoLT inquiries are often 'quite pragmatic questions' (Hutchings 2000: 2), such as why a particular intervention is not working optimally or whether an innovation has led to better learning. As Prosser (2008: 1) points out, much of this work is 'evidence based critical reflection on practice to improve practice'. Indeed, these inquiries 'may be hard to distinguish from teaching itself' and may entail a 'moving target' (Hutchings 2000: 8) as the action research evolves. Such reflections will inevitably vary in content and form as the different SoLT genres, for example, identified in the *Scholarship of Teaching and Learning Online Tutorial* (ISSOTL n.d.) demonstrate.[2] Hutchings (2000: 4–5) has also suggested a loose taxonomy of questions that include:

- questions about 'what works';
- questions focusing on 'what is' or 'what does [the student experience] look like';
- 'visions of the possible'; and
- 'formulating a new conceptual framework for shaping thought about practice'.

In my own work, I have investigated questions across this spectrum. Some examples of my scholarship inquiries, organized according to Hutchings' taxonomy, various of the *Tutorial*'s genres (ISSOTL n.d.), and two groupings of my own, are set out in Table 21.1. Many of these grew out of a desire to test or improve current practice from the perspective of either 'translat[ing] ... research and theory into effective practice' (Tinto 2006–07: 2; Kift 2008a) or working from practice to theory through evaluation and reflection-in-action (for example Kift 2003b, 2004a).

Table 21.1   SoLT questions and SoLT examples

Scholarship questions	Illustrative scholarship examples
'What works' (Hutchings 2000: 4) Analyses of particular teaching interventions: e.g. methodical case studies of what worked well, or evaluations of change in practice by way of quantitative and/or qualitative assessment of 'before and after' interventions. (ISSOTL n.d., Unit 3A: 4; Nelson n.d.)	• Research-based inquiry into what works in generic and discipline-specific skills development in legal education (Kift 1997; Christensen and Kift 2000) • What works to enhance the student experience of teamwork; how to monitor for students at risk of not succeeding in the first undergraduate year (Nelson *et al.* 2007) • Analysis of a teaching intervention to situate knowledge and skills development in core undergraduate curriculum in a cognitive apprenticeship model (Kift and Airo-Farulla 1995) • A case study of several iterations of using audience response systems (clickers) in large undergraduate orientation sessions (Kift 2006)
'What is' or 'What does [the student experience] look like' (Hutchings 2000: 4)	• Examining the attitudinal attainment of ethical values in legal education (Kift 2001, 2008b) • How we might engage students better in active learning (Kift 2002b, 2003c, 2005a, 2008b) • Investigating the entering expectations of diverse first-year cohorts to assess for potential mismatches with the experienced reality (Nelson *et al.* 2008)

(Continued overleaf)

Table 21.1 Continued

Scholarship questions	Illustrative scholarship examples
'Visions of the possible' (Hutchings 2000: 4–5)	• Investigating 'visions of the possible' to 'formulate a new conceptual framework', namely a taxonomy for the integrated and incremental development of generic and discipline-specific skills in legal education (Christensen and Kift 2000; Kift 2002a, 2008b, 2008c) • Exploring a future vision for legal education in the current climate of change in higher education and the legal services industry (Kift 2008b)
'Formulating a new conceptual framework for shaping thought about practice' (Hutchings 2000: 5)	• Shaping conceptions about the FYE of diverse commencing cohorts by articulating a 'transition pedagogy' (Kift and Nelson 2005) to support learning, success and retention (Kift 2004b, 2005a, 2008a, 2009a, 2009c) • Building on first-year curriculum renewal to conceptualize optimal final-year learning environments in legal education (Kift *et al.* 2008)
'Reflections on . . . years of teaching experience . . . informed by other scholarship on teaching' (Nelson n.d.; ISSOTL n.d., Unit 3A: 5)	• Invitations to speak and write on legal education for both the academy and legal profession (Kift 2003d, 2005b, 2007, 2008b, 2008c)
'Larger contexts: comparisons across courses and student change over time' (ISSOTL n.d., Unit 3A: 6; Nelson n.d.)	• Exploration of the pedagogical possibilities presented by online and blended learning environments (Kift 2003e, 2004c, 2005a; Nelson *et al.* 2005a, 2005b; Field and Kift 2006) • ALTC Senior Fellowship on generic first-year curriculum design (Kift 2008a, 2009a, 2009c)
'Summaries and [meta] analyses of sets of prior studies' (Nelson n.d.; ISSOTL n.d., Unit 3A: 8)	For example: • to conceptualize and then advance the graduate attribute agenda (Kift 1997) • to renew first-year approaches in a discipline (Kift 2003c) or across an institution (Kift and Nelson 2005; Nelson *et al.* 2006) • to reflect on changes over time in pedagogical approaches in a discipline (Kift 2005–06)

Investigations of different teaching contexts	For example: • investigating good practice in first-year curriculum design (Kift 2003c, 2004b, 2005a, 2008a, 2009a, 2009c) • developing a framework for graduate attribute assessment (Kift 2002a) • examining good practice to support sessional teaching staff (Kift 2003b) • analysing the emerging leadership role and desirable capabilities of faculty Assistant Deans, Learning and Teaching (Kift 2004a) • conceptualizing how to make teaching 'count' for women academics in the research domain through pursuit of the SoLT (Kift 2003a)
Investigating different perspectives on learning and teaching (for example Indigenous perspectives, interdisciplinarity, work-integrated learning, meta-theory analyses)	• Harnessing ePortfolio in aid of student learning (Kift *et al.* 2007; Kift 2009b) • Investigation of the implications of globalization for legal education and transnational curriculum design (Kift 2004d)

These varied public and peer-reviewed accounts of scholarly activities are characterized by all the usual hallmarks of high-quality research and commonly 'tie into their disciplines' histories, pedagogies and investigative styles' (Huber 2001: 26). Glassick *et al.* (1997: 36) have usefully identified six common standards against which *all* scholarship – the scholarships of discovery, application, integration and teaching (Boyer 1990) – should be evaluated:

- clear goals;
- adequate preparation;
- appropriate methods;
- significant results;
- effective presentation; and
- reflective critique.

As the material above seeks to demonstrate, a persuasive case exists for terminating the tired old debate about the status of 'real' research versus the SoLT (after Boyer 1990). As Shulman (2000: 99) posits,

> . . . as the scholarship of teaching and learning takes hold, and as we generate a powerful body of work from the efforts of individual scholars, the distinction traditionally made between the methods of teaching and those of research will gradually disappear. Each will be

understood as a variety of methodologically sophisticated, disciplined inquiry. Each demands activities of design, action, assessment, analysis, and reflection.

Unless it be thought that scholarly activities should always deliver SoLT outputs, I should make clear that many other of my scholarly contributions, while moving practice forward in valuable ways, would not satisfy all of Glassick *et al.*'s metrics (1997: 36). Examples here include: presentations to colleagues on writing to promotion criteria, on funding opportunities and on the SoLT itself; staff development workshops and seminars; websites; and multiple FYE disseminations to discrete interest groups of professional and external colleagues.

Exploiting the synergies of the academic workload

Once we understand how learning and teaching activities can lead to legitimate scholarly outputs then, in the context of fraught academic workloads, it becomes possible to imagine how the synergies of scholarly approaches across the three academic dimensions – of teaching, research *and* service and engagement – might be leveraged into a coherent and sustainable whole across otherwise disparate silos of activity.

> If knowledge-based integration of the three components is the goal [of universities], it is far more effective to build this integration around teaching and learning than to start with either research or service. Trying to do all three independent of each other is a recipe for fragmentation and failure.
>
> (Fullan and Scott 2009: 55)

Recent government policy and performance incentives in Australia (Australian Government 2009), in conjunction with the ALTC's high-profile suite of programmes and awards, have focused attention on the quality of universities' learning and teaching performance. Moreover, academic promotion criteria now recognize scholarly pedagogical endeavour, admittedly with varying degrees of sophistication and reliability. More than ever before, the context and incentive rhetoric is supportive of teachers who seek to align their career trajectories with institutional pedagogical priorities and to use scholarly activities as their work's organizing and integrating device.

The changing nature of academic work makes the potential for effectiveness and efficiency gains in this regard very real: the academic, administrative and management aspects of the role have diffused and blurred and can be harnessed intelligently to plan, design and enact the teaching 'experiment', which is within everyday workload in any event. More satisfyingly, modern pedagogical and whole-of-programme innovation calls for new leadership and management models, as academics and professional staff are required to work cooperatively across organizational silos to blend support, service and technology delivery into coherent, student-focused, learning environments.

This is collaborative, interdisciplinary and highly strategic work (Kift 2005b); exactly the type of research most universities now commend and encourage. Recent articulations of the highly sought-after teaching–research nexus routinely reference the SoLT, 'pedagogic research – enquiring and reflecting on learning' (Jenkins and Healey 2005: 21), as a legitimate, if distinctive, manifestation of the nexus (Krause *et al.* 2008). In multiple ways, therefore, aligning the three academic domains has the 'potential to serve all teachers – and students' well (Hutchings and Shulman 1999: 14). Specifically, by doing that bit extra at the course planning stage – devising an evaluation strategy and obtaining ethics approval to permit later peer-reviewed publication (as represented in Figure 21.1) – all teachers have the opportunity both to improve student learning outcomes *and* to deliver scholarship outputs.

And so to leadership and influence

In this way, I think it is quite possible for all academics to manage their complex workloads better, self-initiated though this must be. As Ramsden and Scott have both said, 'Leadership in universities can and should be exercised by everyone, from the vice chancellor to the casual parking attendant' (Ramsden 1998: 4); 'Every member of staff is a leader of change in their own areas of expertise' (Scott 2004: 42). Teachers who assume such informal leadership roles may enact their leadership potential through the 'practical and everyday process of supporting,

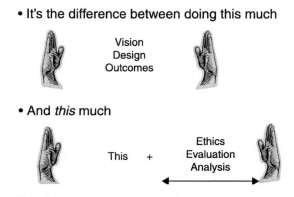

* It's the difference between doing this much

Vision
Design
Outcomes

* And *this* much

This　+　Ethics
Evaluation
Analysis

Figure 21.1　Scholarship of (the extended act of) learning and teaching.

managing, developing and inspiring academic colleagues' (Ramsden 1998: 4) and students.

I have always seen mentoring, modelling and supporting teaching and professional colleagues as an integral component of my learning leader role (Scott *et al.* 2008): whether as subject coordinator supporting sessional staff in their first years of teaching; as Assistant Dean encouraging scholarship outputs from grant team members and supporting their promotion applications; or as ALTC Senior Fellow validating practice and normalizing the complexity of the FYE across the sector. In more formal leadership roles, the type and quality of the scholarly contribution shifts: 'upscaled' influence and leadership may be exercised for a more pervasive 'pedagogical good' (Kift 2004a). Crucially, there is heightened potential to effect systemic culture change and 'get the context right for staff, to get the context right for students' (Hunt 2009). For example, as Assistant Dean and Institutional Director, FYE, important policy enhancements were advanced. The faculty learning leadership role enabled me to establish a research programme specifically to promote (and validate) the SoLT in law and justice education within the mainstream research agenda.

I have sought to explicate this conceptualization in Figure 21.2. Informal learning leadership and influence may be exercised by individual teachers in the immediate ways represented by the lighter, internal quadrants, through:

- the scholarly teaching of their own students;
- working with other teaching and professional staff on scholarly activities (e.g. in teaching teams, on regular quality cycle curriculum improvement);
- operating within the boundaries of existing learning and teaching policy and agitating for change;
- disseminating scholarship and working with colleagues outside their organizational area on scholarly activities (e.g. on learning and teaching grants).

Formal learning leadership offers increased and more pervasive opportunities, as represented by Figure 21.2's encircling, darker quadrants. My interpretation of the leadership model here is a combination of leading through influence and a form of transactional and transformational leadership (Marshall n.d.; Scott *et al.* 2008). Examples here include:

- influencing and guiding pedagogical good practice in curricular and co-curricular design and delivery that benefits *all* students in the faculty (as Assistant Dean), students across all disciplines (institutional role) and across the sector (Fellowship role);
- supporting, developing and motivating greater numbers of academic and professional colleagues across the faculty, disciplines, institution

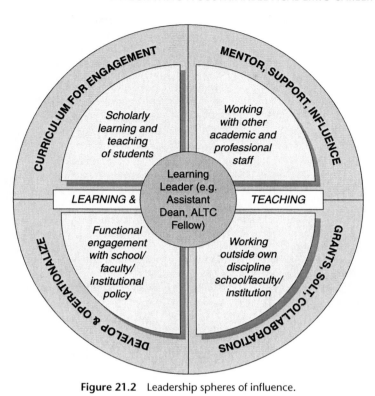

Figure 21.2 Leadership spheres of influence.

and sector through communities of practice and supportive working relationships;

- influencing and initiating policy development and implementation to 'get the context right' for desirable scholarly practice;
- having greater institutional, national and international visibility through grant-getting, publications, invited presentations, staff development activities, auditing activities and the like.

Conclusion

An academic career organized around the integrator of scholarly activities that influence and enhance learning and teaching may present time-poor and change-weary academics with manageable and sustainable career and work-load pathways. I cannot, and do not, suggest that such an approach is entirely risk-free or that it will be warmly embraced in every university. I am, however, cautiously optimistic that current policy, institutional and broader contexts

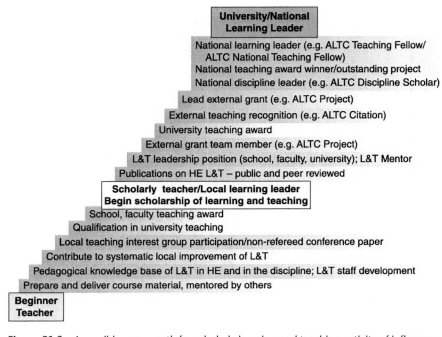

Figure 21.3 A possible career path for scholarly learning and teaching activity of influence.

Source: Kift, adapted from Towers (2006)

augur far more favourably for such an academic focus now than ever before. Any risk involved is manageable and can be substantially mitigated through engagement with the SoLT in the ways here suggested.

In this spirit, I offer finally Figure 21.3 as a possible model for a pedagogical career trajectory, accepting the obvious criticism that career progression will rarely be this linear – mine certainly has not been. On balance, however, what my career has been over the years is collaborative, satisfying, rewarding and energizing. I do actually enjoy my day job and I think that's quite a recommendation!

Notes

1 A fourth attribute implied by these other three is 'question-asking, inquiry, and investigation, particularly around issues of student learning' (Hutchings and Shulman 1999: 13).
2 See especially Unit 3A: How Could I do Scholarship of Teaching and Learning?

References

ACER (Australian Council for Educational Research) (2009) *Attracting, Engaging and Retaining: New Conversations About Learning. Australasian Survey of Student Engagement Report.* http://www.acer.edu.au/documents/AUSSE_ASERReportWebVersion.pdf, accessed 20 July 2009.

ALTC (Australian Learning and Teaching Council) (2009) *Australian Awards for University Teaching – 2009 Guidelines.* http://www.altc.edu.au/awards-how-to-nominate, accessed 20 July 2009.

Australian Government (2009) *Transforming Australia's Higher Education System.* Canberra: DEEWR. http://www.deewr.gov.au/HigherEducation/Documents/PDF/Additional%20Report%20-%20Transforming%20Aus%20Higher%20ED_webaw.pdf, accessed 20 July 2009.

Bass, R. (1999) The scholarship of teaching: what's the problem? *Inventio*, 1(1): 1–9. http://www.doiiit.gmu.edu/Archives/feb98/randybass.htm, accessed 20 July 2009.

Boyer, E.L. (1990) *Scholarship Reconsidered: Priorities of the Professoriate.* Princeton, NJ: The Carnegie Foundation for the Advancement of Teaching.

Brookfield, S.D. (1995) *Becoming a Critically Reflective Teacher.* San Francisco, CA: Jossey-Bass.

Cerbin, W. (1996) Inventing a new genre: the course portfolio at the University of Wisconsin-La Crosse, in P. Hutchings (ed.) *Making Teaching Community Property: A Menu for Peer Collaboration and Peer Review.* Washington, DC: American Association for Higher Education.

Christensen, S. and Kift, S. (2000) Graduate attributes and legal skills: integration or disintegration? *Legal Education Review*, 11(2): 207–37.

Cross, K.P. (1990) Teachers as scholars, *AAHE Bulletin*, 43(4): 3–5.

Field, R. and Kift, S. (2006) Learning on the move: reconciling the needs of students and academics in the fast lane of tertiary education in 2006. Paper presented to Online Learning and Teaching Conference, Learning on the Move, Brisbane, 26 September. http://eprints.qut.edu.au/18052/1/18052.pdf, accessed 20 July 2009.

Fullan, M. and Scott, G. (2009) *Turnaround Leadership for Higher Education.* San Francisco, CA: Jossey-Bass.

Glassick, C., Huber, M. and Maeroff, G. (1997) *Scholarship Assessed: Evaluation of the Professoriate.* San Francisco, CA: Jossey-Bass.

Healey, M. (2000) Developing the scholarship of teaching in higher education: a discipline based approach, *Higher Education Research & Development*, 19(2): 169–89.

Huber, M.T. (2001) Balancing acts: designing careers around the scholarship of teaching, *Change*, 33(4): 21–9.

Huber, M.T. and Morreale, S.P. (2002) Situating the scholarship of teaching and learning: a cross-disciplinary conversation, in M.A. Huber and S. Morreale (eds)

Disciplinary Styles in the Scholarship of Teaching and Learning: Exploring Common Ground. Washington, DC: American Association for Higher Education and The Carnegie Foundation for the Advancement of Teaching.

Hunt, L. (2009) Is it an improvement when a cannibal uses a fork? Critical enquiry into the sustainability of outcomes from first-year experience interventions. Keynote paper presented to FYE Curriculum Design Symposium, Brisbane, 5–6 February. http://www.fyecd2009.qut.edu.au/resources/, accessed 20 July 2009.

Hutchings, P. (2000) Approaching the scholarship of teaching and learning, in P. Hutchings (ed.) *Opening Lines: Approaches to the Scholarship of Teaching and Learning*. Menlo Park, CA: The Carnegie Foundation for the Advancement of Teaching.

Hutchings, P. and Shulman, L.S. (1999) The scholarship of teaching: new elaborations, new developments, *Change*, 31(5): 10–15.

ISSOTL (International Society for the Scholarship of Teaching & Learning) (n.d.) *Scholarship of Teaching and Learning Online Tutorial*. http://www.issotl.org/tutorial/sotltutorial/home.html, accessed 20 July 2009.

Jenkins, A. and Healey, M. (2005) *Institutional Strategies to Link Teaching and Research*. York: The Higher Education Academy. http://www.heacademy.ac.uk/assets/York/documents/ourwork/research/Institutional_strategies.pdf, accessed 20 July 2009.

Kift, S. (1997) Lawyering skills: Finding their place in legal education, *Legal Education Review*, 8: 43–73.

Kift, S. (2001) It's a matter of affecting attitude: influencing law students to embrace higher-order lawyering values. Paper presented to the Australasian Law Teachers Association Conference, Vanuatu, 1–4 July.

Kift, S. (2002a) Harnessing assessment and feedback to assure quality outcomes for graduate capability development: a legal education case study. Paper presented to the Australian Association for Research in Education Conference, Brisbane, 1–5 December. http://www.aare.edu.au/02pap/kif02151.htm, accessed 20 July 2009.

Kift, S. (2002b) Legal education: will modelling engage the learners in the learning? Paper presented to the Australian Technology Network Effective Teaching and Learning Conference, Brisbane, December. http://eprints.qut.edu.au/8270/1/8270.pdf, accessed 20 July 2009.

Kift, S. (2003a) Making teaching count for women in research: the scholarship of teaching. Paper presented to Discovery 2003: Women in Research Conference, Rockhampton, 13–14 November. http://www.wir.cqu.edu.au/FCWViewer/getFile.do?id=5718, accessed 20 July 2009.

Kift, S. (2003b) Assuring quality in the casualisation of teaching, learning and assessment: towards best practice for the first year experience, *UltiBASE*, March. http://ultibase.rmit.edu.au/Articles/march03/kift1.htm, accessed 20 July 2009.

Kift, S. (2003c) The first year renewal to engage learners in law. Paper presented to 7th Pacific Rim First Year in Higher Education Conference, Brisbane, 9–11 July.

http://www.fyhe.qut.edu.au/past_papers/papers03/Refereed%20Papers/Full%
20papers/Kift_paper.doc, accessed 20 July 2009.

Kift, S. (2003d) A tale of two sectors: dynamic curriculum change for a dynamically changing profession, *Journal of Commonwealth Law and Legal Education*, 2(2): 5–22.

Kift, S. (2003e) From bolting on to embedding: how do we progress the seamlessness of online and in-class learning environments to enhance student learning outcomes? Paper presented to Online Learning and Teaching (OLT) 2003, Excellence: Making the Connections, Brisbane, 5 November. http://eprints.qut.edu.au/84/, accessed 20 July 2009.

Kift, S. (2004a) Between a rock and several hard places: where does a Faculty Learning and Teaching Sub-Dean sit and what is that role? *HERDSA News*, 26(3): 8–11.

Kift, S. (2004b) Organising first year engagement around learning: formal and informal curriculum intervention. Keynote paper presented to the 8th Pacific Rim First Year in Higher Education Conference: Dealing with Diversity, Melbourne, 14–16 July. http://www.fyhe.qut.edu.au/past_papers/Papers04/Sally%20Kift_paper.doc, accessed 20 July 2009.

Kift, S. (2004c) A new pedagogy for higher education? Exploring integrated learning environments in legal education. Paper presented to Online Learning and Teaching (OLT) Conference: Exploring Integrated Learning Environments, Brisbane, 3 November. http://eprints.qut.edu.au/24705/, accessed 20 July 2009.

Kift, S. (2004d) Curriculum renewal in law to meet the needs of global practice: embedding and assessing skills acquisition. Paper presented to Association of American Law Schools (AALS) Conference: Educating Lawyers for Translational Challenges, Oahu, 26–29 May. http://www.aals.org/international2004/Papers/KIFT.pdf, accessed 20 July 2009.

Kift, S. (2005a) Transforming the first year experience: a new pedagogy to enable transition. Paper presented to Enhancing Student Success Conference, Newcastle, 11 April.

Kift, S. (2005b) For better or for worse?: 21st century legal education. Paper presented to LAWASIA Downunder, Gold Coast, 20–24 March. http://eprints.qut.edu.au/7439/, accessed 20 July 2009.

Kift, S. (2005–06) My law school – then and now, *Newcastle Law Review*, 9: 1–20.

Kift, S. (2006) Using an audience response system to enhance student engagement in large group orientation: a Law Faculty case study, in D. Banks (ed.) *Audience Response Systems in Higher Education*. New York: Idea Group Inc.

Kift, S. (2007) Launch of Australian Academy of Law. Paper presented to Symposium 2007: Fragmentation or Consolidation? Fostering a Coherent Professional Identity for Lawyers, Brisbane, 17 July. http://www.academyoflaw.org.au/events/sym07.html, accessed 20 July 2009.

Kift, S. (2008a) The next, great first year challenge: sustaining, coordinating and embedding coherent institution-wide approaches to enact the FYE as 'everybody's business'. Keynote paper presented to 11th Pacific Rim First Year in Higher Education Conference: An Apple for the Learner: Celebrating the First Year Experience, Hobart, 30 June–2 July. http://www.fyhe.qut. edu.au/past_papers/papers08/FYHE2008/content/pdfs/Keynote%20-%20Kift. pdf, accessed 20 July 2009.

Kift, S. (2008b) 21st century climate for change: curriculum design for quality learning engagement in law, *Legal Education Review*, 18 (1 & 2): 1–30.

Kift, S. (2008c) Integrating the knowing, the doing and the practice: an early Australian case study of curriculum renewal. Paper presented to International Conference on the Future of Legal Education, Atlanta, 20–24 February. http://www.law.gsu.edu/FutureOfLegalEducationConference/Papers/Kift-SS.pdf, accessed 20 July 2009.

Kift, S. (2009a) A transition pedagogy for first year curriculum design and renewal. Keynote paper presented to FYE Curriculum Design Symposium, Brisbane, 5–6 February. http://www.fyecd2009.qut.edu.au/resources/PRE_SallyKift_5Feb09. pdf, accessed 20 July 2009.

Kift, S. (2009b) Harnessing ePortfolio to support and enhance the first year student experience. Paper presented to the Australian ePortfolio (AeP2) Symposium, Brisbane, 9–10 February. http://www.eportfoliopractice.qut.edu.au/sympo-sium2/program.jsp, accessed 20 July 2009.

Kift, S. (2009c) *Final Report for ALTC Senior Fellowship Program: Articulating a Transition Pedagogy to Scaffold and to Enhance the First Year Student Learning Experience in Australian Higher Education.* http://www.altc.edu.au/resource-first-year-learning-experience-kift-2009, accessed 21 December 2009.

Kift, S. and Airo-Farulla, G. (1995) Throwing students in the deep end or teaching them how to swim: developing 'offices' as a technique of law teaching, *Legal Education Review*, 6: 53–90.

Kift, S. and Nelson, K. (2005) Beyond curriculum reform: embedding the transition experience, in A. Brew and C. Asmar (eds) *Higher Education in a Changing World: Research and Development in Higher Education*, 28: 225–35. Sydney: HERDSA.

Kift, S., Harper, W., Creagh, T. *et al.* (2007) ePortfolios: mediating the minefield of inherent risks and tensions. Paper presented to ePortfolio Australia – Imagining New Literacies, RMIT University, Melbourne, 26–27 March. http://eprints.qut. edu.au/6495/, accessed 20 July 2009.

Kift, S., Field, R. and Wells, I. (2008) Promoting sustainable professional futures for law graduates through curriculum renewal in legal education: a final year experience (FYE2), *eLaw Journal*, 15(2): 145–58.

Kotter, J.P. (1990) *A Force for Change: How Leadership Differs from Management.* New York: Free Press.

Krause, K-L., Arkoudis, S., James, R. *et al.* (2008) *The Academic's and Policy-maker's Guides to the Teaching–Research Nexus.* http://www.altc.edu.au/ project-academics-policymakers-griffith-2006, accessed 20 July 2009.

Kreber, C. (2001) Conceptualizing the scholarship of teaching and identifying unresolved issues: the framework for this volume, *New Directions for Teaching and Learning*, 86: 1–18.

McKenzie, J., Alexander, S., Harper, C. and Anderson, S. (2005) *Dissemination, Adoption and Adaptation of Project Innovations in Higher Education: A Report for the Carrick Institute for Learning and Teaching in Higher Education.* Sydney: UTS. http://www.altc.edu.au/resource-dissemination-adoption-uts-2005, accessed 20 July 2009.

Marshall, S.J. (n.d.) *Issues in the Development of Leadership for Learning and Teaching in Higher Education*, Occasional Paper. Sydney: Carrick Institute for Learning and Teaching in Higher Education. http://www.altc.edu.au/resource-issues-development-leadership-learning-macquarie-2008, accessed 20 July 2009.

Nelson, C. (n.d.) *Selected Examples of Several of the Different Genres of SOTL*. http://www.issotl.org/tutorial/sotltutorial/media/CRAIG1.DOC, accessed 20 July 2009.

Nelson, K., Kift, S. and Harper, W. (2005a) Any portal in a storm? Aligning online engagement patterns with the needs of transition students. Paper presented at Online Learning and Teaching Conference (OLT): Beyond Delivery, Brisbane, 27 September. http://eprints.qut.edu.au/3932/1/3932.pdf, accessed 20 July 2009.

Nelson, K., Kift, S. and Harper, W. (2005b) 'First portal in a storm': a virtual space for transition students. Paper presented to Australasian Society for Computers in Learning in Tertiary Education (ASCILITE) Conference, Brisbane, 4–7 December. http://www.ascilite.org.au/conferences/brisbane05/blogs/proceedings/58_Nelson.pdf, accessed 20 July 2009.

Nelson, K., Kift, S., Humphreys, J. and Harper, W. (2006) A blueprint for enhanced transition: taking an holistic approach to managing student transition into a large university. Paper presented to 9th Pacific Rim First Year in Higher Education Conference: Engaging Students, Gold Coast, 12–14 July. http://www.fyhe.qut.edu.au/past_papers/2006/Papers/Kift.pdf, accessed 20 July 2009.

Nelson, K., Kift, S. and Creagh, T. (2007) Implementing a blueprint for transition success. Paper presented to the 10th Pacific Rim First Year in Higher Education Conference: Regenerate, Engage, Experiment, Brisbane, 4–6 July. http://www.fyhe.qut.edu.au/past_papers/papers07/final_papers/pdfs/4b.pdf, accessed 20 July 2009.

Nelson, K., Kift, S. and Clarke, J. (2008) Expectations and realities for first year students at an Australian university. Paper presented to the 11th Pacific Rim First Year in Higher Education Conference: An Apple for the Learner: Celebrating the First Year Experience, Hobart, 30 June–2 July. http://www.fyhe.qut.edu.au/past_papers/papers08/FYHE2008/content/pdfs/6a.pdf, accessed 20 July 2009.

Prosser, M. (2008) The scholarship of teaching and learning: what is it? A personal view, *International Journal for the Scholarship of Teaching and Learning*, 2(2): 1–4.

Ramsden, P. (1998) *Learning to Lead in Higher Education*. London: Routledge.

Scott, G. (2004) Change matters: making a difference in higher education. Paper presented to the Australian Universities Quality Forum 2004: Quality in a Time of Change, Adelaide, 7–9 July. http://www.auqa.edu.au/files/publications/auqf2004_proceedings.pdf, accessed 20 July 2009.

Scott, G. (2006) *Accessing the Student Voice: Using CEQuery to Identify What Retains Students and Promotes Engagement in Productive Learning in Australian Higher Education*. Canberra: DEST. http://www.dest.gov.au/sectors/higher_education/publications_resources/profiles/access_student_voice.htm, accessed 20 July 2009.

Scott, G., Coates, H. and Anderson, M. (2008) *Learning Leaders in Times of Change: Academic Leadership Capabilities for Australian Higher Education*. Sydney: UWS and ACER. http://www.acer.edu.au/documents/UWSACER_CarrickLeadership Report.pdf, accessed 20 July 2009.

Shulman, L.S. (1993) Teaching as community property, *Change*, 25(6): 6–7.

Shulman, L.S. (1998) Course anatomy: the dissection and analysis of knowledge through teaching, in P. Hutchings (ed.) with L.S. Shulman, *The Course Portfolio: How Faculty Can Examine Their Teaching to Advance Practice and Improve Student Learning*. Washington, DC: American Association for Higher Education.

Shulman, L.S. (2000) Inventing the future, in P. Hutchings (ed.) *Opening Lines: Approaches to the Scholarship of Teaching and Learning*. Menlo Park, CA: The Carnegie Foundation for the Advancement of Teaching.

Tinto, V. (2006–07) Research and practice of student retention: what next? *Journal of College Student Retention*, 8(1): 1–19.

Tinto, V. (2009) Taking student retention seriously: rethinking the first year of university. Keynote paper presented to FYE Curriculum Design Symposium, Brisbane, 5–6 February. http://www.fyecd2009.qut.edu.au/resources/SPE_VincentTinto_5Feb09.pdf, accessed 20 July 2009.

Tomazos, D. (1997) What do university teachers say about improving university teaching? In R. Pospisil and L. Willcoxson (eds) *Learning Through Teaching*. Proceedings of the 6th Annual Teaching Learning Forum, Perth, February. http://lsn.curtin.edu.au/tlf/tlf1997/tomazos.html, accessed 20 July 2009.

Towers, S. (2006) SOTL and the creative industries. Paper presented to QUT Creative Industries Faculty, Brisbane, 9 March.

Trigwell, K., Martin, E., Benjamin, J. and Prosser, M. (2000) Scholarship of teaching: a model, *Higher Education Research and Development*, 19(2): 155–68.

22 Useful sharing

Sally Fincher

Much of my professional life over the past decade has been driven by a problematic rhetoric of 'transfer of practice' or, even worse, 'transfer of *best* practice'. This has proved troublesome for two reasons. First, the phrase is wielded glibly, as if this were an easy and obvious thing to accomplish. Second, it hides within it the idea that teaching knowledge treads the same disciplinary dissemination paths that research knowledge does. It turns out that neither of these things are true, although I have believed them both, once upon a time.

My work now is focused beyond this rhetoric, to examine effective ways that educators may usefully share practice. But I'm going to tell the story backwards, and lay out the argument for my current understanding before outlining how I got there. First, let's unpack what is hidden.

Transfer assumptions

A very common assumption in twenty-first-century UK higher education is that practices disseminate within institutions, but across disciplinary boundaries. This assumption implies that there is either an institutionally distinctive approach to teaching (the distance provision of the Open University or the Oxbridge tutorial system, for example), or that there are themes that transcend subject matter (like 'work-based learning'). As these conditions pertain only rarely, institutional transfer falls on the twin horns of the dilemma of academic development.

The first horn is: specific educators have specific problems. The specific classroom, the details and minutiae of learning auto-ionization, Kant's ethics, or how to program a computer using the language Haskell, are not available to the average institutionally based academic developer and specific subject matter is generally taught by only one or two academics in any institution, so there is little local disciplinary help to be had. The second horn is: some solutions *are* generic. Almost any educator can, for instance, take a 'problem-based learning' approach (Barrows and Tamblyn 1980) or learn classroom assessment techniques (Angelo and Cross 1993). Each of these is applicable to many subjects and many different classrooms. An institutionally based academic developer can have expertise in one (or several) of these sorts of approaches, and deliver it to several educators. But educators have to self-identify that they want to do this/ learn about this, then they have to take that generalized knowledge and adapt it to their own situation, they have to 'work the bugs out' and fill in the gaps on their own. They can't support each other through this implementation process because they're in different disciplines,[1] and they can't find other people doing it in their *own* discipline, because those people are in different institutions, may be difficult to locate, and are working under different constraints.

These assumptions are challenged explicitly by taking an alternative view – that teaching disseminates as research does, across institutional boundaries but within disciplines. This view itself relies on the assumption that practices that constitute a 'discipline' are the same whether they are expressed in research or teaching. This is not so: the relationship of individual academics to their discipline is different in the case of their teaching than it is in the case of their research.

Research in a discipline is characterized by expertise that is not intrinsically necessary to the day-to-day functioning of the institution. It requires knowledge and skills in some particular area of enquiry and a group of peers who acknowledge and value that knowledge and those skills (Collins and Evans 2007). Researchers usually demonstrate their level of knowledge in a discipline via presentation of their work at conferences or publication in journals. Because research work is distributed, the community in which it resides is not governed by the location of any given researcher, and is external to every institution. Research peers, colleagues and collaborators will be scattered in institutions all over the globe in webs of professional association that have been called 'invisible colleges' (Crane 1972). Research activity is highly public, and outputs-based: it is easy to count publications, graduate students and grant income, and it is not very difficult to assess less tangible aspects of success such as the prestige of the places of publication, or invitations to serve on programme committees and editorial boards, or to give invited presentations. However, none of these indicators are granted (or governed) by the employing institution. Researchers gain internal value through activity that is validated by an external community of peers and indicators (papers published, grants awarded, prizes won) over which the institution has no control.

Teaching in a discipline, on the other hand, occurs locally and is of central interest to the institution, contributing directly to revenue and to reputation (although perhaps more obliquely). But teaching activities within any one discipline can be seen to employ markedly similar skills to teaching in any other discipline, while acknowledging differences in subject knowledge. The ability to organize content, deliver lectures, enthuse students and facilitate learning can be seen to be similar whether the educator is teaching French or

Computer Science. Not only that, but teaching of a subject is located in the same place (sometimes literally) as the teaching of other subjects. The skills which make some teaching successful and some not (e.g. enthusiasm, careful formative feedback, pedagogic content knowledge) are invisible as one teacher and one group of students replaces another teacher and another group of students in the same room. The *disciplinary* aspects of a course may be judged by external influences such as choice of textbook, and observed in those distinctive ways of organizing and presenting material that makes learning in the professions similar across institutions – what Shulman (2005) calls 'signature pedagogies' – but for day-to-day purposes a teacher's practice is more likely to be influenced by institutional constraints such as the vicissitudes of timetabling, quality assurance procedures, the quality (or paucity) of physical equipment, the availability and sympathy of colleagues, and the institutional choice of technological environment. It is a highly embodied activity, taking place largely 'behind closed doors' where in lieu of knowledgeable peers the only witnesses are students. Knowledge of teaching practices 'transfers' between institutions only in the heads of individuals, who change employment or who are incidentally exposed to others' work (Fincher 2000).

By stripping away these layers of assumptions, it can be seen that, even though they may work in the same department or within the same discipline, teaching-focused academics have different disciplinary practices and a different relationship to their institution than do research-focused academics. The work itself is different, the community in which it resides is different, and the reward structures for undertaking it (both intrinsic, in terms of motivation, and extrinsic in terms of recognition and reward) are different. These differences have been framed in a theoretical construction, distinguishing two role orientations, 'local' and 'cosmopolitan'. 'The localite largely confines his interests to this community. He is preoccupied with local problems, to the virtual exclusion of the national and international scene. He is, strictly speaking, parochial', while the cosmopolitan has some interest in the local community: 'He is also oriented significantly to the world outside and regards himself as an integral part of that world' (Merton 1957: 447).

Alvin Gouldner took this distinction into a study of 125 academic staff from a mid-range US university he calls 'co-op college' (Gouldner 1957, 1958). He defined his two latent organizational types like this:

> *Cosmopolitans*: those low on loyalty to the employing organization, high on commitment to specialized role skills, and likely to use an outer reference group orientation.
> *Locals*: those high on loyalty to the employing organization, low on commitment to specialized role skills, and likely to use an inner reference group orientation.

> (Gouldner 1957: 290)

Gouldner defines these as 'latent' rather than 'manifest' types because people with ostensibly identical roles (e.g. assistant professor or senior lecturer) may, in fact, have different orientations. Nevertheless, it is clear that researchers are more likely to have a cosmopolitan orientation: they have an external community from which they draw validation and specialized disciplinary skills. Teachers, on the other hand, are more likely to have an orientation to local context and constraints, and draw validation from the institutional community.[2]

My path

I first stepped into this river (although without this understanding) in 1996 when I was employed to run the Computer Science Discipline Network,[3] a project funded to promote and disseminate good practice in the teaching and learning of Computer Science. The implicit expectation was that there was a pent-up force for discussion and exchange on teaching and learning matters which the establishment of channels of communication and dissemination would allow to flow. That proved not to be the case: there was no flood of contributions to the mailing list, workshops were not over-subscribed, and interest when I visited departments was polite rather than eager – a local response, not a cosmopolitan one. Thus I learned that facilitating transfer of practice was not an easy task, and began to suspect that there must be something 'going on', something that was non-obvious and unexplicated (or just plain wrong) in the assumptions we were making.

This suspicion took material form in the FDTL[4] Effective Projectwork in Computer Science (EPCoS) project, 1996–2000. In the course of that project, we planned to undertake deliberate transfers of practice between institutions in the consortium. Practices were to be identified, packaged for export, imported and instantiated, with the whole process recorded in diaries and monitored by third-party observers. This simply didn't work; partners couldn't (or wouldn't) take things on in this way. But as we were struggling to account for this failure (to ourselves and the funders), we noticed that project partners were 'picking up' practices from one another and that 'transfer' was happening under our noses, albeit in a quite different way from our expectations. We were expecting 'exporters' to be able to present teaching and learning ideas as if they were research findings and have 'importers' critically examine them, incorporate them into their own work, and contribute back to the pool of knowledge in parallel to research practice. We were looking for cosmopolitan behaviours where there were none to be seen. At that time, our observations led us down a different path, to characterize ways in which transfer occurred 'naturally', and to devise a form for the presentation of teaching and learning material to facilitate this (Fincher *et al.* 2001).

Treating locals as locals

If you accept the twin associations *local–institutional–teaching* and *cosmopolitan–disciplinary–research* (and I do), it seems clear that treating locals as if they were cosmopolitans, having research-type expectations of teaching and learning transfer of practice, is unlikely to be successful. It calls on inappropriate representations (a journal paper is a terrible way to document teaching), assumes networks of dissemination that do not exist, and ignores the fundamentally situated nature of teaching practice.

> Teachers can teach in the same manner to three classes in a row and experience different consequences each time. Professions (like teaching) deal with that part of the universe where design and chance collide. One cannot resolve that uncertainty by writing new rules. The way forward is to make that collision, that unpredictability in our fields, itself an object of individual and collective investigation. We will never fully remove the uncertainty from teaching any more than we can from such other professions as clinical medicine, architecture, economic planning, or clinical social work. But as a profession, we can grow much wiser about how to anticipate and deal with uncertainty. We can develop new forms of inquiry that both learn from and support the 'wisdom of practice'.
>
> (Shulman 1999: 14)

Conceiving of higher education teaching as professional activity in this way prompts consideration of how other professions deal with 'transfer of practice'. It turns out that most have developed structures for reflection on, and exchange of, practice. Artists and architects have shared studios and 'crits' (Anthony 1991; Doidge *et al.* 2000) where designs are formally critiqued; dancers and musicians have 'master classes', where a visiting expert will come to share special skills and approaches; medical practitioners may have 'Balint groups' (Balint 1993) in which they meet to examine their doctor–patient interactions; and members of the therapeutic professions (counsellors and therapists) have supervision, regular meetings where they engage with a more experienced colleague in structured reflections on their clinical practice. The UKCC *Guidelines for Professional Practice* (UKCC 1996) define supervision as 'a practice-focused professional relationship, involving a practitioner reflecting on practice, guided by a skilled supervisor'.

Taking these considerations seriously, my colleague Josh Tenenberg and I have devised a model of useful sharing called the *Disciplinary Commons* (Tenenberg and Fincher 2007). A *Commons* is composed of educators teaching the same subject – often the same module – but at different institutions. They meet every month over the course of an academic year, to share and document their practice. A *Commons* takes practitioners out of their working environment and creates a structured experience parallel to those found in other professions. Within a *Commons*, meetings parallel the critical practices of the fine arts and studio learning, where practitioners expose their work to a 'coach' and their peers. However, in a *Commons* each participant is a knowledgeable expert, skilled in his or her own practice, there is no 'teacher', and all meet on equal ground. Individuals see their practice reflected in others – and others' in theirs – and inside this 'hall of mirrors' learn their way to new expertise (Schon 1990). Within a *Commons* 'transfer of practice' is never mentioned, but practice is exposed – and transferred, usefully shared – as a matter of course (Fincher and Tenenberg 2007b). While teaching and learning, by its very nature, can never be a cosmopolitan activity, a *Disciplinary Commons* gives an external reference group to institutionally focused teachers, creating a community of 'well-travelled' locals.

The beginning of an answer

So, at this point in my journey, it's still not clear to me what the best mechanisms for 'transfer of practice' might be; we have only just begun to think about these seriously as something separate from institutional models. But to facilitate useful sharing, I have learned that we need to ape research models less simplistically, and look to more nuanced forms of collaboration with regard to teaching and learning.

Notes

1   Although John Websters '4 × 4' model instantiated at the University of Washington, Seattle does address this issue at an institutional level. Some details are available from his website: http://faculty.washington.edu/cicero/SOTL.htm.
2   In Gouldner's study other 'local' orientations included staff who were literally local, that is, were born in the region, and/or who were alumni of the institution. I do not use these distinctions.
3   The Discipline Network programme was funded by the Department for Employment, and instituted 24 subject-based networks across the UK, each with an initial two-year funding.
4   The Fund for Development of Teaching and Learning (FDTL) was funded by the Higher Education Funding Council for England (HEFCE). This funding was for three-year, subject-focused projects. A total of 164 projects was supported over five phases. EPCoS was funded in the first phase.

References

Angelo, T.A. and Cross, K.P. (1993) *Classroom Assessment Techniques: A Handbook for College Teachers*. San Francisco, CA: Jossey-Bass.

Anthony, K.H. (1991) *Design Juries on Trial: The Renaissance of the Design Studio*. New York: Van Nostrand Reinhold; London: Chapman and Hall.

Balint, E. (1993) *The Doctor, the Patient and the Group: Balint Revisited*. New York: Routledge.

Barrows, H.S. and Tamblyn, R.M. (1980) *Problem-Based Learning: An Approach to Medical Education*. New York: Springer Publishing Company.

Collins, H.M. and Evans, R. (2007) *Rethinking Expertise*. Chicago, IL: University of Chicago Press.

Crane, D. (1972) *Invisible Colleges: Diffusion of Knowledge in Scientific Communities*. Chicago, IL: University of Chicago Press.

Doidge, C., Sara, R. and Parnell, R. (2000) *The Crit: An Architecture Student's Handbook*. Oxford: Architectural Press.

Fincher, S. (2000) *From Transfer to Transformation: Towards a Framework for Successful Dissemination of Engineering Education*. Washington, DC: IEEE Computer Society.

Fincher, S. and Tenenberg, J. (2007b) Warren's question. Proceedings of the third international workshop on computing education research (ICER). ACM Special Interest Group on Computer Science Education: 51–60.

Fincher, S., Petre, M. and Clark, M. (eds) (2001) *Computer Science Project Work: Principles and Pragmatics*. London: Springer-Verlag.

Gouldner, A.W. (1957) Cosmopolitans and locals: toward an analysis of latent social roles – I, *Administrative Science Quarterly*, 2(3): 281–306.

Gouldner, A.W. (1958) Cosmopolitans and locals: toward an analysis of latent social roles – II, *Administrative Science Quarterly*, 2(4): 444–80.

Merton, R.K. (1957) *Social Theory and Social Structure*. Glencoe, IL: Free Press of Glencoe.

Schon, D. (1990) *Educating the Reflective Practitioner: Toward a New Design for Teaching and Learning in the Professions*. San Francisco, CA: Jossey-Bass.

Shulman, L. (1999) Taking learning seriously, *Change*, 31(4): 10–17.

Shulman, L. (2005) Signature pedagogies in the professions, *Daedalus*, 134(3): 52–9.

Tenenberg, J. and Fincher, S. (2007) Opening the door of the computer science classroom: the *Disciplinary Commons*. Proceedings of the 38th SIGCSE technical symposium on computer science education. ACM Special Interest Group on Computer Science Education: 514–18.

UKCC (1996) *Guidelines for Professional Practice*. London: United Kingdom Central Council for Nursing, Midwifery and Health Visiting.

23 Excellence and scholarship in teaching: some reflections

Mick Healey

We don't learn from experience; we learn by reflecting on experience.
(Dewey, cited by Bain and Zimmerman 2009: 12)

Beginnings

This is an appropriate time for me to reflect on excellence and scholarship in teaching, because I shall shortly be giving my last class to geographers before I set up as a higher education consultant.

As I write this during the Christmas 2009 break, my younger daughter, Ruth, is coming to the end of her first year teaching geography at a 'research-informed' university (Jenkins and Healey 2007). She is already a better teacher than I am. I may know a little more about what the literature says about effective teaching, learning and assessment and I have researched my own practice and the nature of student learning, but that does not make me an 'excellent' teacher. Nowadays it is my colleagues who are most frequently my 'students', as I run many workshops in universities around the world. It may be my current position, but I feel I relate better to the situations facing my colleagues than I do to those experienced by 18- to 22-year-old students straight from school. Ruth is much better attuned to how to motivate these students and make her classes lively and interesting.

My career to date falls roughly into thirds. In the first third I focused on developing my teaching, research and consultancy as an economic geographer. In the last third I have specialized as an educational researcher and developer. The middle period was one of transition, first into researching and developing teaching and learning in geography and then into undertaking these activities across higher education.

Reading Ernest Boyer's *Scholarship Reconsidered* (1990) introduced me to the scholarship of teaching and learning (SoTL). But it was the work of other members of the Carnegie Foundation for the Advancement of Teaching, particularly Mary Huber, Pat Hutchings and Lee Schulman, and, from the other side of the Atlantic, Graham Gibbs, Carolin Kreber and Alan Jenkins, who challenged and stimulated me to explore and apply the concept further. I was hugely over-ambitious when I said that for my National Teaching Fellowship Scheme (NTFS) project I would investigate the embedding of SoTL in disciplines and institutions. Ten years later I have hardly scratched the surface, but during that period I have been privileged to visit many universities and discuss interesting practices with lots of people, particularly in Australasia and North America, as well as in the UK. I have learnt much from these experiences. But first, before reflecting, we need to clarify some terms.

Clarifications

Following Hutchings and Schulman (1999), whereas striving for *excellence* involves a high level of proficiency in stimulating students and fostering their learning in a variety of appropriate ways, a *scholarly approach to teaching* entails being familiar with the latest ideas in one's subject and also being informed by current ideas for teaching that subject. A scholarly approach also involves evaluating and reflecting on one's teaching practice and the student learning which follows. The *scholarship of teaching*, on the other hand, shares these characteristics of excellent and scholarly teaching, but *in addition* involves communicating and disseminating the teaching and learning practices. It also entails conducting research into aspects of teaching, learning and assessment. Lewis Elton (2005) goes further and argues that if we are going to be professionals we ought to approach our teaching as we do our research. If SoTL is to match that of research there needs to be comparability of rigour, standards and esteem.

I am, however, wary of using the term 'excellent'; I also fight shy of the expression 'best practice', preferring to use terms such as 'good' or 'interesting' practice. Whatever term is used it has little or no meaning unless it is set in a wider political, social and educational agenda. We need to ask, for example, 'excellence of what, for whom, and to what ends?'. Hence we need to recognize that what is excellent teaching varies over time and between national systems, higher education institutions and disciplines. Teaching and learning does not take place in a social vacuum. Excellence is mediated by the social and political circumstances of the time; that is, it is situated and sensitive to context.

Barnett (1992) suggests that before we can understand concepts such as excellent or good practice we need first to have a reasonably clear conception of 'higher education'. For example, Alan Jenkins and I argue that *all students in all higher education* institutions should learn in an environment which goes back to and reaffirms the values advocated by Humboldt who, in founding the University of Berlin in 1810, argued that 'universities should treat learning always as consisting of not yet wholly solved problems and hence always in a research mode' (quoted by Elton 2005: 110). For us, a characteristic of good or excellent university-level teaching is that students will be both the recipients of research through up-to-date curricula, and actively involved in developing their understanding of the provisional and contested nature of knowledge through their involvement in research and inquiry (Healey and Jenkins 2009). We recognize, however, that the ways of achieving this will vary with context (Jenkins and Healey 2007; Trowler and Wareham 2008).

According to Skelton (2005) there appears to be a 'culture of excellence' developing in higher education in many countries. In this view *all* institutions can provide excellence in teaching and *all* teachers can become excellent through continuous improvement; hence different forms of excellence can co-exist and have equal value. I have a lot of sympathy with this more inclusive view of excellence as something to which we should all aspire in pursuing educationally and socially valuable goals for all students and staff in higher education. However, a more critical view of excellence would point out that such a culture of excellence is largely about individuals and individual institutions, rather than systems and structures. A critical view would recognize the imbalance in resources between individuals and institutions in a stratified higher education system. Hence, though we might argue there are different forms of excellence relative to the resources available, the overall quality of student learning across national and institutional systems would be enhanced by reducing inequalities in staff–student ratios, general infrastructure and access to funding to carry out SoTL (Skelton 2005).

Reflections

Reflecting on my own journey, I have learnt much. In particular, I would emphasize the importance of providing and developing: motivation and active engagement; authentic case studies and discipline-based examples; a wide variety of teaching, learning and assessment experiences; an inclusive curriculum; and communities of practice. Below I draw on my experience of researching and facilitating the learning of students and academic staff to illustrate these themes, with examples which may be adaptable to other contexts.

Motivation and active engagement

One of the most successful initiatives introduced by the Centre for Active Learning at the University of Gloucestershire has been the development of discipline-based inquiry projects for new students the week before term begins. In 2007, over 650 students conducted inquiries in small groups through library and field research and presented their findings to tutors in novel ways, such as using digital storytelling, who in turn provided formative feedback. For example, the human geographers and sociologists examined the experience of Gloucester residents in 'the Great Flood of 2007', while the biologists and the psychologists investigated primate behaviour at Bristol Zoo. The activities were designed so that the students began the process of socialization into the nature of inquiry in their discipline in a fun way. I think it is best that the first inquiry-based projects are fairly open-ended projects, as the goal at this stage is to motivate the students; more scaffolded or directed projects can come later when more emphasis can be placed on developing the skills and techniques of knowledge construction (Healey and Jenkins 2009).

I put a similar emphasis on motivation when running workshops for academic staff on SoTL. I find that one of the key ways in which to engage colleagues in their development as critical and reflective teachers, in a way that goes beyond the hints and tips they may need at the beginning of their teaching careers, is to stimulate their intellectual curiosity. After all, asking questions is at the heart of intellectual curiosity and engaging staff in SoTL (Breslow *et al.* 2004).

Authentic case studies and discipline-based examples

I am an advocate of a discipline-based approach to SoTL (Healey 2000, 2003a; Healey and Jenkins 2003). In the first Geography Discipline Network project (1996–98), we produced a set of guides to teaching, learning and assessment in geography and ran 50 department-based workshops across the United Kingdom. We incorporated many mini-case studies in the guides. In running some of the workshops I quickly learnt that my colleagues were far more interested in the case studies than they were in the principles and theories which underpinned their application. This was an 'ah-ha' moment for me, as I realized that if this was how my colleagues were engaged, 'what about my students?' Since then I have usually started my sessions with case studies and later introduced theories and concepts to help interpret them. This approach is vindicated in Bain's (2004) analysis of 33 professors in the United States, who year after year receive high ratings from their students. He found that a pattern emerged in that these outstanding teachers helped their students to adopt deep learning approaches by engaging them inductively, moving them from fascinating and important questions to general principles in their discipline (Bain and Zimmerman 2009).

Wide variety of teaching, learning and assessment experiences

The piece of work for which I am, perhaps, best known, at least to judge by the number of times it has been reproduced, is a model of curriculum design and the research–teaching nexus (Healey 2005). One of the reasons the model seems to attract attention is that it presents an inclusive classification of pedagogies for linking research and teaching. Though I tend to place most emphasis on active pedagogies in which students act as producers of knowledge rather than just consumers, I value all of the methods and I advocate a mixture, accepting that an appropriate balance will vary with level, discipline and type of institution. A variety of experiences are needed to address the range of different learning styles we find among our students (Healey and Jenkins 2000; Healey *et al.* 2005).

Inclusive curriculum

Though I have undertaken several research and development projects in the last decade concerned with supporting the learning of disabled students, my main interest is in learning and teaching rather than disability studies. My motivation comes from a desire to enhance the quality of student learning and I quickly discovered that sound teaching, learning and assessment practices for disabled students generally enhance the quality of learning for all students.

For me, developing an inclusive curriculum is about designing effective learning, teaching and assessment practices for *all* students; focusing on learner *differences*, not learner *difficulties*; valuing differences to enrich learning for all; and making adjustments which are good teaching and learning practices to benefit all students (Healey 2010).

A few years ago I predicted that 'One unintended consequence of this (disability) legislation is that as departments and institutions introduce more flexible learning and alternative ways of assessment for disabled students, demand is likely to rise for giving greater flexibility for all students . . . Disability legislation may prove to be a Trojan horse and, in a decade, the learning experiences of all students may be the subject of greater negotiation' (Healey 2003b: 26). Though change is slow there are now some university courses in Britain where all students are given a choice of assessments, thus no longer requiring some disabled students to ask for reasonable adjustments. I believe that if we want to achieve equality of opportunity for all students we should pay more attention to the variation within the categories by which we traditionally classify students, such as age, disability, gender, race, religion and sexual orientation. Rather than classifying students in these ways we would do better to focus instead on their individual learning needs and entitlements (Healey *et al.* 2006a, 2006b, 2008; Fuller *et al.* 2009).

Communities of practice

Some of my most satisfying and enjoyable learning experiences have been working with colleagues, whether designing and teaching a new course, working on a teaching and learning project, writing or editing a paper, journal or book, or reviewing a course, department or institution. I have drawn on this experience to design and support group activities with my students and to develop networks[1] with my colleagues (e.g. Healey *et al.* 1996; Healey 1998). These networks have acted as my communities of practice. They have had a major influence on sustaining my continuing learning journey. Many opportunities to work on joint projects, give presentations and share experiences would not have occurred without the time invested in developing contacts and building relationships within these communities. We need to think strategically, both for our students and ourselves, as to how we can develop and support such communities of practice to provide opportunities for collaborative learning. Ideally many of these communities will involve students and academic staff co-learning together (e.g. Healey *et al.* 2010a).

End words

In conclusion, I would argue that being prepared to take risks, and as a consequence at times failing, is integral to striving for excellence for both our students and ourselves. As J.K. Rowling (2008) movingly said at the 2008 Harvard Commencement, 'Failure gave me an inner security that I had never attained by passing examinations . . . I discovered that I had a strong will, and more discipline than I had suspected.'

We need to challenge our 'students' to think outside their comfort zone. For Barnett, the central role of the university should be to help *all* students cope with 'supercomplexity'; that is, to appreciate and investigate the *supercomplex* world 'in which the very frameworks by which we orient ourselves to the world are themselves contested' (Barnett 2004: 253).

I agree with Skelton's (2009: 110) paraphrase of Nixon's (2007) argument that 'excellence has to be re-cast as a moral category so that it is not sufficient to think of what "works" in our teaching and support of learning, but rather what is "good" – what is morally defensible and contributes to good in the world'. An example would be teaching for positive social transformations (Wellens *et al.* 2006). Furthermore, as Rowland (2000) argues, the main aim of a culture of excellence is to support and maintain a deep intellectual curiosity in teaching.

I would go a stage further, though, and argue that teaching excellence needs to be seen as part of a whole; we need to bring together the different identities we have as academics, particularly as researchers and as teachers. Too many of the ways universities and funding streams are organized separate these identities. We need to find more ways to bring research and teaching together to develop the synergies between them and to strive *not* just for excellent research and excellent teaching, but primarily for excellent *academic practice*.

As I put the finishing touches to this chapter I received this email:

On behalf of all authors, I would like to thank you for your generous help throughout the peer review process of our article . . . in *JGHE* [*Journal of Geography in Higher Education* (Heller *et al.* forthcoming)]. Your comments and suggestions really helped us to create a paper we are proud of. It is wonderful having one of our first (for some of us) journal submission processes be a timely, encouraging, and educational one. We have all come away from the experience hoping that our future publishing attempts will be as positive!

(Heller 2010)

I hope that as I move into the next phase of my career I can continue to help others, including my daughter Ruth, develop good and interesting practices and strive for teaching that is excellent in the contexts in which they find themselves.

Acknowledgements

Ruth Healey and Alan Jenkins kindly commented on an earlier draft.

Note

1 I have led the Geography Discipline Network since 1996 and co-led the International Network for Learning and Teaching Geography in Higher Education since 1999 (Healey 2003c; Healey *et al.* 2010b). I was also an inaugural member of the UK Geography, Earth and Environmental Sciences Subject Centre, the UK Research and Teaching Forum, and the International Society for the Scholarship of Teaching and Learning.

References

Bain, K. (2004) *What the Best College Teachers Do*. Cambridge, MA: Harvard University Press.

Bain, K. and Zimmerman, J. (2009) Understanding great teaching, *Peer Review*, 11(2): 9–12. www.newsweekshowcase.com/education/us-colleges/articles/understanding-great-teaching, accessed 27 December 2009.

Barnett, R. (1992) Linking teaching and research: a critical inquiry, *Journal of Higher Education*, 63(6): 619–36.

Barnett, R. (2004) Learning for an unknown future, *Higher Education Research and Development*, 23(3): 247–60.

Boyer, E.L. (1990) *Scholarship Reconsidered: Priorities of the Professoriate*. Princeton, NJ: Carnegie Foundation for the Advancement of Teaching.

Breslow, L., Drew, L., Healey, M., Matthew, B. and Norton, L. (2004) Intellectual curiosity: a catalyst for the scholarships of teaching and learning and educational development, in L. Elvidge (ed.) *Exploring Academic Development in Higher Education: Issues of Engagement*. Cambridge: Jill Rogers Associates.

Elton, L. (2005) Scholarship and the research and teaching nexus, in R. Barnett (ed.) *Reshaping the University: New Relationships Between Research, Scholarship and Teaching*. Maidenhead: McGraw-Hill/Open University Press.

Fuller, M., Georgeson, J., Healey, M., Hurst, A., Riddell, S., Roberts, H. and Weedon, E. (2009) *Enhancing the Quality and Outcomes of Disabled Students' Learning in Higher Education*. London: Routledge.

Healey, M. (1998) Editorial I: Developing and internationalising higher education networks in geography, *Journal of Geography in Higher Education*, 22(3): 277–82.

Healey, M. (2000) Developing the scholarship of teaching in higher education: a discipline-based approach, *Higher Education Research & Development*, 19(2): 169–89.

Healey, M. (2003a) The scholarship of teaching: issues around an evolving concept, *Journal on Excellence in College Teaching*, 14(2/3): 5–26.

Healey, M. (2003b) Trojan horse is good bet for all, *Times Higher Education Supplement*, 19 September: 26.

Healey, M. (2003c) Promoting lifelong professional development in geography education: international perspectives on developing the scholarship of teaching in higher education in the 21st century, *The Professional Geographer*, 55(1): 1–17.

Healey, M. (2005) Linking research and teaching exploring disciplinary spaces and the role of inquiry-based learning, in R. Barnett (ed.) *Reshaping the University: New Relationships between Research, Scholarship and Teaching*. Maidenhead: McGraw-Hill/Open University Press.

Healey, M. (2010) Relationships between equity research and practice: reflections on developing an inclusive curriculum, keynote address to Higher Education Academy Research Conference: Promoting Equity in Higher Education, Nottingham, 27–28 January.

Healey, M. and Jenkins, A. (2000) Learning cycles and learning styles: the application of Kolb's experiential learning model in higher education, *Journal of Geography*, 99: 185–95.

Healey, M. and Jenkins, A. (2003) Discipline-based educational development, in H. Eggins and R. Macdonald (eds) *The Scholarship of Academic Development*. Milton Keynes: Open University Press.

Healey, M. and Jenkins, A. (2009) *Developing Undergraduate Research and Inquiry*. York: Higher Education Academy. http://www.heacademy.ac.uk/assets/York/

documents/resources/publications/DevelopingUndergraduate_Final.pdf, accessed 27 December 2009.

Healey, M., Matthews, H., Livingstone, I. and Foster, I. (1996) Learning in small groups in university geography courses: designing a core module around group projects, *Journal of Geography in Higher Education*, 20: 167–80.

Healey, M., Kneale, P., Bradbeer, J. with other members of the INLT Learning Styles and Concepts Group (2005) Learning styles among geography undergraduates: an international comparison, *Area*, 37(1): 30–42.

Healey, M., Fuller, M., Bradley, A. and Hall, T. (2006a) Listening to students: the experiences of disabled students of learning at university, in M. Adams and S. Brown (eds) *Towards Inclusive Learning in Higher Education: Developing Curricula for Disabled Students*. London: Routledge Falmer.

Healey, M., Jenkins, A. and Leach, J. (2006b) *Issues in Developing an Inclusive Curriculum: Examples from Geography, Earth and Environmental Sciences*. Cheltenham: University of Gloucestershire, Geography Discipline Network. http://resources. glos.ac.uk/ceal/gdn/publications/icp/index.cfm, accessed 27 December 2009.

Healey, M., Roberts, H., Fuller, M. *et al.* (2008) Reasonable adjustments and disabled students' experiences of learning, teaching and assessment, *TLA Interchange 2*, http:www.tla.ed.ac.uk/interchange, accessed 27 December 2009.

Healey, M., Mason O'Connor, K. and Broadfoot, P. (2010a) Reflecting on engaging students in the process and product of strategy development for learning, teaching and assessment: an institutional example, *International Journal for Academic Development*, 15(1): 19–32.

Healey, M., Pawson, E. and Solem, M. (eds) (2010b) *Active Learning and Student Engagement: International Perspectives and Practices in Geography in Higher Education*. London: Routledge.

Heller, E. (2010) personal email, 8 January.

Heller, E., Christensen, J., Long, L. *et al.* (forthcoming) Dear diary: early career geographers collectively reflect on their qualitative field research experiences, *Journal of Geography in Higher Education* (in press).

Hutchings, P. and Schulman, L.S. (1999) The scholarship of teaching: new elaborations, new developments, *Change*, September/October, 31: 11–15. http:www. carnegiefoundation.org/eLibrary/sotl1999.htm, accessed 27 December 2009.

Jenkins, A. and Healey, M. (2007) Critiquing excellence: undergraduate research for all students, in A. Skelton, (ed.) *International Perspectives on Teaching Excellence in Higher Education*. London: Routledge.

Nixon, J. (2007) Excellence and the good society, in A. Skelton (ed.) *International Perspectives on Teaching Excellence in Higher Education*. London: Routledge.

Rowland, S. (2000) *The Enquiring University Teacher*. Buckingham: SRHE/Open University Press.

Rowling, J.K. (2008) The fringe benefits of failure, and the importance of imagination. Paper presented to the Annual Meeting of the Harvard Alumni Association, http://harvardmagazine.com/go/jkrowling.html, accessed 27 December 2009.

Skelton, A. (2005) *Understanding Teaching Excellence in Higher Education*. London: Routledge.

Skelton, A. (2009) A 'teaching excellence' for the times we live in? *Teaching in Higher Education*, 14(1): 107–12.

Trowler, P. and Wareham, T. (2008) *Tribes, Territories, Research and Teaching: Enhancing the Teaching–Research Nexus*. York: The Higher Education Academy. http://www.heacademy.ac.uk/assets/York/Trowler_Final_Report.pdf, accessed 27 December 2009.

Wellens, J., Berardi, A., Chalkley, B. *et al.* (2006) Teaching geography for social transformation, *Journal of Geography in Higher Education*, 30(1): 117–31.

24 From fear to flourish

Iain Hay

In commencing this short last chapter, let me make a few remarks about the structure of this volume. As I noted in the Introduction, the book is organized around five areas thought to frame high-quality university teaching and learning. They can be restated very easily as principles of good teaching:

1 Adopt approaches to teaching that influence, motivate and inspire students to learn.
2 Develop curricula and resources that reflect your command of the field.
3 Adopt approaches to assessment and feedback that foster independent learning.
4 Respect and support the development of students as individuals.
5 Participate in scholarly activities that influence and enhance learning and teaching.

These strike me as offering a helpful way of understanding good teaching and extending an appreciation of practice beyond the stereotypical image of a skilled orator with deep and comprehensive disciplinary knowledge (for examples of the continuing prevalence of this view, read comments on internet sites such as http://www.RateMyProfessors.com). However, while the book is built around these five useful elements, I hope it has been clear that its core does not reside there. My purpose in assembling this book was not to examine and scrutinize the worth of these principles; indeed, they have more or less been taken for granted (whether or not that is appropriate is, of course, open to debate!). Instead, the principles or elements have formed a framework for the book's primary focus, which has been setting out a detailed and revealing elaboration of just *how* and *why* high-performing scholars have given those five broad factors life. The emphasis has been on individuals' experiences in professional, personal and conceptual contexts.

By putting this volume together I have tried to make accessible to you as direct and frank an engagement as possible – within the confines of a book format – with the experiences and reflections of talented scholars recognized as being among the world's great university teachers. Through their answers to my 'why' and 'how' questions about their teaching, these 25 contributors have given us insights to both moments and people that have inspired them and to their thoughts on the ways they inspire students. And as I signalled at the outset of the book in my discussion of the role of autoethnography, my aim in putting together these recollections and reflections is to prompt thoughtful contemplation. As these chapters have done for me, I hope they might inspire you to review learning and teaching practice in ways that may work better for you, your students and your institution.

What I would like to do in these closing words is to set out some of my own responses and reactions to parts of the book's content. By way of a somewhat clumsy educational metaphor, one might imagine this contribution to mirror a tutorial in which various invited guests have spoken and now, in the initial awkward silence that sometimes follows splendid presentations, the tutor sets out his or her own reactions as a bridge to support further reflection and to prompt discussion. My comments are not intended to summarize ideas comprehensively nor to be 'indisputable' – they could hardly be that! Indeed, they are likely to be exactly the opposite of that: partial and contestable. They are merely thoughts on a few matters that resonated with my own thinking.

I take some courage in the revelations by several of these distinguished contributors that their teaching career has involved a personal transformation that I characterize as moving from fear to flourish. Kahane, Wesch and Lucas, for example, talk of the fear they experienced of being considered 'inadequate' in their knowledge or skill. And even Nobel Laureate Carl Weiman points to moments in his first-year physics classes when he has not been immediately able to answer students' questions (for a fine, readable discussion of the anxiety of teaching, see Showalter 2003). But rather than being paralysed by fear or pursuing an endless and apparently futile quest to master material and performance to cope with their 'daily exercise in vulnerability' (Palmer 2007: 17), these great teachers have found it more helpful to engage with students mindfully, and even lovingly, to share learning. By opening themselves up to failure, exposing themselves as fallible human beings, working as collaborators with students, and by acknowledging the constant need to learn and develop practice, they sustain outstanding teaching and learning.

In their responses to fearfulness, many of the contributors decry any reduction of teaching to content mastery, suggesting that good teaching is about more than knowing one's stuff (though clearly a bit of this is important!) and having highly developed skills as an orator or entertainer. Good teaching is about much more than having the capacity to stand before a classroom full of students, speaking coherently, advisedly, seamlessly and with humour. Ings, for example, emphasizes the importance of *learning together* – something that in my own experience has been vital to maintaining my enthusiasm for subject material, keeping current, and inspiring students. Schwartz challenges us to dare to be different and several other contributors (e.g. Wesch, Moss, Free, Lucas, Healey) point to risks they have taken in their teaching organizing, for example, courses around real and relevant problems, the answers to which they do not know. Their role is then to join, inspire and support students in the journey for 'answers'. They have learned to accept, acknowledge and work with an appreciation that they simply cannot be omniscient.

Self-evidently, however, risk taking is a perilous pursuit. To be frank, I think this risk needs to be measured. Repeated and unsuccessful risk taking may crush a teacher's self-confidence and undermine any faith students have in their learning guide. So, I take a bet each way, offering the caution of taking well-considered steps while at the same time endorsing the calls for risk taking. And to minimize the prospects of foreseeable harm, 'risk assessment' should include consultation of scholarly work on learning and teaching and, perhaps even more usefully, embrace the kind of collegial 'useful sharing' that Sally Fincher has so helpfully set out in this volume.

Continuing the discussion of the relationship between subject mastery and 'learning togetherness', Rhona Free's reminder that it is critical for us to focus on what students are *learning* – not simply what we believe we are 'teaching' – is very helpful. Her point is well made and it leads to me to offer a caution about the strong emphasis that is being placed on the provision of tangible and formal teaching support resources (e.g. subject benchmark statements, multimedia technologies, immense and detailed topic guides) in institutional education environments worldwide. It can sometimes be easy to get caught up in the cargo cult of constructing and delivering these 'things' and ensuring that they are 'just so', believing that by providing them, good learning and teaching will necessarily follow (for a related and sometimes provocative discussion, see Patience 2008). I have seen that this slavish pursuit of process and perfect resources occurs at all levels: from the painstaking preparation of lecture materials for a single class to the shaping of national educational guidelines. Notwithstanding the real and potential pedagogic or andragogic value of some of these resources, their preparation and delivery should never blind us to the real game: just what and how are our students *learning*?

As a geographer, I cannot help but refer to the point made by both Emerson and Regan that inspiring teaching is also as much about creating *places* where students can learn as it is about the efficacy of specific teaching tools. Certainly the deplorable physical architecture and infrastructure of many teaching spaces – vast tiered rooms, fixed chairs, poor lighting, dysfunctional heating and cooling – works against this, but there is still room for us to give careful attention to ways in which we can shape the complex social geographies of our classrooms. That consideration offers the potential for effective learning-and-teaching places that may even model some processes, such as social justice, that we may seek to advance through our practice (see Hay 2001 for a related discussion).

As well as place and space, scale matters to geographers. Not surprisingly, then, I was impressed by the observations by Dennis Krebs and Roger Moltzen about 'scaling up' our thinking about learning-and-teaching to embrace systemic ways of improving practice, rather than focusing on single students or our own classrooms. Scaling up might be achieved by driving institutional reform or by changing practices and, even more importantly, cultural norms in departments. The shift here is clear: moving us from thinking about academics inspiring students, to academics inspiring colleagues and helping to create the institutional or regulatory circumstances that might, for example, allow scholars to slow down (see the chapter by Jerusha and Brian Detweiler-Bedell), reflect, and seek out new approaches to teaching.

The theme of teaching as a lifelong process of experimentation is taken up in some chapters (e.g. Lucas). One might draw two conclusions from this idea. The first is that such experimentation might converge on or reveal a 'Holy Grail' of good educational practice. And one could read Carl Wieman's chapter in this way. Wieman makes the controversial claim that learning will occur if effective learning principles are put into practice, irrespective of students' cultural or geographical backgrounds. An alternative reading – and the one I favour – is that every class, every subject, every year requires 'experimentation'. Teachers need to gauge each class, assessing different levels of pre-existing knowledge and working with the unique and sometimes perverse dynamics that characterize every class. This diversity and 'unpredictability' is one of the things that makes consistently good teaching so challenging. Certainly, there do exist valuable principles of the sort that Wieman suggests, such as the ones I pointed to at the outset of this chapter, and that other scholars have sought to explicate (Chickering and Gamson 1987; Bain 2004), but each student and every class is unique and will either respond differently to those principles or require their careful tailoring for greatest effectiveness.

It strikes me that many contributors to this collection have maintained their inspiration and inspiring capabilities by reflecting continuously on their practice – gauging their experiences against their own personal and continuing history as a student (e.g. in professional development classes), speaking with their spouse or colleagues, or taking those reflections to the formal literature on the scholarship of teaching and learning. Although these scholars learn from their colleagues' teaching, seeking insights to different philosophies, styles and methods, it is evident that for many (e.g. Cameron, Regan) one of their greatest inspirations has lain in the attitudes and commitment of their own teachers. Some of the authors (e.g. Schwartz) have pointed to the fact that in their early teaching, they had few experiences to call upon, for example, other than the practices and attitudes of their own teachers. They have sought to reproduce the approaches of the best and avoid mimicking the flaws of the worst. It is fortunate that good role models were to be found. But more than that, these recollections of some of today's great university teachers make evident the significant and unanticipated ways in which *every* teacher's practice may inspire future pedagogic/andragogic practice – for better or worse.

As I said on the first page of this book, I started my own journey of teaching development as a 23-year-old brand new Junior Lecturer in New Zealand. I reach the staging post that this book represents in my teaching-and-learning journey as a 50-year-old Professor of Geography in Australia. I am not an educationalist, but I am a university teacher. If I can lay claim to any area of expertise, it is human geography, not pedagogy/andragogy. But over the 27 years since I delivered my first dreadful, hand-shaking, pulse-racing lecture I have felt compelled to think carefully about my teaching, being driven initially by fear and later by both a sense of professional responsibility and a curiosity to find out just how and why successful university teachers approach their vocation. What made or allowed others to flourish? What inspired them? Just how do they inspire others? Rather selfishly, this book has offered me a vehicle to satisfy that personal curiosity. Having disclosed that motive for putting this book together, I should note that I also hope sincerely that you have found the reflections of the distinguished scholars who so kindly contributed to this volume to be as informative, comforting and inspiring as I have found them to be.

References

Bain, K. (2004) *What the Best College Teachers Do*. Cambridge, MA: Harvard University Press.

Chickering, A.W. and Gamson, Z.F. (1987) Seven principles for good practice in undergraduate education, *The American Association for Higher Education Bulletin*, March. http://www.aahea.org/bulletins/articles/sevenprinciples1987. htm, accessed 17 March 2010.

Hay, I. (2001) Engaging lessons. Classrooms as sites of engagement in activist critical geography, *International Research in Geographical and Environmental Education*, 19(2): 55–60.

Palmer, P. (2007) *The Courage to Teach*, 2nd edn. San Francisco, CA: John Wiley and Sons.

Patience, A. (2008) The art of loving in the classroom: a defence of affective pedagogy, *Australian Journal of Teacher Education*, 33(2): 55–67.

Showalter, E. (2003) *Teaching Literature*. Malden, MA: Blackwell.

Index